Crisis in Uganda

The Breakdown of Health Services

edited by

COLE P. DODGE
and
PAUL D. WIEBE

PERGAMON PRESS

OXFORD · NEW YORK · TORONTO · SYDNEY · FRANKFURT

U.K.	Pergamon Press Ltd., Headington Hill Hall, Oxford OX3 0BW, England
U.S.A.	Pergamon Press Inc., Maxwell House, Fairview Park, Elmsford, New York 10523, U.S.A.
CANADA	Pergamon Press Canada Ltd., Suite 104, 150 Consumers Road, Willowdale, Ontario M2J 1P9, Canada
AUSTRALIA	Pergamon Press (Aust.) Pty. Ltd., P.O. Box 544, Potts Point, N.S.W. 2011, Australia
FEDERAL REPUBLIC OF GERMANY	Pergamon Press GmbH, Hammerweg 6, D-6242 Kronberg-Taunus, Federal Republic of Germany

First edition 1985

Library of Congress Cataloging in Publication Data
Crisis in Uganda.
Includes indexes.
1. Public health—Uganda—History. 2. Medical care—Uganda—History. 3. Uganda—History—1971–1979.
I. Dodge, Cole P.   II. Wiebe, Paul D.
RA552.U4C75   1985   362.1'09676'1   85-6492

British Library Cataloguing in Publication Data
Crisis in Uganda : the breakdown of health services.
1. Medical care—Uganda—History
I. Dodge, Cole P.   II. Wiebe, Paul D.
362.1'09676   RA552.U3/
ISBN 0-08-032682-X (Hardcover)
ISBN 0-08-032683-8 (Flexicover)

The views expressed by the authors herein do not necessarily represent the views of the organisations they represent or the views of the editors.

Printed and bound in Great Britain by Biddles Ltd, Guildford and King's Lynn

Acknowledgements

The contributions to this book were all made without agency financial support and by persons with very full schedules. We wish to thank all contributors for their willingness to participate voluntarily in this joint effort, and express here formally our firm and continuing respect for their various contributions in the redevelopment of the health services in Uganda.

Donna Beth Wiebe and Marilyn S. Dodge, our wives, and our children were always supportive as we worked on this project, and Donna Beth helped us imaginatively throughout with editorial and other chores.

Contributors

D. J. Alnwick, M.Sc. (Nutrition) - currently UNICEF Regional Nutrition Officer, Nairobi; from 1981-84 Nutrition Adviser, UNICEF, Uganda, with specific responsibility for Karamoja in 1981-82; prior work in Cameroon and Kenya, with consultancy experience in Malawi, Mozambique and Swaziland.

F. J. Bennett, M.B., Ch.B, D.P.H., F.F.C.M. (Community Health) - for many years Professor of Preventive Medicine at Makerere University, and later Professor of Community Medicine at the University of Dar-es-Salaam and Professor of Community Health at University of Nairobi; well-established writer on health issues in East Africa.

Robin J. Biellik, Dr.P.H. (International Health) - UNICEF consultant on MCH in Uganda; CONCERN field researcher in Karamoja and Teso in 1980; public health consultant to UNHCR in Somalia in 1980; earlier studied refugee relief in Thailand and worked as a nutritionist in Central America.

Mario Cisternino - Postgraduate Diploma in Socioeconomic Planning; Coordinator for Social Services of Moroto Diocese since 1980.

P. S. V. Cox, M.D. (Epidemiology) - missionary founder of Amudat Hospital in southern Karamoja; later served in Marasit and Pokot in Kenya; recently consultant on primary health care in Karamoja.

V. L. B. Dean, Ph.D. (Medical Anthropology) - Visiting Assistant Professor of Afro-American and African Studies at the University of Minnesota; field work and Ph.D. thesis on the Lugbara in West Nile.

C. Dodge - UNICEF Representative in Uganda since 1981; previously OXFAM Field Director in four countries; M.A. in social anthropology, and M.Sc. in public health.

D. Dunlop, Ph.D. (Economics) - research and dissertation on the Ugandan health system; research on the economics of health care; worked under contract with USAID during the period of the research reported here; has written widely on health issues.

Adolf Enns, Ph.D. (Sociology) - Visiting Lecturer in Philosophy and Religion at Makerere University, 1982-84, under the sponsorship of the Mennonite Central Committee.

J. R. Hebert, Sc.D. (Nutritional Epidemiology) - consultant to UNICEF, Uganda, on nutrition in Karamoja, March-May 1983; UNICEF nutrition consultant, 1984; extensive work on relationship between environmental sanitation and malnutrition in South Asia.

Peggy L. Henderson, M.P.H. (International Health) - consultant to UNICEF, Uganda, on monitoring and evaluation; researcher for CONCERN in Karamoja in 1980; public health consultant to UNHCR in Somalia in 1980; earlier studied refugee relief in Thailand and worked as a development programme administrator in Central America.

D. A. Hillman, M.D. (Paediatrics) - Professor of Paediatrics, Memorial University of Newfoundland, Canada; Senior Lecturer in Paediatrics, Makerere University; co-founder in 1983 of CHAMP, an organisation assisting the Department of Paediatrics, Makerere.

E. S. Hillman, M.D. (Paediatrics) - Professor of Paediatrics, Memorial University of Newfoundland, Canada; Senior Lecturer in Paediatrics, Makerere University; co-founder of CHAMP.

Alastair Johnston, M.Sc. (History and Social Studies of Science) - OXFAM coordinator for Luwero relief operations; SCF famine relief worker in Karamoja; UNICEF consultant on the Mbarara and Luwero emergencies.

W. Senteza Kajubi, M.A. (Education) - member and at one time Director of the Institute of Education in Uganda; Vice-Chancellor of Makerere University between 1977 and 1979; travelled to Boston as a visiting scholar in 1980.

Israel Kalyesubula, M.B., Ch.B. (Paediatrics) - Senior Registrar in Paediatrics, Makerere University.

C. A. S. Karamagi, M.B., Ch.B., M. Med. (Paediatrics) - Lecturer in Paediatrics and Coordinator of Social Paediatrics at Makerere University.

Erisa Kironde, M.A. (Anthropology) - Chairman of the Uganda Red Cross Society; civic leader in Kampala as Chairman of the National Theatre and the Nomo Gallery.

Karl-Eric Knutsson, Ph.D. - Assistant Secretary General and Deputy Executive Director of UNICEF; Regional Director for UNICEF in Nairobi, 1980-83.

G. Kyeyune, M.A. (Statistics) - earned the M.A. from Ghana University in 1983; National Officer for UNICEF in Kampala.

F. M. Mburu, Ph.D., M.P.H. (Health Planning) - Senior Lecturer, Department of Community Health, University of Nairobi; health services consultant; community health specialisation.

Klaus K. Minde, M.D., F.R.C.P.(C)(Paediatrics) - WHO consultant to Makerere University, 1971-73; Professor of Psychiatry and Paediatrics at the University of Toronto; with CHAMP in Uganda for two months in 1983-84.

C. Ndugwa, M.B., Ch.B., M.Med., D.C.H. (Paediatrics) - Associate Professor and Chairman, Department of Paediatrics, Makerere University; has given direction to MCH programme development in Uganda.

Mary Okello, B.Sc., Dip.Ed. - Vice-Chairperson of the Family Planning Association of Uganda; intimate knowledge of rural Uganda; has taught in Kenya and Uganda.

Raphael Owor, M.D., F.R.C.Path. - Dean of the Makerere University Medical School.

William Parson, M.D. - Professor of Medicine and Department Chairman, Makerere University Medical School, 1964-72; returned to Uganda in 1977 as an external examiner, again in 1980-82 as a Fulbright scholar.

R. L. Rwakatonera, B.Sc. (Nursing) - professional nurse tutor; has undertaken basic research in the nursing profession in Uganda.

Stanley Scheyer, M.D. (Public and International Health) - founder of Family Health Care, Inc., a consulting firm based in Washington D.C.; extensive work experience in twenty-three countries; currently a consultant.

M. R. Stirling, M.A. (Development Economics) - UNICEF Assistant Project Officer for Health in Kampala, 1981-84; involved in the Karamoja relief operation in 1981; currently UNICEF Resident Programme Officer in Swaziland.

S. Ssentamu, M.Sc. (Engineering) - currently Assistant Commissioner for Water Development in the Ministry of Lands, Minerals and Water Resources; recent interests include a national borehole survey and development of new water sources through spring protection, shallow well construction and new borehole drilling.

D. Stockley, M.D. (Primary Health Care) - doctor at Ngoro Mission Hospital, 1980-83; initiated PHC project in Teso; currently missionary doctor in Kotido, Karamoja.

Melissa Wells, B.Sc. - UNDP Resident Representative in Kampala from 1979 to 1981; Special Representative of the UN Secretary General in the emergency situations in Uganda during this period, and Chairperson of the Relief Coordinating Unit; currently Director of IMPACT in Geneva.

Paul D. Wiebe, Ph.D. (Sociology) - author or co-author of many articles and five books on social and cultural change in South and Southeast Asia; currently Professor of Sociology and Anthropology at Bethel College, St. Paul, Minnesota; field visits to Uganda in July 1972, June 1983 and January 1984.

E. H. Williams, C.B.E., M.D. (Epidemiology) - qualified from St. Bart's Hospital, London, in 1939; proceeded to West Nile in 1941 where, with other members of his family, he founded Kuluva Hospital; worked in West Nile until 1979, then moved to Kenya until 1980 before retiring in U.K.

J. Wilson, B.Sc. (Agriculture) - currently Project Director of the Kapedo Resettlement Project in northern Karamoja where he has worked since 1981 for OXFAM; started his career as District Officer in Moroto in 1951; has studied and published on the soils and vegetation of Karamoja; strong ongoing interests in the culture, language and history of the Karamojong.

Christopher H. Wood, M.D., F.F.C.M. - involved in the start of the medical school in Dar es Salaam where he was Professor of Community Health; moved to the African Medical and Research Foundation (AMREF) to start the Training Department which has developed continuing education and teacher education programmes and a series of health manuals for all levels of health workers; currently Medical Director of AMREF.

K. Wotton, M.D., F.R.C.P.(C)(Community Medicine) - currently working for Africa Medical Research Foundation on continuing medical education; worked with CHAMP at Makerere University and Mulago Hospital in 1983.

Contents

Foreword

Raphael Owor

During the period of military misrule from 1971 to 1979 and in the period
immediately following the liberation war, social services were thrown into
disarray in Uganda. The decline in services, including medical and health
services, became noticeable by the mid-1970s. With increasing insecurity
many members of the medical professions left the country or, as in the case
of the Asians, were ordered to leave. Some professionals were killed.
Medical supplies became scarce and staff morale deteriorated. By 1981 the
breakdown of services was everywhere apparent.

Crisis in Uganda traces the outlines of the medical and health services
before their breakdown, the problems associated with their breakdown and the
beginnings of their rehabilitation. At one time Uganda had one of the most
viable and enviable health service systems in all of Africa. The work at
Makerere University by Professors D. B. Jelliffe and J. P. Stanfield in
nutrition, and Professors D. R. Davies and A. G. Shaper in cardiology, is
indicative of the quality established. So is the classic volume on community health edited by Maurice King, Medical Care in Developing Countries,
the result of a symposium held at Makerere University.

The breakdown of medical and health services occurred at all levels, from
the subdispensary level in remote villages to the national reference and
teaching level at Mulago Hospital. Voluntary mission hospitals as well as
government hospitals were affected. The services provided in particular
units as well as in large geographical areas--for example, Karamoja, the
Luwero "triangle" area and West Nile--deteriorated badly, and in many areas
services ceased to exist.

The breakdown of medical and health services was severe. Literally as well
as figuratively many of the lights of the country went out during the 1970s.
Crisis in Uganda, however, does not concentrate only on Uganda's "dark
ages". While it captures some of the experiences of the country during its
period of turmoil--and in so doing will prove to be invaluable for future
reference--it also throws rays of light and hope into the future. Thus, for
example, as indicted in a number of places in the book, primary health care
is beginning to take root in Uganda, lessons can quickly be drawn from the
experiences of the past decade in the improvement of relief and other services for people in need, baseline data on vital statistics have again been

obtained for a number of areas--with the result that monitoring and planning in the improvement of health services is again becoming practicable--and the implementation of "social paediatrics" in Mulago Hospital has resulted in improvements both in the care of patients and the teaching of paediatrics. Several contributors to the volume make suggestions about how the problems of the Karamojong might be approached.

Ugandans do not wish to put Uganda back into the 1960s. The country must build a new system of providing medical and health services which depends on the participation of the people, emphasises the maintenance of health rather than disease control and encourages the participation of all parties in a position to play a part in the provision of health for all.

Crisis in Uganda brings together a unique collection of articles by persons who have had direct experience with the problems of Uganda in recent years. It cannot be considered an "end" in itself, but as a stimulus. My hope is that it stimulates us to understand that the rehabilitation of health services in the country must go hand in hand with planning for a better future.

Introduction

Cole P. Dodge and Paul D. Wiebe

At independence in 1962 and into the early 1970s, Uganda had one of the most highly developed health service delivery systems in Africa. The services provided in smaller health units in outlying villages and towns were integrated with the services provided in large, regionally located hospitals. The country's network of hospitals, health centres and dispensary and maternity units was well staffed by trained health workers at all levels. Referral systems were well organised. Followup care was routinely encouraged. Few patients in 1972 had to travel more than ten kilometres to their nearest health post.

Then came the troubles associated with the Idi Amin years, the subsequent war of liberation and the aftermath of the war. Amin seized power in Uganda in January 1971. In 1972 he decreed that all noncitizen Asians had just three months to leave, and most of Uganda's 80,000 Asians fled, fearing for their security and lives. As a result the country lost many of its professionals, technicians and middlemen. In 1974, with the economy deteriorating and the security situation worsening, many Ugandan doctors and other professionals left to take up positions outside the country. As the 1970s wore on, the incidence of atrocities mounted, the security situation worsened, goods disappeared from the shelves of stores, coffee exports were sabatoged by army officers and others in the pursuit of personal gain, and the strengths of the country's once respected institutions gave way.

Amin was ousted in April 1979 when Tanzanian and Uganda National Liberation Army (UNLA) troops moved into Entebbe and Kampala.[1] The relief the people first experienced did not last, however, for the ouster did not bring a return to just and stable government. Lawlessness and looting went unchecked. Three weak governments came and went in the period up to December 1980. The UNLA proved to be undisciplined and inexperienced. Magendo (black marketeering) flourished.

Prior to the 1970s Uganda was often referred to as the "pearl" of Africa. By the end of the decade it was one of the world's "least developed coun-

---

[1]Much has been written about the Amin period in Uganda and its end. For a very good summary treatment, see Avirgan and Honey (1982).

1

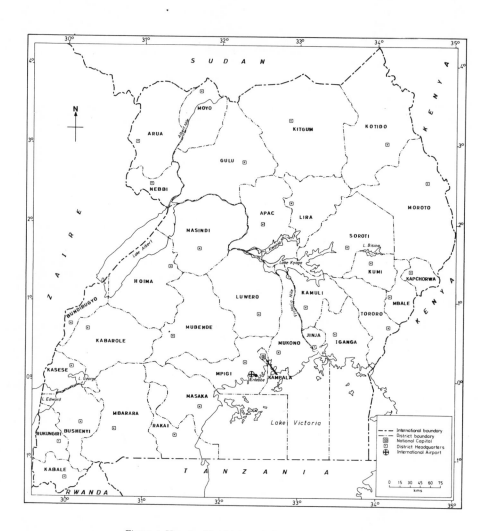

Figure 1 Uganda: District boundaries and main towns

tries". Buildings, roads and other physical infrastructure had deteriorated badly or been destroyed. Spare parts were in short supply or unavailable. Access to clean water and basic sanitation facilities, once possible for a large proportion of the population, had been thoroughly disrupted. Facilities and equipment in most hospitals and other service institutions had been destroyed or looted, and the production of export and food crops had plummeted (see Table 1).

TABLE 1: Production of Principal Crops (in Thousands of Tons), 1970 and 1980[a]

	1970	1980
Export Crops		
Robusta coffee[b]	187.4	130.4
Arabica coffee	14.1	5.1
Cotton[c]	86.4	4.1
Tea	18.2	1.5
Tobacco	3.4	0.4
Sugar (raw)	144.0	2.4
Cocoa	-	0.1
Other Crops		
Maize	388.0	286.0
Finger millet	783.0	459.0
Sorghum	462.0	299.0
Rice	N/A	17.0
Wheat	N/A	17.0
Plantains	7,657.0	5,699.0
Sweet potatoes	1,570.0	1,200.0
Irish potatoes	N/A	213.0
Cassava	2,578.0	2,072.0
Pulses[d]	231.8	183.0
Oil seeds	264.0	93.0

*Source: Adapted from Uganda (1983: 29).
[a]The figures for food crops are estimates of total production, while the figures for export crops are for official purchases only.
[b]Figures are for a twelve-month crop season ending September of the year shown.
[c]Figures are for a twelve-month crop season ending October of the year shown.
[d]Includes beans, field peas, cowpeas, etc.

Milton Obote, President of Uganda before the Amin coup, was returned to power in national elections in December 1980. Gradually, since then, progress has been made in the rehabilitation of administrative, social service, commercial and other sectors, and definite direction has been given in the country's programme of economic recovery. In his period in office in the 1960s Obote encouraged socialism and nationalised a number of enterprises. In his return he turned to a "mixed" economy approach, allowing Asians expelled in 1972 to reclaim seized property or seek compensation and inviting private investment in a number of areas.

Sustained recovery in Uganda is not yet assured. The overall inflation rate fell from around 100 percent in 1979-81, to around 50 percent in 1982 (Africa Now, 1983: 49) and around 30 percent in mid-1983 (Ojulu, 1984: 13).

By 1983-84, as coffee production and coffee export earnings (which make up
the overwhelming share of export earnings in Uganda) rebounded dramatically
from their low points between 1979 and 1981, Uganda had a positive balance
of payments. Mulago Hospital in Kampala, among the best of its kind in
Africa in the 1960s--but plagued by sewage disposal, water and power supply,
maintenance, staff morale and drug supply problems in the late 1970s and
into the 1980s--in early 1984 again had four of its twelve X-ray rooms and
six operating theatres back in action (Pearson, 1984: 25). In the period
1983 and 1984 Uganda's public servants received four- to sevenfold salary
and wage increases.

The problem is that the road to recovery for Uganda will be long and diffi-
cult--not short and easy as predicted optimistically in the immediate post-
Amin period--and that reservations concerning political stability, security
and "displaced peoples" within Uganda are still most legitimately raised.[2]
Furthermore, while salary increases of the kind mentioned above in public
servant salaries are clearly impressive from many viewpoints, in Uganda in
1984 they meant simply that government employees would still not earn nearly
enough to provide for the essentials of life and would have to continue to
work at an additional job or two, and receive the produce of their own or
the shambas (gardens) of their families and friends in order to make ends
meet. Again, the government's "Background to the Budget 1983-84" noted that
the cost of living for low-income earners in Uganda increased by 54 percent
between 1982 and 1983.

"Recovery Programme" figures presented by the Office of the President in
1981 are indicative of the priorities in relation to which efforts were then
directed. Accordingly (Uganda, 1983: 18), "agriculture" was to receive
roughly 30 percent of recovery programme expenditures over the period 1982-
85, "industry" was to receive 29 percent, "transport" 21 percent, "minerals
and energy" 6 percent and "social infrastructure" 15 percent. Expenditures
for the rehabilitation of primary schools and health care facilities, included under expenditures for "social infrastructure", totaled 3.4 percent
over the same period.

In the government's "Revised Recovery Programme 1983-85", industry rather
than agriculture takes the largest share of the resources allocated (35%),
to be followed by agriculture (27%), social infrastructure (20%), transport
and communications (14%) and mining (4%).

The priorities identified in the recovery programmes of the government
reflect basic needs in Uganda. They also reflect the emphases of the development model adopted. The International Monetary Fund, World Bank and
donor country supports necessary for the rehabilitation and reconstruction
efforts identified in the country have been prioritised in favor of the cash
crop export earning sectors. The "Revised Recovery Programme" states the
implications of this orientation for the rehabilitation of social services
as follows (quoted in Pearson, 1984: 25): "Although GDP is expected to grow
at a faster rate than the population during the next five years, resources
available to the social services will remain very limited. Social services

---

[2]Expenditures for "internal affairs, police, prisons, justice and judi-
ciary" and "defence" came to 44 percent of total expenditures in fiscal year
1980-81, to 25 percent of total expenditures in fiscal year in 1981-82
(Uganda, 1983: 20). Questions about "displaced peoples" within Uganda have
been widely raised by members of the international community in the past
several years.

make heavy demands on recurrent expenditure, and the economy cannot sustain any major increase. Thus both the expansion of social services and the level of provision must be restricted to what can be afforded."

None of this means that little is being done to bring social services in Uganda back up to former levels. A National Expanded Programme of Immunisation was launched in 1983 with the hope that immunisation coverage for children under 2 years of age would be increased from 5 percent at the time to 60 percent by 1988. Organisations of many kinds have started to mobilise resources again in the provision of social services, and health units in many parts of the country are now better equipped with medical supplies than they have been for years. The problem is simply that significant as are such developments, without multilateral and bilateral assistance in the rehabilitation of social and health services, far less than has been accomplished would have been accomplished.

PURPOSES

Many doctors, scholars, development and relief workers, aid administrators, consultants and others have paid careful attention to problems and developments in Uganda in recent years. Their perspectives and the results of their analyses, however, have seldom been made available to persons other than those directly responsible for the practical implementation of the projects at hand. Thus we decided in mid-1983 to ask twenty-six persons with direct practical and/or research experience--and preferably long-term experience--with the organisation and delivery of health services in Uganda to write on their own experiences and understandings of the breakdown of health services in recent years. In the end five of the persons we asked originally to contribute could not do so for one or another reason, and six others joined the project. This book is the result of our efforts. Only two of the articles included have been published earlier.

Each of the authors in this collection makes particular and significant contributions to the overall understanding of the topic under consideration. The repeated themes of the volume include the following:

1. The need for basic and continuing emphasis on the development of primary health care capacities in Uganda;

2. The need for further understanding of the relationships between good nutrition, good health and agricultural cropping patterns;

3. The need for adequate monitoring and evaluation of standards of health;

4. The need for the further development of research understandings in the provision of health services;

5. The need for the coordination of agency involvements in disaster situations;

6. The need for the utilisation of Uganda's existing health infrastructure in the rehabilitation of health services;

7. The fact that health services cannot be considered in isolation;

8. The need for a renewal of morale among health professionals;

9. The relationship between political instability and the displace-
    ment of peoples, and poor health;

10. The significance of donor support in the rehabilitation of health
    services in Uganda;

11. The importance of health services initiated "by" and not "for"
    the people, and of community-based rather than vertical interven-
    tions.

In general terms, the articles of Crisis in Uganda were collected in order
to document what has happened to health services in Uganda over the past ten
to fifteen years and to provide overviews of many aspects of the current
health situation in the country. Most of the articles, written as they were
by persons thoroughly involved in the local provision and organisation of
health services, will provide health planners, international and voluntary
agency representatives and health care providers with detailed understandings of how a system of health services was undermined and how such a
system might be rehabilitated. The tone of the articles is not judgemental
of government or other agency involvement in Uganda. Rather it is focused
in the hope that further understandings of the breakdown of services will
somehow help in the development of better services in the future.

                    OVERVIEW

Background to Crisis

Studies from many countries have established that the level of a mother's
education is the key determinant of her children's health (Grant, 1983: 59).
In general, children of more educated mothers have better chances both for
survival and healthy growth than do children of less educated mothers.

Uganda at one time had a well-developed network of schools. In 1983,
however, after a decade of decline, survey findings were that only 53.6 of
age-eligible males in the country, and 41.5 percent of age-eligible females, began P1 (the first year of primary school), and that 51 percent of
the males and 70 percent of the females who had earlier started in P1 had
dropped out by P7 (Serugga and Nsereko, 1984). Projections on the basis of
the survey's results were that, by 1995, only 40.5 percent of adult males
and 27 percent of adult females would be literate, whereas in 1980, about
60 percent of adult males and 40 percent of adult females were literate.

Now the past decade has been a decade of particular crisis for Uganda.
Survey findings a few years from now will no doubt allow a different picture
of literacy in the 1990s, given the reconstruction of the country's primary
schools currently underway. Yet the challenge obviously remains, and it is
the topic with which we begin this collection. Professor Senteza Kajubi
addresses the questions of national integration and development in Uganda
from the viewpoint of education. As he does he shows also how the appropriate reconstruction of Uganda's educational institutions can have important repercussions for other aspects of the country's development, including
health.

The second article, by Drs. Stanley Scheyer and David Dunlop, carefully
traces the story of health services and development in Uganda up to 1971,
then through the 1970s. Special attention is given to health expenditures,
staffing and options the government has considered--and still must consi-

Figure 2 Mulago Hospital, Kampala, as it was
(Photograph courtesy of Medical School)

Figure 3 Destroyed equipment, Maracha Hospital, West Nile, 1981
(Photograph courtesy of UNICEF/C P Dodge)

der--in the development of its health sector.

The last two articles of our first section are by Professors F. J. Bennett and Adolf Enns. Bennett, in a masterful comparison of health services and health status in Uganda, Tanzania and Kenya, shows how different national policies and various crises have affected the delivery of health services. Enns considers reflectively the choices open to Uganda as it seeks to establish again its own balances and directions as a nation.

The Breakdown of Services

Our second section contains articles on the breakdown of services in particular settings. Dr. E. H. Williams writes of how Kuluva Hospital in West Nile was able to continue services throughout the Amin years despite tremendous difficulties. Erisa Kironde reflects on changes in health services from the vantage point of a small village near Kampala, and Rosemary Rwakatonera and Dr. K. Wotton examine particular manifestations of the crisis in health services--problems in the quality of nursing care and the tragically high rate of deaths from measles (easily preventable as many of them might have been) among children--at Mulago Hospital.

Section two also contains an article by D. J. Alnwick, M. R. Stirling and G. Kyeyune on morbidity and mortality in selected Ugandan hosptials during the period 1981-82, in comparison with data for the early 1970s; an article by Dr. F. M. Mburu on the quality of services possible at government rural health centres in 1984; and articles by Alastair Johnston and Cole P. Dodge, respectively, on "emergency operations" and the displacement of peoples in recent years in areas to the north and west of Kampala, and in West Nile.

Dr. J. R. Hebert and S. Ssentamu, in the last article of the second section, examine water supply and sanitation in Uganda and the effects of their breakdown on Uganda's health delivery system. The understandings developed are clearly central in the general discussion of the country's health services. Almost no new sources of water supply were developed during the 1970s. Existing water supply sources and sanitation services deteriorated badly over the same period.

Karamoja Considered

Between mid-1979 and the end of 1980 an estimated 50,000 persons, including perhaps 25,000 children, starved to death or succumbed to disease complicated by malnutrition in Karamoja (Biellik and Henderson, 1981). The famine drew worldwide attention. Doctors, nurses, relief workers, agency heads and others agonised over, and sweated in, the actual provision of relief. Much of what was done was done ineffectively and too late. Much was done well. In any case, the grievous famine of 1979-81 in Karamoja was to a large extent the product of the wider crisis in Uganda.

Our section on Karamoja begins with Alnwick's general consideration of the Karamoja context and the causes of the famine identified. The article by Dr. Robin J. Biellik and Peggy L. Henderson which follows presents the results of their 1980 study of mortality and malnutrition in Karamoja in relation to findings from comparable studies in other famine contexts.

Father Mario Cisternino writes critically about certain aspects of the relief efforts mounted in Karamoja in response to the famine, then argues that cattle restocking is necessary if there is to be a return to economic viability and social stability in the region. John Wilson, in reference to his many years of experience and current efforts in Karamoja, argues forcefully otherwise for resettlment.

Whichever perspective is most appropriate, the problems of the Karamojong were certainly not ended when the famine of 1979-81 subsided. The best armed clans among them now have almost all of the cattle; the others remain socially and economically vulnerable as never before. Furthermore, until current problems of security in the region are settled, it is unlikely that either resettlement or restocking on anything approaching the scale necessary will be possible.

Dr. P. S. V. Cox proposes a "revolution" for the Karamoja health services, arguing that community participation is essential if these services are to prove more viable in the future than they have proven in the past. Melissa Wells and Dr. Karl-Eric Knutsson write about what was learned overall in the relief operation in Karamoja, and about what can be done in preparation for other disaster situations by agencies responsible for the provision of relief.

Perspectives

The Uganda Ministry of Health counted 924 health facilities in the country in January 1984 (Table 2). These form the latent organisational and physical infrastructure in relation to which the country's health services can be rehabilitated, both with reference to secondary and tertiary level medical services and with reference to mounting and supporting effective primary health care programmes.

TABLE 2:   Health Facilities

	Government		Nongovernment		Total
	N	%	N	%	N
Hospitals	46	58	33	42	79
Health centres	101	90	5	10	106
Dispensary/Maternity units	70	75	23	25	93
Dispensaries	48	62	29	38	77
Maternity units	30	73	11	27	41
Subdispensaries	351	96	16	4	367
Aid posts	145	90	16	10	161
Totals	791	86	133	14	924

*Source: Uganda (1984).

The first article of our last section is by Alnwick, Stirling and Kyeyune and gives figures for population access to hospitals, health centres and dispensary/maternity units in 1980. With an estimated 57 percent of the population living within ten kilometres of one such unit--plus the organisation of health facilities at still lower levels (Table 2)--it is clear that health services for most Ugandans could rather quickly be reestablished if political will, finances and personnel were again so directed.

Professor Virginia Dean examines the implications in the introduction of new crops for the nutrition and overall welfare of the Lugbara people of West Nile. Dodge and Henderson next report the results of recent health-status surveys conducted in different parts of Uganda. Some of the findings reported are sketchy at best. Yet they too are important. Very little such information has been collected in recent years.

The articles on the child health crisis at Mulago and Makerere by Professors C. Ndugwa, D. A. Hillman and E. S. Hillman, primary health care in Teso by Dr. D. Stockley, breast-feeding in and around Kampala by Dr. C. Karamagi and family planning in Uganda by Mary Okello all make clear reference to the problems that characterise the provision of health services in contemporary Uganda. Yet all of them allow also a certain sense of guarded optimism. Thus, whatever the difficulties, "social paediatrics" and community-based health systems can be effectively encouraged here, the advantages of breast-feeding are still quickly appreciated (and breast-feeding is still almost universal in and around Kampala) and responses to family planning emphases even in rural areas seem to be increasingly favourable.

Drs. Klaus K. Minde and Israel Kalyesubula, and Dr. William Parson, write in turn about problems in the delivery of primary health care, and medical education, in Uganda today. Dr. Christopher H. Wood, in the final article of our collection, outlines the very significant role the voluntary agency AMREF (African Medical and Research Foundation) has had in the delivery of health services in East Africa, showing simultaneously how such an agency has been able to work effectively in conjunction with other relief and development organisations over the years.

The rate of population growth in Uganda between the census years 1969 and 1980 was approximately 2.7 percent per year. Official estimates assume that Uganda's urban population has subsequently grown by about 3 percent per year, that Uganda's rural population has grown by about 2.8 percent per year, and that the country's population reached 13.9 million by mid-1983.[3] Approximately 47.5 percent of Uganda's population is under 15 years of age. Roughly 8 percent lives in urban areas.

COMMENT

The target of "health for all by the year 2000" which has been set by the World Health Organisation and the World Health Assembly is possible for Uganda, given the country's basic health infrastructure and natural and population resources. But if the target is to be achieved, political will and financial resources will have to be invested appropriately, the participation of the people will have to be encouraged at every juncture and the chance of the people to look with confidence and hope to their tomorrows will have to be assured.

---

[3]The demographic data reported here are "reasonable estimates" from statistics compiled by Uganda Government agencies. They are reported in UNICEF (1984, Annex II).

REFERENCES

Africa Now (1983). Ugandan Economy Slowly Returns to Health.   November.

Avirgan, Tony and Martha Honey (1982). War in Uganda: The Legacy   of Idi Amin. Lawrence Hill,   Westport, Connecticut.

Biellik, Robin J. and Peggy L. Henderson (1981). Mortality, Nutritional Status, and Diet During the Famine in Karamoja, Uganda, 1980. Lancet, ii (12 December): 1330-1333.

Grant, James P. (1983). The State of the World's Children 1984. Oxford University Press.

Ojulu, Epajjar (1984). The Revised Version Has These Main Points. African Business, January.

Pearson, Bryan (1984). Uganda: Picking Up the Pieces. Africa Health, 6 (February/March).

Serugga, S. W. and Munakukaama Nsereko (1984). A Survey of Education at the Primary Level. National Institute of Education, Kampala.

Uganda, Republic of (1983). Uganda 1983 Yearbook. Ministry of Information and Broadcasting, Kampala.

Uganda, Republic of, Ministry of Health (1984). Health Facilities and Manpower Report. Planning Unit, Entebbe.

UNICEF (1984). Child Survival Revolution. Mimeographed, Kampala.

Section 1
Background to Crisis

Integration and National Development
from the Viewpoint of Education in Uganda

Senteza Kajubi

Among the many baffling questions which face Uganda today are the following:
What are the basic needs of the people, most of whom dwell in rural areas?
How can these be met? How can the productive skills of the people be
harnessed, increased and more effectively applied? How can values pertaining to representative democracy, the sanctity of human life, the
supremacy of law and order, the primacy of the country's constitution and an
awareness of the rights and responsibilities of citizens best be taught?
Above all, what is the best means of inspiring love for the country and of
creating a feeling of national identity and belongingness among peoples of
diverse ethnic, cultural and religious backgrounds who were brought together
only recently by colonial accident and who have not interacted together long
enough to evolve a common language, let alone a shared universe of ideals
and values?

My difficult assignment here is to examine integration and the question of
national development in Uganda from the perspective of education. My
responses below will focus on the type of education that will best contribute to national reconstruction. I am aware in beginning that proposals
for the implementation of education for national integration and development, except only as a facade or academic dream, assume a modicum of law and
order and a great deal of political will on the part of both leaders and the
people.

RESOURCES

In order to understand fully how education can contribute to development and
integration in Uganda we must analyse the stock of resources available.

Physical Resources

Uganda, in comparison with many African countries, is extremely well endowed
with natural resources. It is estimated that over 85 percent of its land
area of 236,000 square kilometres is arable. Rainfall over most of the
country exceeds 75 centimetres per annum, and in the fertile lucustrine
crescent in the south of the country is over 125 centimetres and evenly

distributed, making crop growing possible throughout the year. Large areas
of unexploited natural hardwood forest exist, and five major fresh water
lakes teeming with fish could form the basis of an important fish meal or
poultry feed industry.

Although Uganda lies astride the equator it is over 1300 metres above sea
level, so that what would otherwise be debilitating tropical temperatures
are considerably tempered by altitude. Vast areas of swamp land (such as
Kibimba in Busoga District) are ideally suited to rice growing, and the
scope of improving and extending tea and sugar plantations and growing maize
on a commercial basis are enormous. Uganda is not yet fully surveyed for
oil and other mineral resources. But major copper deposits of iron ore,
walfram, chrome, beryllium and other industrially useful minerals such as
asbestos and limestone exist in commercially workable amounts in a number of
areas. The country has vast resources of wildlife in its national parks,
and its terrain is magnificent.

Current global concerns over the possible depletion of known energy resources such as oil, natural gas and coal, and the escalation of world
prices for these resources, particularly oil, has led to concerted efforts
to search for alternative sources of energy. The electric power potential
of the Upper Nile basin is almost inexhaustible and the possibility of
tapping solar energy at the equator is without question. Uganda is capable
of providing hydroelectric power to western Kenya, eastern Zaire, southern
Sudan, Rwanda and Burundi.

Yet, in spite of the natural advantages of the country which Winston
Churchill once described as the "Pearl of Africa", Uganda since independence
has increasingly depended on Kenya, and recently Tanzania, with much less
arable land and reliable rainfall, for the supply of basic commodities such
as sugar, maize meal, cooking oils, rice, milk, butter, soap and textiles.
While 42,000 square kilometres of fresh water in Lake Victoria border
Entebbe and Kampala, the supply of water in even these towns is always
problematic.

Human Resources

The most important resource any country has, however, is its people. As the
Kiswahili saying goes, __Utajiri ya inchi ni wana inchi__--the wealth of a
nation is its people. The population of Uganda in 1980 was estimated to be
12.8 million people. Roughly 90 percent of all Ugandans live in rural
areas; about 50 percent are below the age of fifteen. Such distributional
factors have far-reaching implications for social services.

In 1977 only 48.5 percent of the children of primary school age were
actually enrolled in government-aided schools, and of the children in school
only 39 percent were girls. Among the children who complete the seven-year
primary school cycle, only about 20 percent can proceed to postprimary
institutions, and of the children who proceed only 27 percent are girls.
Each year a rising flood of pupils completes the primary school course, but
for many such children secondary level educational opportunities are not
available. In 1977 some 120,000 youths took the dreaded Primary Leaving
Examination (PLE), but only 23.3 percent continued with some form of postprimary education. In 1980 only about 20 percent of the 150,000 candidates
who faced the PLE could find places in secondary level institutions. The
percentage of primary school leavers continuing to formal schooling has
decreased significantly in recent years as competition has increased.

In 1972 the Government of Uganda spent almost one-quarter (23.5%) of its budget on education. Owing to the increased attention paid to security and defence by the military regime of Idi Amin, expenditures devoted to the Ministry of Education had dropped to 18.7 percent of the recurrent budget in 1976 and to lower figures in 1982. It is not as yet clear whether allocations to education and social services in the future will increase significantly. The one thing that is certain is that with population growing at a rate of 2.8 percent or more per annum, and continuing problems with stagnation or recession in the economy, it will be difficult for Uganda to democratise and make more participatory its educational and social processes without the radical transformation of some of the institutional and ideological patterns with which Uganda is currently encumbered. In The Common Man's Charter (1970), Dr. Milton Obote phrases the challenge like this: "We cannot afford to build two nations within the territorial boundaries of one country: one rich, educated, African in appearance but mentally foreign; and the other, which constitutes the majority of the population, poor and illiterate." New strategies are required.

COHESION AND IDENTITY

Throughout the developing world, and particularly in Africa, people are impatient with the slow rate of development and the maldistribution of social and economic opportunities that have often accompanied the changes that have occurred. The founding fathers of African nationalism such as Nkrumah and Kenyatta during the struggle for freedom promised their people: "Seek ye first the political kingdom and the rest will be added unto you." After two decades of independence, little if anything seems to have been added to the majority of the people in most African countries, and judging by the widespread occurrence of famines, economic stagnation, rampant inflation, political instability, coups d'etat and the refugee syndrome in much of the continent, one can rightly say that even the very little that the people once had has often been taken away. The Matunda ya Uhuru--the Fruits of Independence--have taken so long to appear in so many places, let alone ripen, that the revolution of rising expectations for very many has turned into a counterrevolution of rising frustrations. Okot p'Bitek (1973) laments the situation with a verse:

> And those who have
> Fallen into things
> Throw themselves into soft beds
> But the hip bones of the voters
> Grow painful
> Sleeping on the same earth
> They slept
> Before Uhuru.

Uhuru, concludes p'Bitek, has all too often meant the replacement of foreign rule by native dictatorship. Unfortunately, in this assessment he has been all too accurate.

One of the major problems in educational reform in Africa is the lack in many countries of a national philosophy or ideology which unites the different groups--whether ethnic, tribal, religious or cultural, military or civilian--into a "social order with a collective common purpose" and with suitable core values that would animate and guide the new education broadly understood. Poverty, ignorance and disease are merely symptoms, and not the

real causes, of the malady of African underdevelopment. At the tap root is
the lack of national unity. The problems of underdevelopment throughout the
Third World are first and foremost social rather than physical.

Uganda was created by colonial accident as recently as 1894. The country's
problems today can be associated in part with its colonial heritage; they
can certainly be associated with the ways in which international economic,
political and informational relationships are structured to the advantage of
particular countries; they are certainly often manifested in poverty,
ignorance and disease. But without doubt Uganda's most crucial problem
today is the lack of national cohesion and identity. Those who defined
Uganda's boundaries did not pay sufficient attention to cultural differences. Through the system of indirect rule under the colonial system
various parts of the country were administered separately through traditional local institutions, with the result that people in adjacent
territories frequently had few dealings with the emerging central power
systems of the country or with other parts of the country. There is not as
yet a national language which is understood by all the people. Over thirty
different languages are spoken, and Radio Uganda broadcasts in at least
twenty languages. Police and army officers frequently find it difficult to
communicate with the people under their authority. The result is often a
lack of trust, mutual suspicion and antagonism. Interethnic, religious and
regional rivalries still exist to such a degree that economic, social and
other forms of development are seriously hampered.

Needed today in Uganda is a new empathy, a spirit of love for country, a
feeling of national identity and belongingness and a shared universe of
national ideals and values. Needed is continued socialisation in the
customs, mores, values and traditions that allow progress along the path
from government through force and repression to government through consent.
The contributions of many institutions will be significant as changes along
the lines specified are introduced. Among the institutions critically
important in the entire process will be the institution of education.

A CURRICULUM FOR NATIONAL INTEGRATION AND DEVELOPMENT

Curriculum does not refer merely to syllabi or materials contained in
subjects and textbooks. Broadly conceived it refers to the total spectrum
of experiences which influence the lives of students as they go through the
educational programme. As treated here it includes almost everything that
impinges on learning and on how the school affects or alters a pupil's
capacity and will to do things. To consider the curriculum to be
encouraged, in short, is to speak of the kind of society we would like to
build in Uganda.

Education and Community

Uganda is one nation. All of its people, no matter how different their
backgrounds, must be encouraged to work together for common goals and
ideals. The Ugandan child, however, like a small stone dropped into a pool
of water, is surrounded by many ripples or circles of loyalty and citizenship. At the core of these ever-widening circles is the family into which a
child is born. The second circle is the clan to which the family belongs
and in which members trace their origin to a common ancestor and share a
common symbol. The third circle of the age group (or nowadays school group)
is surrounded by the fourth circle of the village or community.

Beyond the village is the fifth circle, the ethnic or cultural/language group to which the family belongs, while the sixth circle is the circle of national loyalty. The seventh and eighth circles, respectively, are the circles of Africanness--which Nkrumah called the "African Personality" and Sengoh called "Negritude"--and membership in and loyalty to the human race and the world community.

These circles or ripples of loyalty are not complete and separate circles. Rather they are interrelated and interconnected like the spirals made by a watch spring, or a rolled mat, which start from the centre and roll themselves into ever larger spirals. Thus loyalty and pride in one's ethnic group and culture need not lend distrust or detraction to one's identity with the nation as a whole or his church, just as love for or membership in one's family should not lead to separation from one's culture or the people of one's village or community. On the contrary, an individual who has no pride and respect for his own family, community, religion or culture, or for life in general, or is otherwise rootless, is not capable of valuing and respecting the families, communities, religions, cultures and even the lives of others.

The core value of traditional African life was that of community life, and the principal aim of African education was to produce men and women "who put the interests of the group above personal interest, whose hearts were warm towards the members of family and kinfolk" (Busia, 1964: 17). Teaching individuals to interact harmoniously with others in the community was a central concern of the traditional educational system. The Baganda and the Basoga, for example, emphasise obuntubulamu, which in Runyankole is put simply as obuntu--that is, qualities of decency and humanness--as the main aim of education. What Mulago (1969: 169) termed "vital participation" and Nyerere calls ujamaa is the "cornerstone" of Bantu traditional society. The educated person in traditional African life, as Majasan has written from West Africa (1975: 429), is one who is "philosophical in his outlook, human in his dealings with other people, cooperative as a member of society, refined and capable as an individual."

Another important theme which goes through African philosophy and religion is the idea of life as a cyclical or continuous process; one's family includes the unborn and the living as well as the dead. Reverence for the sanctity of life was always emphasised, as Busia (1964: 17) states: "There was always the awareness that human life was the greatest value and increase in the number of the members of the community, the greatest blessing the gods and spirits and the supernatural powers could confer on the living."

The curricula inherited from the preindependence period ignored values such as those referred to above, and instead emphasised the acquisition of knowledge for the purpose of passing examinations and obtaining certificates, diplomas or degrees which the socioeconomic system recognised and rewarded highly. This phenomenon which has variously been referred to as "qualification syndrome" or "diploma disease" is one of the greatest dilemmas in African education today. However, to ignore the family, clan, community and culture in African education is like watering a plant whose tap root has already been cut. Every effort should be directed toward the revival, preservation and further growth, development and refinement of traditional African values as curricular reforms are introduced.

In view of the foregoing considerations the immediate concern of the educational system to be encouraged, and indeed of all development agencies in Uganda, should be:

- to foster national unity and integration;

- to build a democratic society rooted in liberty, brotherhood, e-quality and justice, a society in which human rights are respected and guaranteed;

- to develop a society which is appreciative of and rooted in its different cultures but at the same time is innovative and oriented to the future;

- to build a self-reliant nation that should take its rightful place and play a dynamic and constructive role in the promotion of African unity, international understanding and world peace.

General Content

In order to promote the aims and values mentioned above, the curricula of the schools and nonformal education should recognise and respect the different circles of citizenship and loyalty surrounding the individual, and their interrelatedness. Education should lay stress not only on knowledge and information but also on learning skills, values and attitudes. While the basic learning needs of individuals will inevitably differ from one community to another, and in accordance with different age groups and occupations, the following elements are essential in the education of all citizens:

- positive attitudes towards and functional knowledge of social justice, community cooperation and the ethical values of integrity, interdependence and service to and with others;

- knowledge and skills for raising a family and managing a household (including child care, family health, sanitary food preparation and storage, and the making and repairing of clothing, furniture and tools), and for primary health care and recreation;

- knowledge and skills for effective civic participation;

- knowledge and skills to enable one to earn a living;

- a rational and scientific approach to the environment and problem-solving, and the capacity to apply such understandings in daily work and life;

- skills of communication;

- a personal philosophy and code of values giving meaning and guidance to life.

Action-Based Education

In the traditional African setting infants from about the age of three or four were integrated into the economic activities of the family. Youngsters looked after babies while older children gathered firewood or vegetables from the garden, or fetched water. Work was regarded as natural. Even today you can see a young Karamojong or Masai boy of eight or nine in charge of a herd of cattle whose capital value would startle many bank managers.

On the other hand, in schools work is usually assigned as punishment to those who come late or misbehave. Youths who have received formal schooling for seven years are still helpless and are considered too young to enter productively into the real world of work and toil. Those who are "fortunate" enough to continue with university education can grow into men and women while still playing the roles of onlookers and spectators in community and national affairs. Their meals are served to them in dining halls, their dishes are removed by paid servants and the weeds around their residence halls grow into bushes unless they are cut by porters. At school children are seldom allowed to make any significant decisions, not even to elect prefects, class monitors, or sports captains, and they seldom have any say in community activities. Their only social responsibility is to learn their lesson notes and pass examinations.

In a country like Uganda where about half of the population is composed of people below the age of fifteen, book learning divorced and completely separated from useful and productive work deprives the society of a large reservoir of would-be productive energies. School learning must be integrated with productive work much more thoroughly than it is.

The difficulty here is that the socioeconomic reward system is heavily weighted in favour of the individual with a certificate. Governments in Uganda have overtaxed coffee and cotton farmers in Uganda for decades to provide social amenities, not in rural areas where so many of the country's people live, but in towns. Thus tax monies have not been used to purchase hoes or tractors for villagers, but to provide additional amenities for townspeople, particularly those at the highest levels. Necessary now is a reevaluation of the purposes of education and a new recognition of how the people of Uganda can build a new nation together.

A Future Orientation

Images of the future influence the way people behave. People who believe the future is a chancy prospect, or already fixed like a motion picture--and therefore something that just unfolds--need not make much effort to influence or ask questions about what tomorrow will bring. They tend to regard calamities--whether these are the consequences of droughts or political tyranny--as inevitable or God given in the same way as the sunrise or the flow of water down a valley.

More optimistic people endeavour to influence the future, and it is important that our educational system in Uganda further this orientation. John Mbiti (1969: 159-64), writing about the concept of time among the members of a number of African societies, concludes that Africans are more Zamani or past oriented than future oriented, as follows: "As it happened in the past, it is happening now and it will do so forever. There is no end . . . People neither worry about the future nor build castles in the air." Clearly there is overstatement in this. But Mbiti's central message is significant all the same. A general past orientation is strong in African culture.

But if we continue to base our perspectives in Uganda on a rear view or myopic laissez faire image of the future, we will betray our children. The Uganda Education Commission (1963: 12) drew attention to this problem when commenting on the general education of primary school teachers in the country as follows: "Themselves educated in the past, (teachers) have to teach children in the present for a life in the future which is unknown."

Now it is neither possible nor desirable to equip the individual with all
the knowledge or intellectual baggage needed to board the ship into the
twenty-first century. Much of the knowledge that will be necessary then
has not yet even been produced. But one thing we do know is that individuals who will cope effectively in the future do not need to burden their
minds today with mere facts and information for mere examination certificate
purposes. Required are appropriate values, attitudes, habits and skills
that allow new combinations and see education as a process in inquiry. In
other words today more than ever our students need to _learn_ how to _learn_,
not learn how to pass examinations. Research into the problems and prospects of our country with reference to patterns of social life, mortality
and morbidity and cropping must be encouraged. Without research the practical decisions that will of necessity be made in the future will be far less
appropriate for the needs of the people than they should be.

STOP THE BRAIN DRAIN

One of the greatest resources of any country is in the brains of its trained
people. Countries like Switzerland, the banking capital of the world, and
Japan, one of the most technologically developed of all countries, have no
substantial actual resources of their own. They rely mainly on their human
resources and the ingenuity and resolve of their people working together.

After 1971 Uganda suffered a crippling outflow of its high level manpower to
other countries. Many men and women left in search of greener pastures or
to get away from the discomfort of severe shortages of essential commodities
and amenities, or because of the lack of certain fundamental freedoms. But
most of those who fled the country fled in order to save their lives. At
the end of the Mutukula War between Tanzania and Amin in April 1979 there
were 100 Ugandan university teachers at the University of Nairobi and
Kenyatta College, fifty at the University of Zambia in Lusaka and a similar
number at the University of Dar-es-Salaam and other universities in southern
Africa, to say nothing of doctors and other high level personnel in those
countries, the United States and the United Kingdom. Of a total of 728
established posts at Makerere University at the end of 1979, only 332 were
filled. The situation was more critical in certain faculties than in
others. In the Faculty of Medicine only forty-five of an establishment of
172 positions were filled, leaving twenty-four professorial, thirty-four
senior lecturer and sixty lecturer positions vacant. In the Faculty of
Sciences, only forty-six of 103 established positions were filled.

A Staff Development Programme was initiated in Uganda in 1962 in order to
promote the orderly East Africanisation of university staff. Of the many
graduate assistants who were subsequently sent abroad to pursue postgraduate
studies in various fields, however, many decided to stay abroad upon the
completion of their degrees, as did many members of staff who went to
conferences or short missions of various types. By now it is axiomatic that
no amount of mere expansion of the Development Programme will produce the
required results to arrest shortages of university staff, doctors, teachers
and other high level manpower, unless with the expansion of training in
Uganda and abroad there are definite concomitant and tangible steps taken
to stop the brain drain and to retrieve those who are already outside the
country. Preventing the brain drain is not merely a question of instituting
competitive salary structures and conditions of service, for we will never
be able to compete favourably with the United Kingdom, the United States or
even with our neighbour Kenya. Salaries are of course important, but more
important are the individuals concerned, and concrete steps must be taken to

reduce the insecurity of staff and to assure them unfettered freedom in their activities. It is an important responsibility of government and university authorities to convince all Ugandans outside the country that the institutions of Uganda are their institutions and that Uganda is their country, and that it is in their promises that the people of Uganda have invested so much.

Soon after the war university administrators at Makerere wrote to all Ugandans who previously had been on its Staff Development Programme to return to Uganda. The vice-chancellor and the academic registrar visited Nairobi and Lusaka and held meetings with Ugandans urging them to return to their homeland. That exercise had a great impact and many individuals returned, although some of them soon had to leave again for exile because of the political turmoil which soon followed. This kind of exercise, however, should be repeated by appropriate officials from time to time.

International agencies and persons from other countries are doing much for Uganda and will continue to do so. But they can never build our country for us. This we will have to do ourselves.

CONCLUSION

The social institutions of Uganda were left in disarray after the despotic and destructive misrule of the 1970s. In this paper we have examined questions of integration and national development in Uganda from the viewpoint of education. Education must be conceived not merely as schooling for young people alone but as _learning_ for the entire population. It must aim at promoting a heightened sense of being in the individual as a member of his family and community as well as of the country. Education should be community centred, taking the school to the community around it and the community into the school, and it must link theory with fact in the real world in a sense that corresponds with the best interests of national development. Problem-solving approaches must be promoted along with orientations that identify the possibilities of the future. Above all, education must be directed towards the promotion of national integration.

In order to be effective the institutional kinds of changes suggested here will require changes of heart and a spirit of give-and-take. The point is that the people of Uganda must come to understand that development is essential and _possible_ and that it is through them, by them and for them that it can and _should_ be brought about.

Not all readers will agree with all of the views expressed here. Some will argue that the ideals are utopian. Others will say that Uganda is a country badly torn by ethnic divisions and that the more urgent tasks of fighting poverty, disease and starvation preclude the encouragement now of participatory and democratic emphases. Some no doubt will argue that democracy, human rights and civil liberties can only be established after freedom is won through armed struggle. Others will contend that the emphases placed on indigenous cultural values is reminiscent of cultural relativism and a return to the _magimbo_ or regionalism or tribalism of the 1960s.

Such reservations are understandable, and perhaps it is overly optimistic to expect a young country like Uganda, hardly twenty years old, to attempt to attain national integration based on the principle of profound mutual respect and belief in equal opportunity. After all, even wealthy countries with well-established traditions of democracy continue to struggle with just such issues. National integration must be conceived as an urgent objective, however, and at the same time as an ongoing process and an ideal towards which always to strive. If there is no agreement on the means but there is unanimity on the development of a democratic society based on freedom, equality, brotherhood and justice, all is well, for we shall have a common goal towards which to strive.

REFERENCES

Busia, Kofi (1964). Purposeful Education. Mouton, The Hague.
Majasan, J. A. (1975). Traditional Education and Its Contribution to Modern Education. West African Journal of Education, XIX: 420-429.
Mbiti, John (1969). Eschatology. In K. A. Dickson and S. Ellingworth (Eds.), Biblical Revelation and African Beliefs. Butterworth, London.
Obote, A. M.(1970). The Common Man's Charter. Government Printers, Entebbe.
p'Bitek, Okot (1973). Africa's Cultural Revolution. Macmillan Books for Africa, Nairobi.
Uganda, Republic of, Education Commission (1963). Education in Uganda. Government Printers, Entebbe.

Health Services and Development
in Uganda

Stanley Scheyer and David Dunlop

Health and health services play an important role in socioeconomic
development because of the cumulative and mutually reinforcing manner in
which health improvements interact with development processes. This theory
underlies the rationale for the increasing emphasis given to "basic human
needs" by development planners in some developing countries, and it
recognises increasing evidence that simultaneous improvements in nutrition
and health, declines in fertility and increases in income are necessary
prerequisites (as well as being benefits) of overall socioeconomic development.

The situation in Uganda provides poignant evidence both of the strength of
health and development linkages and the importance that a national
development strategy must ultimately invest in health improvements. Uganda
is a unique case in this regard, because the developments in its health
services system and its people's health status during the past three decades
show evidence of cumulative and synergistic interaction of health and de-
velopment--firstly, in progressive advancement and then, since 1971, in
steady deterioration of social and economic well-being, culminating in the
war of 1978-79.

Before the turning point of Amin's takeover in 1971, Uganda's health status
and health system had reached an impressive level, given its means, having
been developed in parallel with national economic development strategy.
During Amin's regime, Ugandan society was subjected to repeated political
disruptions and economic policies which led to serious deterioration of
health and social services. By the beginning of the war in 1978, staffs and
budgets of health centres and hospitals were seriously depleted, drugs and
supplies were in short supply, and a nearly total breakdown of the health
services administration had occurred.   Public health problems which had
previously been all but eliminated from most of the country began to
reappear as a result of the social and economic decline.   An improvement in
the pattern and distribution of diseases was reversed. Moreover, the effect
of the war was to accelerate the reemergence of certain epidemic diseases in

---

*Editors' note: This article was first published in **Rural Africana**, 11
(Fall 1981): 37-57.

certain parts of the country, particularly cholera, malaria, measles and trypanosomiasis (sleeping sickness).

The discussion which follows will provide a theoretical and factual background to the state of health emergency which currently exists in Uganda. An examination of the dynamics of health improvements and development processes, both before and since 1971, will provide the necessary foundation for suggesting a strategy for rehabilitating the Ugandan health system and for assisting the government in that process. An understanding of the development context of health and health services is a necessary perspective from which to judge the resources which should be and can be developed to meet the health needs of the country.

HEALTH AND DEVELOPMENT PRIOR TO 1971

The Economy

Like in most sub-Saharan African countries, Uganda's economy is based on agriculture which in 1970 accounted for about half of the gross domestic product (GDP) and for 90 percent of all employment and income. Coffee, cotton and tea have been the main cash crops and have contributed a substantial share of the country's foreign exchange earnings which generally relied heavily on agricultural exports. Smallholder farmers are an important segment of the economically active population (about 20 percent of the total) and are engaged both in subsistence farming and in cash crop production (agriculture production was about evenly divided between subsistence and monetary sectors in 1970).

Until 1971 the monetary economy had been steadily growing so that about 70 percent of the GDP originated in that sector (about half of which was industrial and service output). The rate of growth of the GDP, which fluctuated over the years according to world prices for coffee and cotton, averaged 4.2 percent per year during 1954-1965 and 4.8 percent per year during 1966-1970.

Overall development of Uganda was keyed to increasing agricultural output because the modern industrial sector was dominated by agricultural processing industries such as coffee curing, cotton ginning, textile production and the processing of cooking oils, sugar and tea.

Attempts were made during the 1960s to diversify agricultural production away from the primary crops of coffee and cotton toward tea, tobacco and sugar production. During the Second Plan period, tea production expanded rapidly, primarily due to the successful introduction of smallholder tea programmes in the western highland areas. During the Third Plan period, the tea programme, as well as new projects in tobacco and sugar, were expected to result in rapid output increases. In addition, substantial efforts were to be made to increase food and livestock production. A strong commitment to rural development was made in the Third Five-Year Plan, not only in terms of increasing total output but also in terms of improving the distribution of social amenities and the standard of living in rural areas.

Ugandan Development Policy Related to Health

The role of health in Uganda's development was given high priority in the 1960s. This was reflected in the country's planning strategies, Work for

Progress (1966-71) and Plan III (1971-76). During the second development
period (1966-71), the development strategy "aimed to change the structure of
the economy so as to lessen its dependence on the existing export crops."
The campaign to develop the economy had "three spearheads: (1) agricultural
development, (2) industrialisation and (3) expansion and improvement of
education and health services."

The government's concern for the third "spearhead"--the improvement of
education and health services--was manifested during the 1966-71 plan by a
combined expenditure of USh 380.6 million which comprised approximately 18
percent of all development expenditures during the period with health
receiving slightly more than half of the total (USh 191.3 million).

During the third five-year planning period (1971-72 to 1975/76), the
government's concern for health continued, although its priority, in terms
of the proportion of the total development expenditures, declined from about
9.1 percent to 5.7 percent. The absolute expenditure was estimated to have
remained constant (USh 183.5 million); however, with inflation taken into
consideration, this figure represented only 80 percent of the Second Plan's
expenditure on health services. This decline in total expenditures can be
explained by a shift in the nature of expenditures: the construction of
twenty-three hundred-bed hospitals was targeted during the second development plan, while improvement of rural health facilities such as health
centres and training more health workers was the target ot the Third Plan.
In addition, a substantial increase was projected for two preventive health
programmes: water supplies (to a level of USh 159.8 million) and population
control (a nominal USh 1.0 million allocated from government funds).

The development of rural areas clearly had high priority during Plan III.
By its statements in the Plan, the government recognised that (1) its
resource endownment required the development of rural areas and (2) rural
living conditions, including health services, had to be improved in order to
increase agricultural production and to minimise the rate of rural urban
migration.

Uganda's Financial Commitment to Health Services

Uganda maintained a fairly large development commitment to health services
for some time. From the mid-1930s to 1970, the central government consistently allocated a minimum of 6.5 percent of the total recurrent and capital
budget to health services during years of minor capital improvements. In
addition to this central government commitment, local government expenditures on health increased substantially in later years. Since 1947 the
percentage of total district administration expenditures allocated to health
has risen from approximately 3.5 percent to nearly 20 percent.

The first upward shift (1956-57) was related directly to the implementation
of the so-called Frazer Report, one of whose main recommendations was the
improvement of rural health services. The second major shift occurred near
the time of independence, 9 October 1962; the major cost increase at that
time was due to shifts in power and political relationships between the
central and various local governments. Finally, the launching of the Second
Five-Year Plan in 1966-67 gave emphasis to the expansion of health services.
This expansion occurred not only in hospital facilities but also in rural
health facilities such as health centres and dispensaries. The combined
expenditures of local governments on health services increased from USh 22
million in 1965 to USh 35 million in 1970, in spite of a large decline in

expenditures recorded in Buganda District. As a share of total local government expenditures, health services increased during this period from 8
percent in 1966 to approximately 20 percent in 1970.

Finally, it is important to point out that approximately 75 to 80 percent of
expenditures on health services in Uganda have been directed toward curative
as opposed to preventive services.

The Health Service System in Uganda

The curative health service system that had developed in Uganda by 1971 was
characterised by a number of different types of health facilities, as well
as several administrative structures through which services are delivered.
The government provided curative services, without charge, in hospitals,
health centres, dispensaries, subdispensaries, maternity centres and aid
posts. The Catholic and Protestant Church Medical Bureaus also provided
curative health services, for a small fee, through hospitals, subdispensaries and maternity centres. Curative health facilities were also operated
by large commercial firms for employees and their families. The type of
facility maintained by the firm was determined primarily by legal requirement: firms employing more than 1000 persons had to have a hospital, whereas smaller firms could either operate a dispensary or contract with a private physician for service as required. The army and prisons also offered
curative health services to their specialised populations through dispensaries and, in the case of the army, a hospital. Finally, there were a
number of private practitioners in the larger cities and towns who provided
a range of curative services to those willing to pay.

Government health facilities were integrated in such a way that an individual could be referred to a facility providing more intensive care or
treatment than that offered by the facility originally attended. It was
theoretically possible for an individual who initially attended a weekly
outpatient clinic in a rural aid post to eventually receive treatment at
Mulago Hospital in Kampala, the country's national referral, teaching and
research hospital. In addition, private physicians, mission facilities and
other population-specific facilities could refer individuals to government
facilities for certain specialised services. The most common referral
relationship, however, existed between rural government health facilities
and government district hospitals.

Preventive health services in Uganda were usually provided by local govern-
ments--district administrations, municipalities and townships. Environmental health services such as sanitation, waste disposal, vector control and
clean water supplies were administered by special health manpower headed by
the health inspector. Other preventive services, such as antenatal clinics,
young child clinics and immunisations, were usually delivered through weekly
clinics held at local health facilities. The central government also supported an immunisation team which travelled throughout the country and
conducted daily immunisation clinics. In one district the preventive
services of static facilities were supplemented by a mobile health team
which brought immunisation, young child, antenatal and health education
services to thirty different locations in the area one day each month.

Health Status

At the outset of Plan III in 1971, Uganda enjoyed a level of health services

far superior to many other developing countries. With a total of well over
four hundred health units (ranging from rural subdispensaries to large
reference hospitals) dispersed all over the country, there was some form of
medical centre within a reasonable distance of every household, and the
records showed that a rapidly increasing number of people did actually make
use of these facilities. The basic health services were provided free to
all. A number of once major health scourges such as smallpox, sleeping
sickness, meningitis and certain venereal diseases had been reduced to only
occasional incidence, while others such as tuberculosis, poliomylitis, river
blindness and leprosy were under control. The preliminary analysis of the
1969 Census revealed that the infant mortality rate may have fallen by as
much as 25 to 30 percent between 1959 and 1969. Although the overall infant
mortality stoodin the neighbourhood of 120 per thousand live births, in
certain areas this rate was reduced below one hundred. The Census also
revealed that overall life expectancy at birth was appreciably higher than
forty years, and as high as forty-six years in some regions of the country.
Although precise quantitative comparisons were difficult to make, these
indicators pointed to considerably improved health conditions compared to
those of a decade or so earlier.

HEALTH AND DEVELOPMENT SINCE 1971

The Economy

While the Ugandan economy was still expanding in early 1970, virtually all
economic indicators showed a downward trend from that point onwards, with
some acceleration downward after 1973 when all Asians, who comprised the
majority of traders and merchants in urban centres, were expelled from the
country. Government figures showed that the total GDP per capita in 1966
prices declined from USh 745 in 1970 to USh 672 in 1974, an average annual
decline of 2.7 percent. From the mid-1970s, GDP data became increasingly
unreliable and were not even calculated after 1976-77.

Indicators of industrial, export and financial activity, however, all show
evidence of a steady contraction of activity in the organised, legal and
monetary sector of the overall economy. Real investment fell sharply,
inflation surged and production declines accelerated in the modern sector
particularly, as imports decreased. As farmers turned increasingly to
subsistence agriculture for essential food crops, production of cash crops
dropped and exports declined correspondingly. From 1974 to 1978, according
to World Bank estimates, both exports and imports declined in real terms by
more than 40 percent. Whereas Uganda in 1970 enjoyed one of the highest
per capita incomes in East Africa, by 1978 it had experienced a real decline
estimated by the World Bank at about 25 percent.

The government's attempt to exercise greater and greater control over the
economy during this period of contraction exacerbated inflation, discouraged
investment and participation in the modern sector and caused a rapid surge
of economic transactions occurring in the nonformal sector. Magendo (black
market activities) became an increasingly important source of income for
people whose regular wages could buy only a fraction of their basic
consumption needs. Production of domestic manufactured goods declined substantially from 1970 to 1978, with some essential consumer goods experiencing near total elimination of output: as a percentage of 1970 production, 1978 production of soap was 9 percent; 1978 production of cooking oil
was 11 percent; and 1978 production of blankets was 14 percent. Imported
consumer goods, when available in 1978, were prohibitively expensive to all

but the very rich. Production of some cash crops experienced similar output reductions: as a percentage of 1970 output, 1978 production of sugar was 8 percent; and 1978 production of cotton was 15 percent. Subsistence agriculture increased as a proportion of total output as people returned to their land to produce only what they themselves could consume or needed.

Health Services Development During the 1970s

At the beginning of the decade, the government was in the midst of expanding its already extensive network of hospitals and health centres. At the time Plan III was published, the targets of the Second Plan had only been partly achieved; of the planned addition of twenty-three hundred-bed rural hospitals, only eleven had been completed (the rest were scheduled for completion by the end of 1971); of the original target 327 rural health centres, few were completed even though the target had been revised downward to only thirty-six. Including the 1200 beds to be added from the completion of rural hospitals, Plan III established a target of 3400 additional beds during the plan period, mostly in district and urban hospitals. Important additional objectives of Plan III were the assumption of direct responsibilities for district medical administration (of rural health centres and local administrations) and significant expansion of training capacity of various types of health manpower.

The political and economic policies introduced by the Amin regime, however, caused serious disruption of plans in all ministries, not the least of them in health. By mid-1974 only 1183 hospital beds had been added in government hospitals in the four years since 1970. Shortages of foreign exchange led to reductions in the availability of supplies and equipment, and a steady deterioration in physical facilities as lack of spare parts inhibited proper maintenance. The effects, as well as budgetary cutbacks, led to staff attrition, as trained medical personnel of all types left the country for employment elsewhere. This development was accelerated by the expulsion of Asians in 1973 which was followed by the departure of many expatriate physicians and technicians. By 1975 the importation of drugs and medical supplies had slowed to a trickle, and the administrations and general management of government health facilities were becoming increasingly hampered by a host of fiscal, personnel and logistical difficulties.

In sum, instead of expanding its health services or even maintaining the existing network of services, the government services deteriorated. In many areas of the country the partially staffed and faltering facilities were abandoned completely during the final days of the war, and the frenzy of looting which followed eliminated whatever was left of the drugs, supplies and equipment. The government health services were thus totally unable to respond to the increasingly critical health problems of the people which had been brought on by the dissolution of the previous structure of the economy and the society.

Health Status During the 1970s

The deterioration of the health status of Uganda's people that occurred during the 1970s (and which is discussed in detail in the next section) was partly related to the decline in available services and drugs and partly to the abrupt appearance of the particularly adverse social and economic conditions that are the underlying causes of ill health. In regard to decreasing availability of health services, the almost total breakdown of immunisation and MCH services had far more serious impact on the population than the decline in general diagnostic and treatment services. In terms of the effects of the breakdown of the economy and of social services and amenities, some of the dynamic processes which led to greater public health problems were as follows:

> In urban areas, social services and amenities were gradually eliminated or drastically reduced; waste and sewage disposal services functioned poorly or not at all; the water system deteriorated from lack of maintenance; the resulting unsanitary conditions and unsafe drinking water led to an increase in waterborne and fecal-borne gastrointestinal diseases.

> In rural areas, immigration from the towns and cities put pressure on the capacity of small farmers to feed extended families which were growing rapidly; malnutrition and related diseases increased, particularly among low-income families.

> Almost 80 percent of all hand-pump-operated boreholes were out of operation by 1979 due to lack of maintenance; thus, rural families suffered increased incidence of waterborne diseases when forced to use polluted sources of drinking water.

> Steady and substantial declines in per capita income associated with increased unemployment led to increased crime and psychosocial disorders.

> Lower standards of living made it increasingly difficult for families to buy the food and shelter fundamental to maintaining physical well-being.

In terms of health status, the years of Amin's regime have caused the kinds and incidences of diseases that were characteristic of the Uganda of thirty years ago. Reversing such a rapid (and still continuing) decline in health status will be a considerable task--one that will involve far more than the rehabilitation of the relatively intact (and extensive) physical infrastructure of medical care facilities throughout the country. A return to health status of 1970 will require the alleviation of that complex of social and economic ills that underlie the current cuases of poor health. Curing these ills requires an overall strategy and plan for the long-term socioeconomic development of the country.

HEALTH SERVICES IN THE 1970S

At the beginning of the decade, Uganda's health services delivery system had developed far beyond the level reached by other developing countries at an equivalent stage of economic development. A former Minister of Health described the situation as follows:

> The country has inherited a fine medical system. There was a good foundation of forty-eight government hospitals, twenty-eight mission hospitals, one hundred and fifty health centres (small units with about thirty beds each) and three hundred dispensaries. The government hospitals were administered in British fashion. Treatment was free. Doctors could, however, set aside part of their time and some of their beds for private practice. The mission hospitals levied a small charge; the government defrayed their running costs. At the time of the coup, these institutions were staffed by experienced teams of doctors, nurses and paramedical staff. By 1974 Uganda's excellent medical infrastructure was in a steep decline (Kyemba, 1977: 129).

As in other sectors of the economy and society, the Amin regime led to a degenerative cycle in the health sector in which available resources contracted while the demands on the system mushroomed. Critically needed health manpower fled the country, revenues and expenditures needed to maintain the system stagnated, and facilities deteriorated from neglect. The sequences of events which most affected the health system were as follows:

After eighteen months in power, Amin announced that all Asians would be expelled from Uganda. When the order became effective in November of 1972, Uganda had lost what had been an important base of the economy and a large segment of the professional and technical class. The social consequences of the economic chaos which ensued led to the departure of virtually all expatriate professionals, including doctors. During 1973 the departure of perhaps half of the some thousand physicians in the country created, needless to say, serious problems in the health care delivery system, particularly in mission hospitals which lost the most doctors. In addition, for virtually the entire calendar year 1974, Amin did not appoint a Minister of Health after Dr. Justin Gesa resigned at the end of 1973. Attempts were made by the Ministry of Health to remedy the doctor shortage by appealing to other countries for help; the Russians sent twenty physicians, and the Egyptians sent thirty-six physicians, seven dentists and one pharmacist. Nevertheless, the government health services were tremendously overburdened with demand for services--demand which could not be, and increasingly was not, met.

When Amin placed a ban on private practice of medicine in late 1974, the situation was made still worse, and even more physicians left the country, even though the ban was eased after several weeks by allowing private practice by those who held no government employment. After several years all but a few of the Egyptian and Russian doctors had left.

Immediately preceding the doctor shortage was a dramatic increase in outpatient and inpatient numbers at government hospitals. From 1971-72 to 1972-73, the number of admissions at government hospitals increased 2.5 times, and the average number of cases treated per person per year rose from 2.08 to 2.63. The opening of a dozen new hospitals combined with a 15 percent drop in admissions to voluntary hospitals was an important factor underlying this increase. However, with the continuous decline in the number of physicians, staffing hospitals and clinics, the numbers visiting hospitals plummeted. Admissions at voluntary hospitals declined from the 1971-72 high of 106,000 to a low of 64,000 in 1975-76. For government hospitals the high patient totals of 1972-73 (almost 28 million cases seen) had dropped to half that two years later (see Table 1).

In summary, the current delivery capacity of the Uganda health care system is roughly half of what it was at the beginning of the decade--equal to what it was in the early 1960s. Just as significant in this reduction of capacity and the shortage in trained manpower, however, is the drastic reduction in the fiscal and physical resources possessed by the system. Following the late 1960s, when the real resources applied for recurrent health expenditure had almost doubled (because staffing and bed capacity also almost doubled), the last decade has seen the real purchasing power of the health budget dwindle to 6 percent of what it was in 1968-69 (see Table 2).

Health Manpower

In 1969 there were approximately 17,700 persons employed in Uganda providing

TABLE 1:   Utilization of Governmental Health Facilities

Year	Estimated Total Population (000)[b]	Total Number of Cases (000)	Total No. of New Outpatient Cases (000)	Total No. of Out- patient Re- attendances (000)	Total No. Inpatient Admissions (000)	Estimated Average No. of Cases Per Person Per Year
1951	5,322.0	4,873.0	2,329.0	2,422.0	122.0	0.92
1955	5,874.0	5,459.7	2,732.3	2,597.1	130.3	0.93
1960[a]	6,573.0	7,784.8	4,335.2	3,245.4	204.2	1.18
1965/ 66	8,221.0	13,083.9	7,178.6	5,658.6	246.7	1.59
1968/ 69	9,191.0	17,826.5	9,537.3	7,884.0	405.2	1.94
1971/ 72	10,292.0	21,497.9	11,569.2	9,543.9	384.8	2.08
1972/ 73	10,634.0	27,990.9	14,696.3	12,345.0	949.6	2.63
1973/ 74	10,991.0	13,773.7	7,000.7	5,985.0	788.0	1.25
1974/ 75	11,354.0	14,538.7	7,180.3	7,007.3	351.1	1.28
1975/ 76	11,728.0	19,049.0	10,485.8	8,116.0	447.2	1.62
1976/ 77	12,115.0	18,361.1	10,357.3	7,551.7	452.1	1.52

*Source: Republic of Uganda, Ministry of Health, Annual Reports and Statis-
tical Records (Government Printers, Entebbe), selected years.
[a]The figures shown for 1960 are estimated from the data reported for the
first six months of the year.   In 1960 the government changed from a calendar to a fiscal reporting year.
[b]Total population estimates were derived from estimated rates of population
growth between censuses.

**TABLE 2: Central Government Recurrent Expenditures on Health
Services by the Ministry of Health**

Year		Amount in Shillings (million) (current prices)	Amount in Shillings (million) (constant prices)[a]
1959	Actual expenditure	52.5	53.8
1963-64	"	52.6	48.7
1968-69	"	118.4	92.5
1969-70	"	103.6	73.0
1970-71	"	115.9	73.8
1973-74	"	119.9	34.3
1978-79	Approved expenditure	327.1	14.8
1979-80	"	287.2	5.7

[a]Constant prices.   Deflated by implicit GOP deflator with 1960 = 100 and
adjusted by low income Kampala index.   For the recent period prices are
rising daily, and the figures are only shown to indicate trends.

health and medical care services in all delivery systems (Dunlop, 1973). The government was employing approximately 15,500 (the Ministry of Health establishment was 3954 in 1968-69) with the remaining employed by mission and private facilities and pharmacies. Further, approximately 3800 employees in other sectors and industries were employed as a consequence of the derived demand for health care services. A large proportion of that number were employed in the construction industry which was involved in the construction of twenty-three rural hospitals and many rural facilities at that time. The figure on total employment in the health sector today is unavailable, but there are some data on trends in the supply of skilled health manpower which provide an indication of the present situation.

In Table 3 the number of registered health manpower in Uganda is presented for the period 1951 to 1979. As the data show there was a continual increase in the number of physicians, dentists, midwives, nurses and pharmacists through 1968. Further, the Third Five-Year Plan, 1971-1976, addressed the health manpower issue in light of the expanding number of hospitals and rural facilities and made a number of recommendations to expand the existing training schools and build new ones to increase output (see Table 4 which shows the envisioned expanded training programme as of 1969). Virtually every cadre of staff from physicians, medical assistants, various levels of nurses and midwives, assistant health visitors, public health dental assistants to medical records officers, were to be expanded during the planning period through expansion of existing or creation of new training schools in order to staff the rapidly expanding hospital and rural health facilities. However, as can be seen in Table 3, by 1978 the number of doctors registered or licensed in the country had declined to a level approximating 60 percent of the earlier levels. The decline in the number of dentists and pharmacists also registered a significant decline. Only the nurse and midwife cadres did not register a significant decline. Given the fact that sizable training programmes were operating in all cadres at the outset of the period, the substantial declines in certain cadres and no increase in the female-dominated cadres of midwives and nurses is even more significant.

TABLE 3: Medical Manpower Registered to Practise in Uganda

| Year | Doctors | | | Dentists | Midwives[a] | Nurses[b] | Pharmacists |
	Registered	Licensed	Total				
1951	151	81	232	10	732		
1960-61	476	52	528	18	1060	410	61
1961-62	479	73	552	28	1156	1354[c]	72
1962-63	504	80	584	22	1290	1557	84
1963-64	538	113	651	28	1430	1748	95
1964-65	588	140	728	31	1565	2271	85
1965-66	642	171	813	39	1911	2682	61
1966-67	727	214	941	40	2199	3040	104
1967-68	797	181	978	42	2551	3277	116
1979	508	66	574	24	2404	3532	15

*Source: Republic of Uganda, _Statistical Abstract_ (Government Printers, Entebbe), selected years.
[a]A new ordinance for the registration of midwives was initiated in 1958. As a result the series is discontinuous from that date.
[b]State registered nurses only.
[c]Includes state registered nurses, enrolled nurses and male nurses.

TABLE 4:   Planned Expansion in Health Care Training

Category of Staff	Number Available (1969-end)	Additional Output from Existing Local Training Facilities at Current Rates (1970-1976 inclusive)	Requirements (1976-end)	Indicated Shortage (1976-end)[b]
Medical officers and specialists	588	335	1225	420
Dental surgeons	31	-	60	30
Medical assistants	407	350	900	285
Registered nurses[a]	473	540	1100	180
Registered midwives	183	250	na	na
Registered mental nurses	25	75	140	45
Enrolled nurses[a]	1015	1440	2970	720
Enrolled midwives	955	1720	2060	40
Enrolled mental nurses	36	110	235	95
Health visitors	19	-	45	30
Assistant health visitors	42	280	880	565
Health inspectors	115	130	470	250
Health assistants	474	250	1595	965
Public health dental assistants	5	90	175	85
Pharmacists	51	-	115	70
Entomologists	3	na	5	na
Medical social workers	-	25	25	-
Psychiatric social workers	2	5	5	-
Health education specialists	-	-	20	20
Dispensers	120	125	225	-
Laboratory technicians	18	35	140	90
Radiographers	46	75	200	90
Physiotherapists	21	-	30	75
Anaesthetic assistants	49	55	235	140
Orthopaedic assistants	44	80	120	-
Dental technicians	12	20	15	-
Occupational therapists	4	-	25	25
Entomological field assistants/officers	11	15	35	15
Medical records officers	2	na	60	60
Health staff tutors	33	35	115	60

*Source: Uganda (1972). All figures in vertical columns are rounded to the nearest five.
[a]Including nurse-midwives.
[b]With allowance for attrition.

The declines in critical cadres have largely been due to the facts that (1) in 1973 President Amin expelled all Asians and (2) many people suspected of views antithetical to the regime were killed and many others who feared for their lives emigrated to Kenya, Tanzania, the United Kingdom and other places. At the present time there are perhaps forty Ugandan physicians occupying academic posts in Nairobi, and a number reside in Lusaka, Zambia. While there have been a number of appeals to them to return home, many have remained at their present posts for many reasons, including (1) continued insecurity for physicians (several have been killed by certain extremists groups operating in the country in the last six months); (2) salaries are too low in Uganda, given alternative salaries and the rate of inflation in Uganda; (3) housing is unavailable; (4) other complementary staff, materials, drugs, supplies and equipment are unavailable or in short supply; or (5) personal concern for family living, children's education or spouse's employment. Similar reasons exist for the non-return of other cadres of Ugandan personnel. The Ministry of Planning and Economic Development has recently established a Manpower Planning Division which is expected to deal with many of the general problems facing the country in recruiting its nationals back to the country.

Health Training Institutes

As can be ascertained from Table 5, the number of training programmes, institutions and courses is considerable. The exact status of all of these courses and programmes is mixed, with many operating at less than full capacity, without tutors, or with many other problems including lack of housing, food, training materials or transport. The training schools for medical assistants, for assistant health visitors and for health inspectors have been particularly hard hit. AMREF has proposed to rehabilitate and redesign the curriculum of the health inspectors' school at Mbale. DANIDA has indicated its willingness to assist the Dental School. CARE discussed its concern about the assistant health visitor training schools in light of a primary health care strategy. However, its plans are sketchy at present. Given that the medical assistants still comprise the primary diagnostic and

TABLE 5:   **Selected Health Training Institutions in Uganda, 1977**

Manpower Cadre	Number	Location	Potential Output/Yr	Control Govt	Control Mission
Doctors	1	Mulago/Makerere	100-120	1	0
Medical assistants	2	Fort Portal, Mbale	120-150	2	0
Registered nurses	1	Mulago	45	1	0
Enrolled nurses and midwives	15	Jinja, Masaka, Gulu, Lira, Mbarara, Arua Soroti, Kabale, Nsambya, Rubaga, Mengo, Virika, Kamuli, Kalongo, Ngora	320 nurses 300 m/wives	8	7
Assistant health visitors	6	Entebbe, Mbarara, Arua, Mulago, Gulu, Jinja	100	6	0
Health inspectors	1	Mbale	150	1	0

*Source: Uganda (1977).
*Note: There are a number of other health manpower training courses which have been discussed in previous planning documents and which may have operated for various periods. The courses include ones for health manpower trainers (tutors), anaesthetic assistants, lab technicians, radiographers, dispensers, pharmacists, health and hospital administrators, social workers, occupational therapists, orthopaedic assistants and psychiatric workers.

medical care treatment cadre, particularly in rural facilities, a careful
analysis of the rehabilitation problems faced by the two training schools is
critical. Subsequent analysis of the curriculum, practical training and
supervision is also required.

As if budget cutbacks and staff shortages were not enough of a burden,
Uganda's hospitals have been beset by water shortage (a chronic problem in
some urban areas since 1974) and periodic lack of food and critical supplies. Even before the war, Uganda's health care system had been reduced to
a state where the "care" delivered may have been worse than no care at all.
Again in the words of the former health member, Henry Kyemba: "By 1974
there was not enough water for cleaning floors, for washing, for sterili-
sing, for bathing or for flushing toilets. We had to hire tankers (we later
bought our own) to bring water to Mulago Hospital from standpipes near Lake
Victoria. On more than one occasion, we seriously thought of closing the
hospital for fear of infection" (Kyemba, 1977: 130). Since liberation from
Amin in April 1979 the situation in Uganda's hospitals and clinics has, if
anything, become worse.

NATIONAL HEALTH POLICY AND FUTURE OPTIONS

The government of Uganda faces a number of critical decisions as to the
future development of its health sector. The government's immediate response in the ten months following liberation from the Amin regime has been
to seek immediate relief assistance from a number of external donors in the
form of drugs, vaccines and food. In the past few months the process of
assessing the current status of facilities, manpower, equipment, supplies
and needs has begun both within the Ministry of Health and the Ministry of
Local Administrations.

Preliminary health budgets for both national and district administration
have been drawn up. The crisis nature of getting the ministries back functioning, of developing new leadership and of coping with the enormous constraints under which they are operating has left little time for officials
to rethink the future direction of health policy and the strategic allocation of scarce resources. Perhaps more importantly, the Ugandan government to date has not been able to formulate a strategic coordinated plan for
external donor assistance in the health sector.

The statement of economic and social policy released by the United National
Liberation Front (UNLF) does not mention health (UNLF, 1979). The government's "White Paper" (Uganda, 1979), responding to the report of the
Commonwealth Team of Experts, merely notes that the serious health needs of
the devastated areas of Masaka and Mbarara had not been addressed by the
report. In all documents itemising the health sector needs of the
country, be they ministry-specific or institution-specific, the orientation
is toward "lists of requirements" to replace what was broken, lost or stolen
during the past ten years.

The exclusive focus on material needs of the health care delivery system
(which is evident in all discussions with officials, managers and providers)
is based on an assumption (a memory of the 1960s) that the physical infrastructure and capacity of the health care delivery system remains as it was
in 1971. However, the evidence is clear that there has been a significant
shift—by several orders of magnitude—in both the needs faced by the health
system and the resources that are now available to it. The reversal of the
upward trend in health status has altered the pattern of diseases and re-

quires a different kind of response than the health system was designed (in the 1960s) to deliver. Moreover, the real and substantial decline in the standard of living within Uganda has impoverished the health sector.

During the decade the country experienced a roughly 25 percent drop in per capita income and roughly 1200 percent increase in consumer prices. Even if one assumes that health will continue to be allocated the same share of the government budget as in the 1960s, and that the government budget remains an equivalent share of national income (both dubious assumptions), it seems clear that the real purchasing power of the government health budget is only a fraction (probably 10-20 percent) of what it was in 1971. Thus, even if the government could obtain donor assistance to rehabilitate completely its physical health infrastructure to what it was in 1971, government fiscal capacity would be unable to sustain the operating costs of more than a part of it. In short, the government can no longer afford to give the public the kind, quality or amount of free health care that it could offer in the 1960s, and if it attempts to do so it may do so at the measures that would be highly cost-effective in improving previously prevented (but now resurgent) public health problems. It is this predicament of the government's health care delivery system that points to the priority need for an early and concerted effort to examine national health policies in the context of needs, available resources and the overall development strategy of the government.

During the 1960s, prior to the Amin regime, the Ugandan government developed, and effectively utilised, policy planning mechanisms for health which were successful in designing national health programmes which met the particular health problems facing the country and also were affordable within the development context. Significant achievements were the use of curative care facilities in rural areas in establishing a broad campaign for community-oriented, public health measures emphasising immunisations, MCH and child care, and sanitation.

At the time Amin took power, the Ugandan government was in the last states of completing construction of twenty-three district hospitals, with one hundred beds each (implemented by the Ministry of Health), and was in the early stages of an upgrading and expansion of the rural health care delivery systems. During the Amin years the operation of the twenty-three new hospitals was hampered by inadequate operating budgets which led to neglect and decline of the technical capacity the hospitals had had; the planned development of the rural health delivery systems was never implemented. Planning ceased to be a function either in the Ministry of Health or in the Ministry of Local Administrations, and all efforts had to be focused on solving immediate shortages and difficulties.

The need to reestablish national health policy planning mechanisms has been quite evident during the months since liberation when coordination of donor assistance with government policies has been lacking, and when policies of the government themselves have been less than clear--at least in health. An evident need is to coordinate better the activities of the Ministry of Health which administers the rural health care delivery system; each has launched independent efforts to gather roughly the same kinds of information about facilities and personnel as they stand following the war. Moreover, the Ministry of Health recently experienced an internal policy debate over a major expenditure of foreign exchange on new capital equipment. The argument made against the purchase (which was executed) was that existing capital infrastructure will remain--in its current deteriorated condition--a liability to the recurrent budget (reduced effectiveness at constant opera-

ting--mostly personnel--costs) while the new equipment would add a liability
to the recurrent budget (questionable effectiveness of added or diverted
personnel). Donors who are interested in the effective utilisation of
assistance cannot afford to be indifferent to the policy, management and
budgetary issues raised--apparently in ad hoc fashion--by these kinds of
decisions made in the absence of any planning.

As has been well documented in the previous section, the number of government health facility visits per capita dropped since the early 1970s from
2.50 to around 1.50 in 1976-77, just before the last of Amin's atrocities
and the subsequent war of liberation. After the war the number of visits
per capita has declined even more due to a lack of drugs, transport, water
and, to a lesser extent, staff.

At present the government has not taken any firm policy position with respect to the extent of rehabilitation of the system developed in the past,
but normalising conditions and future political considerations suggest additional resources will be allocated to rebuild the system. Recently the
government has demonstrated its interest in rebuilding the system; newspaper
stories have appeared about the purchase of vehicles, other equipment and
supplies, and about the opening of previously closed hospitals and other
rural facilities (see Uganda _Times_, 1980). An important aspect of the
present issues facing the government are the budgetary implications of a
fully established health care system.

While it is difficult to estimate the capital recurrent costs precisely, it
is feasible to define the order of magnitude. The Ministry of Health has
estimated that it would require an initial capital rehabilitation of USh
773.7 million (USh 615.3 million in foreign exchange). The Ministry of
Local Administrations, in their memo to DANIDA, has detailed an additional
USh 47 million, not counting a backlog of unfinished rural health facility
construction and a totally depleted set of medical stores. Mulago Hospital
and Makerere Medical School had produced similar lists.

Once the entire government health system has been rehabilitated, not counting the envisioned additional rural facilities not constructed earlier, the
recurrent costs to both the central and district governments will rise
considerably. The question of how much recurrent cost would rise was addressed in the following way. Firstly, the question was posed as follows:
"What would have been the collective government of Uganda expenditures in
1979 if the health care system, as functioning in 1968-69, was still in
existence?" This question can be answered in at least three ways, depending
upon which alternative programme objective one may wish to attain.

There were three alternatives considered (summarised in Table 6). The first
was to equalise the constant shilling expenditure per visit in 1979 to the
level in 1968-69. There was no adjustment in this estimate for differential
utilisation rates in existence in 1968-69 compared to the assumed rate for
1979. In 1968-69 the combined (central and local) governments in Uganda
spent about USh 6.78 per visit in 1960, whereas the estimated expenditure
per visit in 1979 was about USh 1.16 (1960). (Assuming a 1979 system
utilisation rate of 12 million visits which was similar to 1973-74--a period
of civil and political disturbance) In order to retain the previous level
of expenditure existing in 1968-69, it would be necessary to increase total
expenditures in 1979 by 5.84 times what they actually were (6.78 divided by
1.16 equals 5.84), or to USh 2440 million.

The second possible alternative was to calculate the size of budget needed

TABLE 6:   Estimates of Government Recurrent and Capital Expenditures to Regain Previous Government Health Care System as of 1968-69

Year	Government Recurrent Expenditure MOH & Local Admin. Current Shs (millions)	Estimated Government Recurrent Expenditure MOH & Local Admin. Est. Constant 1960 Shs (millions)	Recurrent Per Capita Expenditure in Current Shs	Estimated Recurrent Per Capita Exp. in Constant 1960 Shs	Estimated Expenditure Per Visit in Constant Shs[a]
1968-69	149.9	117.1	15.8	12.3	6.78
1979	417.6 E	13.9	31.6	1.1	1.16 E[b]

*1979 Estimates - Recurrent
A. Equal per capita   2440.0   (5.84 fold increase over actual)
B. Equal per capita   4670.0   (11.20 fold increase over actual)
C. Equal per visit ad-
        just for utilisation   5200.0   (12.45 fold increase over actual)
Capital rehabilitation
1979   773.7[c]

[a]Visit = total number of new and reattendance outpatients plus inpatient admissions in government health facilities
[b]Estimated number of visits is assumed to equal 12 million which is based on previous low attendances in 1973-74 due to civil strife, the war of liberation and shortages of drugs and other essentials.
[c]Per memorandum from MOH. This figure requires 615.3 million Shs of foreign exchange.

to equalise the per capita recurrent health expenditure level for 1979 to that level prevailing in 1968-69. This objective takes into consideration the dynamics of population growth on social and human service programmes. In 1968-69 the expenditure per capita was about USh 1.1 (1960 = 100). Thus, to equalise 1979 per capita expenditures to 1968-69 levels would require an expenditure in 1979 (current prices) 11.2 times larger than it actually was, or approximately equal to USh 4.670 million.

The third plausible objective considered was that of equalising the expenditure per visit and the utilisation rate per capita that was in existence in 1968-69 (thus also taking into consideration population growth). In this case, the system in 1979 was assumed to have a total number of cases around 12 million which approximated 0.91 visits per capita. In 1968-69 the number of visits per capita was 2.13 times as large (1.94 visits per capita). Thus, it would be necessary to increase total expenditure in 1979 by 12.45 times (5.84 x 2.13 = 12.45) or to 5200 million shillings.

This latter estimate may be considered as an extreme, given the fact that there are many economies of scale involved in the expanded utilisation of each facility in the system. However, since the rate of utilisation taken as the target is not as large as in 1972-73 (2.63 visits per capita), this estimate may not be as large as potentially possible.

Basically the range of estimates ranges from nearly 6 to 12.5 times as large as were the approved estimates for the 1979 period. The magnitude of these figures raises serious questions about the extent to which the original expenditure pattern and thus the configuration of that earlier delivery system can be retained. While the pattern of diseases has been altered to one of more infectious parasitic diseases such that the cost of treatment per case may now be lower, perhaps by as much as 10-15 percent (Dunlop, 1973), the fact remains that the previous expenditure levels for health care by the government are not economically feasible in the near-to-medium period even if the government, via other policies, stimulates a rapid economic recovery.

This view is supported in at least three following ways. Firstly, combined expenditures on health in the period prior to 1971 were never more than 10 percent of the central government recurrent budget or approximately 25 percent of the combined district administration budgets. If health expenditures were to rise in the order of magnitude discussed above, a considerable reallocation of government budgets would be implied. Other ministries would find this most difficult to accept.

Secondly, even if government tax revenues from Uganda exports were to rise to approximately 1970 levels in the next two years, which is optimistic, the population of the country has expanded by 40 percent in the interim. Therefore, expenditures would need to be distributed in ways that would reduce overall health expenditures per capita.

Thirdly, in order to expand crop- and commodity-specific production levels which can begin to increase government revenue at all levels, in the short-to-medium term available foreign exchange must be allocated primarily to agriculture, and possibly education, which will significantly compromise current Ministry of Health hopes and ability to improve, rehabilitate or expand operations requiring new technology.

REFERENCES

Dunlop, David Wallace (1973). The Economics of Uganda's Health Service System: Implications for Health and Economic Planning. PhD dissertation, Department of Economics, Michigan State University.

Kyembe, Henry (1977). State of Blood: The Inside Story of Idi Amin's Reign of Terror. Gorgi, London.

Uganda, Republic of (February 1972). Uganda Plan Three: Third Five-Year Development Plan, 1971-76. Government Printers, Entebbe.

Uganda, Republic of (1977). Uganda Plan Three: Third Year Interim Plan, 1977-80. Government Printers, Entebbe.

Uganda, Republic of (October 1979). White Paper on the Report by the Commonwealth Team of Experts. Government Printers, Entebbe.

Uganda Times (January and February 1980).

United National Liberation Front (UNLF)(October 1979). The Economic and Social Policy of the UNLF.

A Comparison of Community Health in Uganda with Its Two East African Neighbours in the Period 1970–1979

F. J. Bennett

A comparison of health services and health status in the three adjacent countries of Uganda, Tanzania and Kenya over a decade is difficult but perhaps even a rough attempt is useful. It will show the impact of differing policies and social and economic crises against a background of rising populations in a largely tropical setting.

The vital statistics show the broad picture at the start and end of this important decade but, of course, they do not indicate the differences concealed within the national averages and the local fluctuations with times of famine or civil disturbance.

TABLE 1: Vital Statistics 1970 and 1979

	1970			1979		
	Kenya	Tanzania	Uganda	Kenya	Tanzania	Uganda
Infant mortality rate	119	160	120	104 (119)[a]	110 (125)[a]	116 (136)[a]
Crude birth rate	52	47	48	54	43	47
Crude death rate	19	17	19	14	16	15
Annual growth rates	3.3	3.0	2.9	4.0	2.7	3.2
Total fertility	7.6	6.3	7.1	8.1	?	?
Population (millions)	11.2	13.5	9.5	16	18	12.6
% Growth in Period				43	33	33

*Source: These figures are largely from a table by Bennett (1980) derived from several sources. Many of the figures are estimations.
[a] Alternative figures from 1979 World Population Data Sheet (Population Reference Bureau, Washington D. C.).

Kenya has managed to reduce infant mortality rate much more than Uganda although starting the period at the same level. However, Kenya still has areas of high infant mortality at the coast and the lake shore, these being

areas where mothers have less education and where malaria is endemic. No
doubt the average rate in Uganda also conceals very great differences
between areas. Uganda at least did not have to deal with as rapid a rate of
population increase as Kenya where the population increased by 43 percent in
the decade.

DISTRIBUTION OF HEALTH SERVICES

In this particular decade, while expansion of the health services in Uganda
was confined to the opening of a few one-hundred-bed hospitals (which had
been initiated by the first Obote Government), the other two countries were
concerned with bringing services closer to the rural population by increasing the number of small health units.

Tanzania went through a social reorganisation of people into ujamaa villages
with a specific aim of making it possible to provide services such as water,
health and education to a previously scattered population.

In 1970 the central government in Kenya took over the health services in
rural areas from the county councils, a system which Uganda still retains.

Kenya, with external aid, developed a system of rural health units--
demarcated geographical areas with a population of 50-70,000 served by a
health centre and a number of supporting and linked dispensaries. Six large
training health centres were set up in different ecological areas and the
staff trained as a team to teach management and teamwork, community
diagnosis and the new community orientation for the health units teams.
These training centres were also responsible for reorienting staff to provide integrated maternal and child health services including immunisation
and family spacing.

Tanzania had developed a policy of expanding the rural infrastructure rather
than spending more and more on urban hospitals, but Kenya was not able to
curtail this spiral as the new twelve-floor Kenyatta National Hospital was
opened. Hospital services in Kenya continue to absorb a large part of the
health budget.

COMMUNITY-BASED HEALTH CARE

Uganda in the late 1960s had some community-oriented health programmes such
as those at Kasangati and Lutete. In the late 1970s some community-based
activities were initiated and supported by nongovernmental organisations
(NGOs) such as the Kayunga Nutrition Scouts Project supported by UNICEF,
Kagando (Church) and Busoga (Church). The Uganda Ministry of Health convened an interministerial workshop on PHC and then not much happened for
some time.

Kenya developed many PHC projects run by nongovernmental organisations
including one by the African Medical Research Foundation (AMREF) at Kibwezi.
This organisation had been developing a primary health care support unit
for PHC training and support in Kenya, Uganda, Tanzania and southern Sudan.
This was possible because AMREF also operated the Flying Doctor Service out
of Wilson Airport in Nairobi. AMREF was also active in the production of
textbooks for auxiliaries and recently started producing texts for community health workers. In Kenya, staff of the Department of Community
Health of the University Faculty of Medicine, directed three PHC projects

including the National Pilot Project in western Kenya sponsored by the Ministry of Health with assistance from UNICEF. All of these projects in Kenya were community based with the establishment of health committees sponsoring health workers and with integration of other activities such as agriculture, education and water development. Links with the health services for supervision, training, continuing education, supplies and referral are important, and Kenya is fortunate that it has concentrated on developing a well-distributed infrastructure of training health centres, health units and smaller clinics. The pilot project in western Kenya produced a model for regional and district level activities required to promote and support PHC at village level, and a national plan which will receive UNICEF assistance has been made based on the report of the project (Were, 1980). Projects assisted by other NGOs are still developing and will be incorporated into the national programme but are encouraged to be innovative and address their own local problems.

Tanzania started training village health workers in the early 1970s. This is described in a chapter in the WHO publication **Health by the People** (Chagula and Tarimo, 1975: 145-168), a book which helped to lay the foundation for the Alma Ata Conference on PHC. In this chapter significantly titled "Meeting Basic Health Needs in Tanzania", the authors describe the sociopolitical situation in Tanzania. This included (among others) decentralisation, the concept of the ujamaa village, an emphasis on rural development, government mobilisation of all national resources to eliminate the priority problems of poverty, ignorance and disease, local contribution as an instrument for self-liberation and socioeconomic development. Special concern was expressed to ensure improved access to health care (no more than a two-hour walk to a health facility), more emphasis was placed on disease prevention, on community involvement, on mass health education and on training of auxiliaries. Even more important was the fact that these policies and the shift to rural areas were reflected in manpower and budget figures.

In 1971, 70 percent of the hospital service expenditure was in the capital city, but by 1973 this had been altered. These very impressive changes were due to political will and this example from Uganda's neighbour emphasises the progress that was possible under favourable circumstances in this decade.

Some of the significant changes in this period (Table 2) were greater emphasis on maternal and child health and the training of MCH aids, and the creation of village health posts in ujamaa villages. These were manned by village medical helpers who were selected by the village, had primary education and then had six months of training at the district hospital. However, after this good start primary health care in Tanzania faltered and most of the village health workers left for towns, joined rural medical aid training schools or just gave up their work. This was largely because of poor support both by their communities and by the health services and also because of poor selection. Recently a new programme has been planned which aims at better selection and more support of the primary health workers, which will now include both community health workers and traditional birth attendants.

In summary, as far as primary health care is concerned Tanzania during the early 1970s was in the forefront of thinking largely due to political will, Uganda was not taking visible steps to improve rural health, and Kenya was laying the foundation of an improved structure while allowing nongovernment initiative to assist small community-based health care projects. Uganda's

TABLE 2a: Tanzania Expenditure 1970–71 and 1978–79

	1970–71		1978–79	
	Shillings (million)	Percent	Shillings (million)	Percent
Hospitals	5.5	34	26.5	32
Health centres	0.8	5	19.5	23
Dispensaries	3.5	22	8.1	10
Preventive services	0.3	2	8.7	10
Training	5.1	3.2	12.4	15

*Source: Ministry of Health, United Republic of Tanzania Evaluation of the Health Sector 1979 (October 1980).
#In 1975 Hospital expenditure had gone down to 12.9 million shillings (20%), Training expenditure had risen to 18.9 million shillings (29%) and Preventive services had also risen to 9 percent.

TABLE 2b: Tanzania Health Personnel 1972–73 and 1978–79

	1972–73	1978–79
Total dispensary staff	3,303	5,625
Maternal and child health aids in dispensaries	–	310
Rural medical aids in dispensaries	383	769
Total health centre staff	2,333	3,803
MCHA in health centres	–	134
Rural medical aids in health centres	96	231
Medical assistants in health centres	90	170

*Source: Evaluation of Health Sector 1979.

health services continued to deteriorate in the second half of the 1970s, Tanzania's PHC efforts faltered and only one or two NGO projects flourished, while Kenya started a National Pilot PHC Project but then, apart from continued NGO activities, little happened for several years. In the meanwhile, other nearby countries such as Ethiopia were developing extensive national primary health care plans and starting to implement them, a task made easier by political endorsement and mass organisation within a socialist system.

MATERNAL AND CHILD HEALTH SERVICES

Uganda had been in the forefront during the 1960s with services for mothers and children. Cook (1967) and subsequently others had been working in Ankole District on the Oxfam and Save the Children Fund-sponsored Preschool Protection Programme (PPP) which through mobile clinics brought immunisation, growth monitoring and treatment of minor ailments to all children in the district. This focus on child care had come from the stimulus of the paediatric department in Makerere University where the professor was especially concerned with community child health, nutrition, breastfeeding and management of diarrhoea. Several books had come out of this department aimed at adequate management of child health problems by auxiliaries—for example Child Health in the Tropics (Jelliffe, 1974), which has gone through many reprints and editions. A book from Uganda on community nursing for auxiliary nurses (Byrne and Bennett, 1973) also stressed child health problems. Emphasis on risk factors in antenatal care was also prominent in Uganda and speedy referral systems were being set up to cut maternal mortality.

In the 1970s Uganda's leading role in maternal and child health was usurped by Kenya and Tanzania which now forged ahead in eliminating the fragmentation of services. For example, antenatal clinics had been run by midwives, immunisation was done on separate days by nurses, sick children had to see a medical assistant in a morbidity clinic, and family planning was often done outside the health service by a voluntary organisation. In Kenya the concept of a "supermarket MCH clinic" had evolved from the work of staff of the University Department of Community Health (Vogel and associates, 1974; Dissevelt, 1978; and Malone, 1977) in a management and operations research unit in Kiambu and also in Machakos. In this method all services for mother and child are provided daily by the same staff. Kenya now calls these comprehensive MCH services "Service Delivery Points". Tanzania had also (with USAID assistance) set up new training for MCH aids and the Kilimanjaro Christian Medical Centre at Moshi became well known for its books dealing with child health (see Balldin and associates, 1975).

In Uganda, family planning was more or less banned, and in spite of a drive in the other countries under the new name "family spacing" (indicating the acceptable political view) there was little real progress. Population boomed.

In Kenya it seems "exposure to primary education makes it possible for a woman to be more conscious of hygiene and nutrition and this helps prevent pregnancy wastage, while exposure to secondary education appears to be a prerequisite for a change in attitude towards family size" (Kenya, 1979a). Only 10 percent of Kenya women at risk to pregnancy were using any effective family planning methods by 1979. Kenya, however, started to take the increase in population more seriously as rates of increase approached 4 percent--a population centre was set up to do demographic studies, and an enlarged family health unit in the ministry now put greater emphasis on making the population aware of family spacing and on making the methods available through better oriented staff.

NUTRITION

All three countries had ongoing programmes of research, training and services in nutrition. Uganda had the once very active Infant Malnutrition Research Centre in Kampala where some of the initial work on kwashiorkor was done. The rehabilitation of malnourished children was done in what was then quite an innovative nutrition rehabilitation unit (NRU) called Mwanamugimu (see Amann and associates, 1972). The use of centres for rehabilitation of kwashiorkor spread to other countries of East Africa but they often had other names such as "family life training centres" (Ministry of Social Services) in Kenya where there was an emphasis also on use of appropriate technology. While Mwanamugimu languished in the 1970s from the general faltering of the economy, the similar units in Kenya equally had difficulties but rather due to problems of supervision and the fact that they were perhaps not altogether the correct solution to the problem in Kenya. However, a NRU at Nangina Catholic Mission Hospital which was linked with follow-up in the home and visits from community health workers was more successful and had a similar barrage of nutrition learning experiences in appropriate surroundings which had been the hallmark of the Uganda unit.

Tanzania started a food and nutrition centre in 1974 which is a parastatal body affiliated to the Ministry of Health. It was charged with nutrition planning, coordination, research and training and conducted many surveys of malnutrition. Tanzania in 1975 had a mass nutrition campaign called "Chakula ni Uhai" (food is life). This campaign was necessitated by a national food shortage due to poor rains coupled with the move to ujamaa villages. Such a mass media campaign used "participatory radio", a technique which had been developed in an early campaign--"Mtu ni Afya" which had been concerned mostly with improved environmental sanitation. Uganda made little use of its mass media for health education.

In Kenya the Medical Research Centre (with aid from the Netherlands) had commenced a series of research activities as well as the training of nutrition workers. Nationwide nutrition surveys were undertaken by the Central Bureau of Statistics, Ministry of Economic Planning, Nairobi (Kenya, 1978 and 1979b), so that Kenya steadily built up a very complete picture of the nutritional status of its various communities.

While much of the 1970s' nutrition literature from East Africa was coming from Kenya and Tanzania, Uganda was singularly silent. It can be assumed that the Nutrition Research Unit was no longer taking the lead in research, and that what was once one of the best nutrition laboratories in the Commonwealth was now little used.

During the 1970s there was more realisation of the significance of various anthropometric measurements in terms of chronic stunting and acute wasting for categorising the type of malnutrition, and computerized survey material was becoming more useful in providing a clear picture of the nutritional status of the country. If Uganda had had the capacity or political will to undertake nutritional surveillance, then perhaps the tragedy of Karamoja would not have been so great.

CONTROL OF COMMUNICABLE DISEASES

During the 1960s there had been periodic epidemics of smallpox in all the three countries of East Africa, but the WHO-assisted vertically executed eradication programme was carried out equally well in each country. The disease was eradicated and in Nairobi on 26 October 1979 the world was declared to be free of smallpox.

Other communicable diseases, however, have not been so dramatically dealt with. Expanded Programmes of Immunisation (EPI) have been started which aim at bringing the important immunisations to every child by the year 1990. Smallpox immunisation required only one shot of a freeze-dried more stable vaccine done easily with a bifurcated needle. Now, however, small children need three to five contacts at the correct ages for administration of six antigens dependent on an efficient "cold chain" for their potency. This requires an educated public, good management, logistic support and constantly functioning refrigerators.

Uganda, with its failing services, lack of kerosene and demoralised staff, has been the last of the three countries to be able to make any headway with EPI although Tanzania is also experiencing difficulties. In Tanzania, with its village organisation in ten house cells, each with a chairman and good ability to mobilise populations, there is every hope that once the logistic and cold chain problems are overcome, good coverage of immunisation will be relatively easy. Kenya has developed a good infrastructure and with an outreach strategy rather than mobile clinics, should be able to achieve the EPI objectives.

Sexually transmitted diseases (STD) had started on their epidemic explosion in the late 1960s and Uganda developed what was then a model service with laboratory diagnosis and effective treatment. Scientific papers were produced on social factors, treatment regimes and the value of health education in control programmes. Although the incidence must have increased exponentially during the military regime, it appears that inadequate drug supplies and deterioration of laboratory services led to decreasing control measures. In Kenya, however, research and control programmes for STD gained ground so that now international conferences are held in Kenya which has also developed specialised laboratory facilities and is now publishing papers on these diseases.

Some of the major communicable diseases in East Africa previously had vertical programmes. Malaria eradication was temporarily successful in Kigezi in Uganda and in Zanzibar but then failed. The environmental control measures need to be reinstituted by the staff of local health units, but little was done in the 1970s and reliance placed on chloroquine prophylaxis and treatment which was fortunately still effective. In Uganda, however, supplies of chloroquine were seldom available so even the acute cases could not always be treated. The disease is presumably now as endemic and serious as it was in the 1950s. Leprosy and tuberculosis control have remained as more or less vertical programmes with their own centralised administration and specialised staff although leprosy is no longer dealt with exclusively in special hospitals run by church organisations. Supervision in Kenya was tightened up by starting a new course for training special clinical officers for TB and leprosy. Kenya also was in the forefront with successful clinical trials of new short courses for tuberculosis using more costly drugs (eg. Rifampicin). The Leprosy Research Centre at Alupe in Kenya continued to function after the breakup of the East Africa Community.

Uganda in 1970 had a very successful and efficient trypanosomiasis control programme run almost on paramilitary lines, but during the military regimes this broke down and trypanosomiasis is again spreading in the southeastern border. In the meanwhile, the disease had been limited to one small area of Kenya.

EPIDEMICS

Cholera has been coming and going in all three countries so it is now characterised by a state of hidden endemicity with sudden epidemics. When it first arrived in East Africa, emphasis was on immunisation and prophylactic tetracycline and the setting up of rehydration centres. In Kenya, with better ability to investigate and control epidemics, the emphasis changed to one of involving the community in environmental improvement and having early notification and rehydration and treatment with tetracycline. Outbreaks are now controlled within two to three months rather than smouldering on for six months. In Tanzania too, community participation is easy to obtain in the face of an epidemic.

Kenya has developed a very good vector-borne disease section with laboratories in different parts of the country so that an outbreak of Kala-azar in Machakos District with a new pattern of disease in younger age groups was quickly investigated. Karamoja was always an endemic area for Kala-azar but as trained staff and laboratory are required to identify the disease, it might be that it continues unabated in this corner of Uganda.

Epidemics of plague have occurred in Kenya and been controlled, and one case of Marburg disease was acquired in western Kenya. It is possible that some serious epidemics did occur in Uganda in the 1970s as there were always rumours of epidemics with high case fatality, but notifications and the record and information system also suffered from the general weakening of the whole health service.

ENDEMIC DISEASE

"Vertical" centrally administered separate programmes for endemic disease are slowly disappearing as the basic infrastructure of health services is now able to deal with cases on a more routine basis. Schistosomiasis, however, is becoming an increasing problem in irrigation areas so it is partly related to agricultural development and dam construction. In Kenya the newer effective drugs are available for treatment and the vector-borne division assists in undertaking surveys and initiating control measures.

In Tanzania the Mwanza Schistosomiasis Research Station, which previously fell under the East African Community, has continued to do work and to deal with the problem on the southern lake shore.

Schistosomiasis mansoni infection in Uganda was serious in West Nile where V. Ongom (1973) and D. Bradley (1973) had done much work in assessing morbidity, but in the 1970s, presumably, this problem was neglected.

Trachoma, an eye disease, is a problem in all three countries, and in Kenya the International Eye Foundation has done a lot to prevent blindness using mobile teams and training staff of health units.

Other endemic diseases in East Africa include onchocerciasis, filariasis and hookworm. All of these diseases, whether vector borne or not, require good epidemiological research, often expensive drugs or insecticides and the specialised staff to guide local service or community control measures. External aid from international organisations has been required. It is in all these aspects that Uganda fell behind its neighbours.

MENTAL HEALTH

In the late 1960s Uganda had established itself as one of the countries in Africa with the most effective and innovative programmes for control of mental illness. Research into the epidemiology of maternal mental illness, child psychiatry, mental health problems of university students and day care management of psychoses and psychoneuroses was undertaken. Training programmes were instituted for medical students and psychiatric nurses, and postgraduate education was commenced. A mental health association was formed and public health education to change adverse attitudes was started. There was progress in decentralisation of management of cases and small psychiatric units were established at district hospitals. What happened in the 1970s is not clear but certainly the focus of activity shifted to Tanzania when psychiatric villages were started and where C. Swift published several books (Swift and Asuni, 1975, and Swift, 1977), and subsequently to Kenya where several of the Uganda psychiatrists took up university posts.

THE PROSPECTS FOR THE 1980s

The health problems of Uganda were well documented--the Uganda Atlas of Disease Distribution first published in 1968 (Makerere) was a model for the similar book Health and Disease in Kenya published in 1974 (Vogel and associates). In Uganda a remarkable spectrum of almost all the tropical diseases occurs. Now the ill health due to war, drought and social chaos has been added together with the problems of collapse or stagnation of previously fairly effective health and social services. In the meanwhile, neighbouring countries have been rethinking their health services and are starting to embrace the primary health care strategy with its objective of health for all and its involvement of communities and other sectors. The need for political commitment, new administrative, financial and management structures, decentralisation and the reorientation of health and other social sector workers has become apparent. All of the neighbouring countries are now busy fulfilling these needs.

The question facing Uganda is how to achieve health for all by the year 2000. Only with very careful planning will the country be able to obtain the best balance between restoring the quality of existing services while at the same time building the new structures necessary to meet the needs of the PHC approach.

REFERENCES

Amann, V., D. Belshaw and J. Stanfield (Eds.)(1972). Nutrition and Food in an African Economy. Department of Rural Economy, Makerere University. (Section IV (pp. 242-306) is devoted to nutrition rehabilitation based on hospital and health centre services.)

Balldin, B., R. Hart, R. Huenges and Z. Versluys (1975). Child Health--A Manual for Medical Assistants and Other Rural Health Workers. AMREF, Nairobi.

Bennett, F. J. (1980). Community Health in East Africa 1970-1979 and Future Prospects. East African Medical Journal, 57: 434-447.

Bradley, D. J.(1973). Schistosomiasis. In Hall, S. A. and B. W. Langlands, Uganda Atlas of Disease Distribution. East Africa Publishing House, Nairobi.

Byrne, M. and F. J. Bennett (1973). Community, Nursing in Developing Countries--A Manual for the Auxiliary Public Health Nurse. Oxford University Press.

Chagula, W. K. and E. Tarimo (1975). Meeting Basic Health Needs in Tanzania. In K. W. Newell, Health By the People. WHO, Geneva.

Cook, R. (1967). The Health of Preschool Children in Ankole: The Ankole Preschool Protection Programme, 1964-67. Department of Paediatrics, Makerere University (mimeographed).

Dissevelt, A. G. (1978). Integrated Maternal and Child Health Services--A Study at the Rural Health Centre in Kenya. Amsterdam: Royal Tropical Institute, Amsterdam.

Jelliffe, D. B. (Ed.) (1974). Child Health in the Tropics (4th edition). Edward Arnold, London.

Kenya, Republic of, Ministry of Economic Planning and Community Affairs (1978). Child Nutrition in Kenya. Government Printers, Nairobi.

Kenya, Republic of, Ministry of Economic Planning and Community Affairs (1979a). Economic Survey. Government Printers, Nairobi.

Kenya, Republic of, Ministry of Economic Planning and Community Affairs (1979b). Report of the Child Nutrition Survey, 1978-79. Government

Printers, Nairobi.

Makerere University, Department of Preventive Medicine and Department of Geography (1968). Uganda Atlas of Disease Distribution. Makerere University College, Kampala.

Malone, M. I. (1977). Quality of Care Assessment in the Outpatient Services of a District Hospital in Kenya. MD Thesis, University of Dublin. (This thesis contains a bibliography of the operations research carried out in Kenya in the 1970s.)

Ongom, V.L. (1973). A Study to Determine the Medical Significance of Schistosoma Mansoni Infection in the Jonam of West Nile. MD Thesis, Makerere University.

Swift, C. R. (1977). Mental Health--A Manual for Medical Assistants and Other Rural Health Workers. AMREF, Nairobi.

Swift, C. R. and T. Asuni (1975). Mental Health and Disease in Africa: Medicine in the Tropics. Churchill Livingston, London.

Vogel, L. and associates (Eds.) (1974). Health and Disease in Kenya. East African Literature Bureau, Nairobi.

Were, M. (1980). Organisation and Management of Community Based Health Care. UNICEF, Nairobi.

The Clocks Have Stopped in Uganda

Adolf Enns

The clock at the prestigious Mulago Hospital's eye-nose-throat clinic reads 4:56. On the tower of Makerere University's administration building the clock reads 12:20. Above the main entrance to the high court in downtown Kampala it reads 11:14. Inside the main post office it reads 12:27. All over Kampala clocks have stopped--at different times.

The clocks are Western mechanical or electrical devices. During the past ten years they have broken down or worn out, and so far it has not been on anyone's priority list to get them fixed. The broken clocks are symbolic. Clock consciousness represents Western values. The broken clocks not only testify to their unimportance in the present system of values in Uganda, but also to the lack of spare parts.

Mulago Hospital, built by the British at the close of the colonial era, is a white elephant rather than a prestigious institution to many Ugandans. While walking through its wards I have noted at least six clocks, all of them stopped, all showing different times. But nobody complains.

If you need an injection the nurse swabs you with water, since the hospital supply of alcohol ran out some time ago. But nobody complains--except for recently arrived Western doctors who are disturbed by the resulting skin infections at injection points. Ugandan staff members do not complain because the alcohol ran out when one of the clocks stopped.

There is no penicillin, but no one complains about that either since that clock stopped some time ago. And when you do not have soap, water, bandages, cottonwool, toilet paper, bed linens or blankets, how can you complain about the lack of tetracycline?

Reports of people resorting to traditional medicine are on the increase. Academicians are debating among themselves what an appropriate African philosophy of sickness and healing might be. When the academicians have finished their debate, perhaps the clocks will be fixed; or perhaps they will be removed. Meanwhile, the hospitals are treating gunshot wounds and the effects of malnutrition. Measles has become the number one killer among children.

Makerere University, once the best university by Western standards between Cairo and the Cape, remains the strongest national symbol of Western ideology. It is not the most visible symbol of Western ideology, nor the one affecting most people; that is still, unfortunately, the AK-47 and related weaponry. At Makerere many remain committed to Western academic ideals.

The university budget was drastically cut this year, but no howl of protest was heard from the administration. Its clock still reads 12:00. It takes two months to get a new light bulb installed in a classroom and four months to get enough seats, even backless benches, for students to be able to sit in class.

In the arts building everyone is expected to use the washroom marked for women students. The washroom has a trickle of water about two-thirds of the time. The university, like most of society at large, is caught somewhere between two ideologies: flush toilets into which water is carried by jerry can; decreasing faculty ranks and increasing student numbers; people doing graduate studies in a library that has no current periodicals and virtually no book additions in over a decade; administrators driving their Mercedes on the sidewalk right up to the door of their office building; no paper available for faculty to prepare a class syllabus or duplicate faculty minutes.

The clocks have stopped at different times. The abandonment of Western ideology, a carry-over from colonial times, has halted at various points. It will take time to invent an ideology that can work in Uganda.

But the clocks are running in two places in Uganda. The solar energised clock at the Wandegeya roundabout is running. The sun continues to shine despite all political and ideological upheaval. One segment of Uganda's economy that flourishes is solar-powered basic food production.

The clock in the SB supermarket is also running. The supermarket is operated by Asians whose exile by Amin represented a rejection of their Western economic ideology. But the clock in the supermarket is an ironically anachronistic clock.

My colleague at the university earns 6000 shillings a month. He could spend one-third of his monthly salary at the supermarket to buy one tin of British potato salad for 1700 shillings. The SB supermarket clock, as well as the Mercedes of the VIP, is out of step with the rest of the country.

Who will get the clocks in Uganda moving? Should they be started again? Will they ever be synchronised again unless they are set on sun time? Which way is forward?

Section 2

The Breakdown of Services

The Health Crisis in Uganda as It Affected Kuluva Hospital

E. H. Williams

Kuluva Hospital was established by my doctor brother and myself and our wives and parents in 1951 and is situated six miles south of Arua, the capital of West Nile. My wife and I had established a small hospital two miles from Arua in 1941; our joint move to Kuluva was made in order to expand our work to include the development of a leprosy control scheme. Kuluva Hospital was first operated under the auspices of the Africa Inland Mission, later under the auspices of the Church of Uganda. A total of some twenty medical missionaries worked with us in the hospital over the years to 1979.

Three major bus routes converged near Kuluva Hospital and brought many patients from the area lying to the south. Other patients came from the north via Arua but in smaller numbers because of the location of the Government Hospital in Arua. Many patients were attracted by the specialities we offered in ophthalmology, gynaecology and oncology. Approximately 20,000 people lived within walking distance of the hospital, and over the years the hospital clearly had an influence in the area in the promotion of certain aspects of community health. Hospital buildings were constructed as far as possible with local materials in order to save expense and in recognition of the fact that changes in layout and design would probably be called for in the future.

The popularity of the hospital increased slowly during the 1950s, then surged in the 1960s in common with other hospitals in West Nile. This change was generally thought to be due to a public realisation of the greater efficacy of Western medicine as compared with traditional varieties. The work at Kuluva reached its zenith during the 1960s and diminished during the Amin era of the 1970s. The hospital had a small X-ray unit (the fourth to be installed in Uganda), its own electricity supply from diesel-run generators and a piped water supply from a borehole. Surgical and laboratory equipment at the hospital was basic but adequate.

THE "DISEASE" SITUATION

Inpatient registers, outpatient daily records, operation registers and annual reports were kept over the years at Kuluva. These form the bases of the comments made below.[1]

Malaria

Malaria was hyper- to holoendemic in the area and probably the major cause
of death among young children. It also tended to complicate other conditions, especially those which were pyrexial. We tended to follow Morley's
precepts in dealing with the prevention of malaria since most patients with
acute malaria were from nearby. Towards the end of the 1960s we noticed
chloroquin resistance in our treatments of malaria cases.

Measles

A major epidemic of measles occurred in the Kuluva area in 1976-77 and
resulted in high death rates among children. As indicated in the figure
below, our hospital admissions rates reflected the problem that emerged.

The outbreak of measles was followed by a prolonged period during which
malnutrition rates increased among children. Another major epidemic of
measles occurred in 1943-44; fairly frequent minor epidemics occurred over
the years with lower resultant death rates.[2]

Malnutrition

Malnutrition was not as great a problem in our area as it was in other parts
of Uganda and was most commonly noted among children three to four years of
age. Its occurrence was probably linked in part with the habit of giving
small children a gruel made of cassava flour which was filling but not
particularly nutritious. Other factors in the fluctuating incidence of
malnutrition were linked to poor rainfall, crop failures and the lack of
cultivating tools. Cultivating tools were hard to obtain by the end of the
Amin era. The willful destruction of crops by units of the Uganda army
contributed to an increase in malnutrition in the early 1980s.

Infestations

Schistosomiasis mansoni was exceedingly common in our area, and 500 to 800
patients were treated annually at Kuluva. But the incidence of schistosomiasis did not change as a result of Amin's rule. Nor did the incidence of
ankylostomiasis and ascariasis change as a result of Amin's rule, though a
gradual increase of the latter infestation was noticed during the 1970s.
Since infestation by the ascariasis ova probably resulted from contamination
of food by hands, during preparation, it might be conjectured that the
shortage of soap during the 1970s played a role in the increase observed in
this infestation.

---

[1]Further publications on the basis of the records preserved are planned
as analyses are completed.
[2]It is interesting to wonder whether or not there are patterns in the
background and occurrence of measles epidemics in West Nile and elsewhere,
and whether or not vaccination campaigns might be planned so that such
epidemics could be warded off in the future.

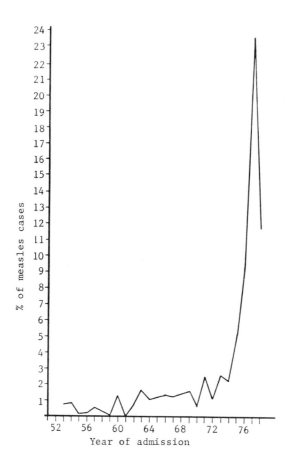

Measles cases represented as percentage of total admissions.

Gonorrhoea

Gonorrhoea was once very uncommon in West Nile, found mostly among members
of the police force and their wives. It spread slowly during the 1960s,
however, and more rapidly during the 1970s when perhaps the army was responsible. During the 1970s ectopic gestation and pelvic sepsis became much
more common than they had been. Many unhappy men with nonspecific posterior
urethritis during this time wandered from medical unit to medical unit in
search of penicillin and other antibiotics.

Inguinal and Femoral Hernias

Inguinal and femoral hernias were common, with the latter probably associated with onchocerciasis. A policy of repairing all hernias which presented was in effect at Kuluva and undoubtedly had a preventive effect on
the incidence of strangulated hernias in the area.

Tuberculosis

Tuberculosis was almost unknown in West Nile during the 1940s but became
more common during the 1950s. The Uganda Ministry of Health set up an
excellent treatment and follow-up programme for tuberculosis patients based
at the hospital in Arua. Lack of drugs, discouragment among staff members
and other factors during the 1970s, however, caused a serious deterioration
in this service.

Tetanus

The incidence of tetanus among adults has remained relatively uncommon in
recent years, but its incidence among children increased dramatically in the
1970s as tetanus toxoid became unobtainable and could not be given to pregnant women.

Leprosy

Kuluva was established as a leprosy treatment centre and during the 1950s
had 400 patients resident in seven surrounding villages. In the realisation
that there were several thousand patients with leprosy in West Nile, that
treatment was a privilege and that treatment was rather easily accomplished
if patient attendance at the centre was as encouraged, two simple bylaws
were introduced in 1958. The first introduced a small penalty for persons
who suspected they had leprosy lesions but failed to come to the clinic, the
second introduced a small penalty for those who were supposed to attend the
centre for treatment of their condition but failed to do so. Both bylaws
were soon forgotten. Yet both were helpful in inculcating habits of attendance at the centre and district clinics.

By 1978, with the extension of our Kuluva programme, some eighty leprosy
clinics had been established throughout West Nile, and some 2000 active
cases were being treated under the supervision of seventeen trained leprosy
assistants and one leprosy supervisor, all of them Ugandans. By 1978 the
leprosy population at Kuluva had been reduced to 160 with a high proportion of lepromatous cases.

In 1978 the admission of new patients to our scheme was lower than the
number of patients discharged because they no longer needed treatment. By
the end of the 1970s and into the 1980s, however, drugs needed for the
treatment of leprosy patients were difficult to obtain and the situation
deteriorated.

THE AMIN "COUP" AND THE RESULTING HEALTH CRISIS

Many responsible observers contend that the deterioration of health services
in Uganda began much earlier. In any case there were few noticeable differences in the two or three years immediately following Amin's coup in January
1971, relatively easily identifiable consequences not long thereafter. Many
factors were involved.

The expulsion of Asians in 1972 badly decimated the ranks of medical personnel in the country and badly undermined access to services. Prior to the
expulsion there had been approximately 1200 doctors in Uganda, and the
pharmaceutical industry had been almost entirely in Asian hands. After the

expulsion the number of doctors was reduced by half and only half a dozen registered pharmacists remained.

Transport facilities of all kinds deteriorated from 1973 onwards making it increasingly difficult for patients to travel in search of medical help.

With the uncertainty of the security situation, banditry by members of the army and the presence of many roadblocks, people were discouraged from moving around. The number of doctors was further reduced from its already low number as doctors who were members of tribes in disfavour were either killed or forced to flee in order to save their lives.[3] Similarly, the numbers and work conditions of nurses, midwives and other ancillary medical workers were very severely affected.

Expatriate staff members at Kuluva were also adversely affected. About every nine months Amin would utter threats against expatriates. At one time he declared his intention to rid Uganda of them by 1975. Roadblock encounters became very unpleasant experiences especially for parents with children. As a result of the deteriorating situation expatriates started to leave, and in 1974 Kuluva was left with one expatriate doctor, his wife and two expatriate nurses. The evil reputation of Uganda at the time discouraged the recruitment of new expatriate staff. Yet two doctors came short-term in 1975 and 1976. In 1977 the murder of Archbishop Luwum served to convince Ugandans, finally, of the desperate situation in their country. Expatriates soon thereafter left Kuluva on holiday for a period of five months.

FACTORS IN THE SURVIVAL AND CONTINUANCE OF KULUVA HOSPITAL

Upon their return to Kuluva expatriate staff members found that Ugandan nursing aids and others had maintained a dispensary during their absence and had behaved very responsibly indeed in the diagnosis of illness and treatment of patients and in the maintenance of the hospital and its grounds. It was obvious immediately that Ugandan staff members were capable of taking much more responsibility than had been thought. This in turn paved the way for the initiation of an intensive training programme to prepare Ugandans for the possibility that expatriates might have to leave again.

Many factors contributed to the survival and continuance of Kuluva during the years of crisis. Among these, firstly, Kuluva was a Christian hospital established under a mission agency, taken over later by a board of governors appointed by the Church of Uganda. At the end of the 1970s there were more than 100,000 adherents of the Church of Uganda in West Nile organised in some 600 churches. These adherents looked upon Kuluva as their hospital. They were concerned for its survival. The hospital's solid core of dedicated and hard-working Christian staff members maintained high standards in caring for patients, whatever their backgrounds, and always projected a favourable image to those who came to them for treatment.

Secondly, there was continuity among the expatriate and the Ugandan staffs up until the period of crisis. Most of the Ugandan members of staff had already served for twenty to thirty years by this time and were trained in

---

[3]I was told at the end of the 1970s by an official of the Kenya Ministry of Health that it was then employing some 100 Ugandan doctors.

all basic hospital procedures. They knew exactly what to do when they found themselves on their own.

Thirdly, stocks of essential medicines were always maintained at adequate levels. When the last expatriate doctor left in 1979 a two years' supply of essential medicines remained in stock.

Fourthly, it was policy at the hospital to keep income and expenditure under constant review in order to facilitate economies. Income was derived as follows: half from fees, one-quarter from government grants-in-aid and one-quarter from other sources. The level of hospital fees charged was considered one of the lowest in Africa. This was necessary in order that the hospital's services should cater for the lowest income groups in the predominantly rural community within easy reach of the hospital. Missionaries received their incomes through the parent missionary society. Ugandan staff were paid at basic government rates but expected to work only thirty to thirty-five hours per week for this. They were then paid at overtime rates for additional work, thus enabling them to have better incomes.

The implementation of our policies involved careful planning, the restriction of times when nonurgent outpatient cases were seen and the avoidance of whole days occupied in specialised activities such as surgery. Surgical operations at Kuluva were performed daily in ones and twos. Our aim in organisation was that all staff members and departments should be utilised as fully and continuously as possible.

Fifthly, willing and caring relatives of patients were used to watch patients, carry out simple nursing duties and provide and cook food for them. Custom in West Nile demanded that no sick person should be left unattended by relatives. Only special diets were the financial responsibility of the hospital.

Sixthly, expatriate staff members all spoke one or more local languages. This enabled direct doctor-patient communication, saved time and made for the preparation of much better clinical histories in the avoidance of the need for interpretation. Doctors at Kuluva generally screened outpatients by themselves, delegating duties in the laboratory and treatment departments to others. Direct doctor-patient relationships were especially appreciated by women patients with gynaecological complaints. Such complaints were often not understood and not diagnosed in other medical units.

Seventhly, our records system was appropriate for the local setting. A patient attending for the first time went to the records clerk, paid the requested fee and received a card or piece of metal which was to be retained indefinitely and upon which was stamped an identifying number. The patient at this time would also be handed a record card (not a piece of paper) to be presented to the doctor on duty in "outpatients". The doctor would write brief notes of history, signs, diagnosis and treatment on the card and place it in an appropriate docket from which it would be collected and taken to the department where the patient would receive treatment or be further investigated or admitted. Finally the card would be returned to the records room and filed, to be withdrawn again the next time the patient came to the hospital and presented his or her permanent number. Some 100,000 patients were enrolled in Kuluva between 1951 and 1978.

Finally, we were able to control patient numbers effectively without in any way jeopardising patient services. Alarming increases in patient numbers

during the 1960s threatened to disrupt the smooth running of the hospital.
In recognition of the fact that it was unnecessary to require most patients
to attend the hospital frequently, even daily, for treatment, it was decided
to make a sustained effort to provide treatment for as many patients as
possible for up to three weeks by utilising tablets packaged in small
plastic bags. In this way the average number of reattendances per patient
was reduced from six to two, and the total number of patients who attended
the hospital remained about the same as it had been even while the number
of new patients trebled.

One of the departments that showed signs of swamping other activities was
the maternity department. The number of women who came for delivery--
especially the number who came from further away--increased during the
1960s. With the midwives at the hospital at the time almost all expatriates, and the number of expatriates diminishing over time, the situation
became increasingly acute.

As the Uganda Medical Service opened up a number of maternity units throughout West Nile, however, our problem subsided; we simply decided to refer
women back to the unit nearest their homes whenever possible. Meanwhile, we
encouraged women from nearby areas to attend antenatal clinics, and decided
to introduce a tripartite policy according to which we 1) identified patients for whom delivery in hospital would be mandatory, 2) monitored
primapara carefully for signs of possible complications during delivery and
encouraged women with potential problems to come to the hospital when
labour began and 3) advised women whose pregnancies were proceeding normally
to deliver at home, while at the same time advising them that if labour was
prolonged for more than six hours they should come to the hospital.

THE POST-AMIN PERIOD

I was the one remaining doctor at Kuluva as the Amin era drew to an end. I
was nearing retirement age, had not had adequate overseas leave for many
years and realised that I could not much longer carry on the clinical,
clerical, administrative and maintenance work for which I was responsible,
without experienced assistants. In May 1978 I slipped while doing a ward
round and sustained a fractured hip. I was flown to Kenya for operation,
returned later to Kuluva on crutches to supervise the imminent partial
closure of the work. The two expatriate nurses at the hospital were also due
for overseas leave. The final impetus in my own departure was provided by a
severe attack of tick typhus. By March 1979 all expatriate staff had left
Kuluva, leaving behind the long-serving and reasonably competent Ugandan
staff to carry on as best it could with the assistance of a recently qualified Ugandan medical assistant.

A year later one expatriate nurse returned. Then in October 1980 the Acholi
members of the Uganda army found opportunity to invade West Nile to wreak
vengeance on the Lugbara, Kakwa and Madi tribes for being associates of
Amin, a Kakwa. A period of unrestrained terror, violence and slaughter resulted. The Kakwas and large numbers of Lugbaras and Madis fled en masse
into Sudan and Zaire. Arua and its hospital were destroyed. So were the
hospitals at Maraca, Yumbe and Moyo. Kuluva remained relatively unmolested,
though a number of people were summarily executed in the area. The Alur
tribe, with its affinities with the Acholi tribe, was left untouched as
were the Angal and Nebi hospitals in its area. The Red Cross and a German
emergency medical team later occupied Kuluva. Then in mid-1982 Dr. Johnson
Lulua, a Lugbara himself, took over the management of the hospital. Dr.

Keith Waddell, an expatriate, arrived at Kuluva in early 1983 and is seeking to build up again the opthalmology and leprosy work at the hospital.

CONCLUSIONS AND IMPLICATIONS

An attempt has been made here, albeit cursorily, to outline the effects of the health crisis of recent years upon one small voluntary agency hospital in the northwest corner of Uganda. Many restrictions on the functioning of medical centres occurred during the period of Amin's rule. But seven medical centres remained functioning at its end in West Nile. Unfortunately, following "liberation" in 1979 a tribe from outside West Nile which had suffered greatly under Amin's rule attacked and decimated four of the seven centres. Kuluva Hospital was forced to maintain a reduced level of functioning but did not close. An account has been given here of the policies and ideas which were implemented over thirty years at Kuluva and which may have contributed to its survival. It is hoped that this account will provide suggestions and ideas for other hospitals which may be faced with similar situations.

A Village Perspective of Health Services in Buganda

Erisa Kironde

My viewpoint of health services in Uganda is rooted in my home village, Busozi, only ten miles from Kampala. Being in this central location and in close proximity to the capital, my family and I have benefited from the medical services introduced and developed by missionaries over the past one hundred years. My mother delivered me at the mission maternity unit at Mukono eight miles distant from Busozi in 1926, almost sixty years ago. In 1928 my younger brother was born in a similar unit in Kira, a mere two miles away. Neither of these maternity centres has survived as improved roads and transport have allowed more centralised services. People from our village today usually use the mission health centre at Namugongo, three miles away.

Government medical services in my home area have suffered greatly in recent years. Staff morale has been shattered by low salaries and lack of supervision, and medicines and supplies have been very difficult to obtain. Services are technically free to all at all locations, but there are major hassles in obtaining them as various abuses have recently emerged. A sick person or his relative has to grease so many hands to get to the point of treatment, and pay even more bribes after diagnosis in order to get supposedly free drugs, that on balance most people in despair resort to private practitioners or unlicensed pharmacists thereby saving time if not money.

Practices such as these have eroded the confidence of the local people in government medical services. Also, the bridge connecting our village to the teaching health centre at Kasangati was broken three years ago, and the bus service once provided has been discontinued. Such developments have further cut off our access to medical services in places close to our village.

Currently there are several fee-for-service private practices in my village where illnesses are treated and maternity care is provided. In adjacent villages two miles on either side of Busozi qualified nurses have opened home-based clinics. Similarly, a medical assistant has opened a practice in Namugongo three miles away. These local practices regularly refer complicated cases to private doctors in Kampala. They refer serious cases to any one of the three hospitals in Kampala, but usually to one of the mission hospitals. Our people have more confidence in mission hospitals.

Self-care is also evident. My grandmother was a locally famed traditional

65

birth attendant. She died sixteen years ago but passed on her knowledge and
training to a male cousin of mine who was more receptive to her teachings
than any of her female relatives. This cousin has delivered his own wife of
six children--the most recent in May 1984--though he does not otherwise
regularly practise his skill.

For minor crises there is a wealth of local traditional lore. Recently I
observed a sixteen-year-old girl mixing a poultice of leaves for the treatment of a burn on her four-year-old sister. Many such practices are no
doubt helpful. The herbal poultice, for example, may be suitable in the
relief of the pain from minor burns. But unfortunately sometimes the result
is not so good. A self-styled traditional practitioner in the area treats
diarrhoea in young children by extracting incipient incisor teeth. This old
woman's treatment has seen many babies die from sepsis and bleeding after
the crude operation.

There are three traditional healers in the vicinity of my village. One is
the old woman just referred to. The other two handle cases generally
thought to be beyond the scope of Western medicine. The conditions these
healers treat include impotency among men and barrenness in women. They also
include possession by devils and symptoms of madness.

Since health services can only be viewed in the totality of services in
general, a digression is necessary. My area was transversed in the 1960s by
a bus service provided by the country's largest bus company. This service
was later suspended. But luckier than in most areas, a truncated service
now stops midway in the area where the tarmac ends in Namugongo.

In any case no sensible operator would today trust his vehicles to traverse
the area as the roads are in such a bad state. They have not been graded
for at least fifteen years. One of the main access roads is impossible even
with a Land Rover while another through-road lost a bridge in 1980. The
bridge has since been patched up, but most of the time drivers continue to
shun the road on which it lies.

Fortunately, there are a lot of footpaths in the area. In the 1930s and
1940s, when Uganda was famed for bicycles, we used the footpaths for ease of
communication and transportation. The bicycle was then a popular and prestigious form of transport, a priority for which individual young men saved
even before saving for a wife. The bicycle's status value dropped in favour
of easily acquired motorbikes, scooters and even cars in the 1950s and 60s,
but prices have now ruled these out. Even the humble bicycle, when available, is no longer affordable.

Given the general health breakdown in our area, it would appear that the
tradition of local chiefs exerting their influence to maintain roads and
such things might be encouraged. Also it would appear that the church could
provide the catalyst for the introduction of something like primary health
care. But while the churches thrive in popularity, collectively they are
vehicles of conservatism. They are much more interested in bewailing the
loss of the glorious past than in encouraging much needed changes and new
developments in leadership.

Local schools are numerous and education is now the only opportunity for
upward social mobility. Hence schools have ample local support. But what
do schools teach that is of benefit to village people as regards health and
welfare? In the 1930s and 40s catalytic subjects on hygiene and nutrition
were a standard part of the curriculum. Today education is examination

oriented and hygiene and nutrition have been dropped in favour of English, mathematics and the other subjects required for entrance to higher education.

For much of this century it was accepted in our area that hygiene was a subject to be practised. Each household had to have a pit latrine in addition to a separate kitchen. Standards and specifications were established. For example, the latrine had to be at least fifteen feet deep and sited a considerable distance from the house. The locally domiciled chief, backed by a considerable hierarchy of authority, was charged with ensuring that each house had a latrine. Today all that has changed.

Since independence in 1962 hardly any local elections have been held. The top end of the local hierarchy of authority has collapsed and only a truncated hierarchy of authority at the subparish, parish and county level has continued. These levels have been drawn into the national political arena and have been increasingly concerned with politics rather than the needs of our local communities.

Insecurity is another problem. It is a sad fact that in my immediate area, at the lowest subparish level, two chiefs were shot and killed in 1983. The newly appointed subparish chief hails originally from another district with a different mother tongue and resides eight miles away. Hence he is uninterested in such mundane matters as hygiene in our village. Meanwhile, our parish chief was killed three years ago and his post has not been filled.

Local chiefs were traditionally responsible for organised communal work, be it staving off an imminent danger or clearing paths and digging shallow wells. Drum calls were used to communicate the need for communal work. Today the social basis for such authority has been badly undermined.

What I'm trying to say is that despite the breakdown of nationally organised services, there exists a precedent in rural Uganda through the role of the church in the early provision of medical services, the role of schools in teaching hygiene and proper nutrition and encouraging good health practices, and the role of local chiefs in ensuring the implementation of public health measures. It seems to me that such practices, organisations and positions could be revived today in meeting current challenges.

The run-down in health services in Uganda is not isolated. It is symptomatic of a general deterioration of all of the services previously assumed and has resulted in communal disillusionment about what to expect. Many Ugandans have come to condemn the deterioration of moral fibre they see all around them both in individuals and in society.

All the same, some compensatory qualities have emerged. Where previously overreliance was placed on a paternalistic hierarchy, a new spirit of self-reliance is becoming discernible. Some services like funerals are still run communally, which of course is good. But otherwise individualism is more and more the order of the day. As everywhere in Uganda, the recent financial arrangements including the floating of the Ugandan shilling have benefited the countryman farmer. He now guffaws at the previously envied office worker who, wearing a tie and often a suit, works for a mere pittance.

Just a few weeks ago I was delighted to talk with Kefa in our village. Last year he took his O level examinations in school and failed. He was offered a job in Kampala at USh 800 a month but immediately turned down the offer in

favour of growing cabbages on his father's patch of ground. This cavalier
attitude to authority, hierarchies and salaried employment, unknown a few
years ago, further manifests itself in astuteness in joining voluntary
organisations. Many of the people in our area have joined organisations
where few benefits can be identified individually but where much is possible
for the common good.

It is my hope that by a clear definition of the benefits to the individual
and the community the health services too can join current trends and work
with communities and not, as has too often been the case, for them. Many of
the institutions of Uganda have been severely undermined in recent years but
the people of Uganda now, as in the past, have shown themselves resilient in
the face of the challenges.

Factors Affecting the Quality of Nursing Care at Mulago

Rosemary Lynda Rwakatonera

The quality of nursing care given to patients, particularly children, in Uganda's government hospitals has been questioned by members of the medical profession as well as members of the public since early in the 1970s. In this paper I will outline some of the common problems affecting nursing care on the paediatraic wards of Mulago Hospital in Kampala in 1983.[1]

One hundred and eight persons worked as nurses on the six paediatric wards and units at Mulago in early 1983: ten as Grade I nursing officers, thirty-six as Grade II nursing officers, fifty as enrolled nurses/midwives and twelve as student nurses.[2] Fifty-four nurses worked on the morning shift, twenty-seven on the evening shift and twenty-seven on the night shift. Patient numbers during the period under consideration ranged from 240 to 600, meaning that the nurse/patient ratio ranged from 1:5-12 on the morning shift and 1:9-22 on the evening and night shifts. The data in relation to which the outlines of this study were drawn were collected in three principal ways: a review of records, observation on the wards and interview. All of the twenty-five nurses interviewed were female; all but three were between twenty and forty years of age. Four were Grade I nursing officers, six Grade II nursing officers, ten staff nurses and five student nurses.

DISCUSSION

Most of the children admitted to the paediatric wards and units at Mulago Hospital are younger than five years of age. Most are admitted acutely ill with measles, bronchopneumonia, diarrhoeal disorders, severe dehydration and other such problems.

---

[1]Dr. J. W. Owange Iraka read through an early draft of this paper and offered valuable advice on how it might be improved. Professor E. S. Hillman gave me much help in the study's initial stages. I am grateful to my colleagues on Mulago's paediatric wards and units for their help in my collection of data.
[2]The Department of Paediatrics in Mulago Hospital included the following six units: Ward I C, Ward II C, Ward 15 (MRC), Ward 3 (Nutrition), Special Care Unit, Acute Care Unit.

Unfortunately, the nursing care the children received after admission was
likely to be far from satisfactory. Quite frequently the following routine
nursing care procedures were either done incorrectly or not at all during
the period of my observation:
- the receiving of ward reports on each shift
- ward cleaning, bed making and dusting
- care of the skin and treatment of pressure areas of patients
- care of the eyes, nose and mouth of patients
- preparation for and attendance during doctor rounds
- collection of specimens for laboratory examination
- administration of drugs
- the feeding of children
- care of emergency cases
- observations and records
- prevention of cross infection

Many factors help explain the inadequate provision of nursing care on the
paediatric wards at Mulago. The more important of these are identified
below.

Lack of Cooperation between Doctors and Nurses

Little cooperation was evident between doctors and nurses on the wards as
far as the management of patients was concerned. The doctors were observed
to be overly demanding in their directions to nurses and unwilling to listen
to the suggestions of the nurses under their authority.

Lack of Facilities

Table 1 identifies some of the items of equipment necessary for basic paediatric nursing care, plus the number of wards/units (of a total of six) not
well equipped with reference to each in early 1983. The standards used in
making judgements of adequacy were the standards officially identified as
acceptable at Mulago at the time.

Table 1 makes it clear that there are many serious shortages of some of the
basic facilities necessary in caring for sick children at Mulago. With most
of the medical equipment out of order, relatively routine nursing procedures
have become problematic. Nurses on evening and night duty cannot work
effectively without adequate lighting, and many ward areas are in darkness
at night. Instruments cannot be sterilised properly without sterilisers.
The heads of oxygen cylinders frequently do not work properly. Mechanical
suction apparatuses in three of Mulago's paediatric wards were out of order
at the time of study and had been out of order for a long time.

Staffing

A nurse/child ratio of 1:2 is often recommended for paediatric wards and is
considered optimal at Mulago. The day duty 1:5-12 ratio and the evening and
night duty 1:9-22 ratios that in fact exist are far below the optimal
standard. Furthermore, most of the nurses on the paediatric wards are
general or midwives, not nurses with particular training in paediatric
nursing. In fact there were only three nurses with paediatric training
working on the paediatric wards during the period of this study, and two of
these three were ward sisters. Problems in staffing have been due to the

large number of dropouts from nursing over the years. The shortage has led
to overworked nurses and problems of inefficiency in the provision of health
services.

TABLE 1:   Equipment Shortages

Item	Number of wards (of 6) not well equipped
Thermometers	3
Torch	4
Tongue depressor	3
Examination couch	2
Urine testing equipment	6
Resuscitation drug tray	6
Oxygen cylinder or piped oxygen	3
Mechanical suction apparatus	3
Blood pressure machine	6
Airways	4
Artery forceps	3
Medicine utensils	4
Feeding utensils	5
Adequate handwashing facilities	6
Blankets	4
Mattresses	2
Cot sheets	4
Heating facilities	5
Electric or steam steriliser	2
Bowls, kidney dishes and gallipots	4
Bed bathing facilities	5
Adequate lighting	6
Cotton wool, gauze swabs and adhesive plaster	5
Weighing scales	3

Overcrowding

The number of children per ward varied over time, of course. But occasionally overcrowding was severe and a ward designed to cater to   forty-nine
patients held eighty to 100. Additionally, due to shortages of beds and
mattresses, two to three children at times had to share the same mattress,
quite possibly each with a different illness. As a result cross infection
frequently occurred.

Mothers and Attendants on the Ward

Mothers and attendants are often extremely helpful in the care of sick
children at Mulago. At times, however, they pose problems for the nurses.
Mothers with very sick children are often mentally depressed and, in consequence, are unable to cooperate with nurses. Mothers frequently discharge
their children without the knowledge of a nurse or doctor, upon learning
that their children may require intravenous infusion, oxygen, nasal-gastric
feeding or other such special attention, only to return later with their
children in worse condition than before. Mothers are not separable from
their traditional beliefs about health and illness and sometimes bring
native medicines to the hospital and administer these to their children even

as the doctors prescribe other drugs.

Ward Administration

In wards in which administrators and supervisors tended to be creative,
responsive to the needs of nurses and organised in their procedures, morale
among nurses tended to be relatively high. In wards in which administrators
were ineffective and uncommunicative, morale tended to be low. Overall,
administrative procedures were not nearly as effective as they might have
been. As indicated in the data recorded in Table 2, on-duty and off-duty
reporting times among nurses ranged widely (though they were precisely
defined and standardised), and often resulted in gaps in the provision of
nursing care on the wards. In illustration, during the period of research
night nurses reported off-duty between 6:30 and 7:30 a.m. and morning nurses
only reported on-duty between 8:30 and 10:30 a.m. More effective administration could have solved the problem obvious in this and similar situations.

TABLE 2: Reporting Times

Time of reporting on-duty	
Morning nurses	8:30 a.m. - 10:30 a.m.
Evening nurses	3:00 p.m. - 3:30 p.m.
Night nurses	6:00 p.m. - 8:00 p.m.
Time of reporting off-duty	
Morning nurses	2:00 p.m. - 4:30 p.m.
Evening nurses	5:30 p.m. - 7:00 p.m.
Night nurses	6:30 a.m. - 7:30 a.m.

Lack of Incentives for Nurses

Promotion exercises among nurses at Mulago have not been carried out since
1976. A few nurses are taken each year for post-basic courses in nursing.
The majority of those selected for such privileges, however, are selected
arbitrarily in relation to personalistic considerations, not in relation to
performance records. One of the consequences of the lack of recognition
implied in such considerations is the fact of low morale among the nurses,
especially among those who are conscientious in the performance of their
responsibilities.

Recruitment in Nursing

Up until 1976 individuals were recruited for training in nursing in consideration of their interests, promise in nursing and academic ability. Since
that time individuals have often been recruited purely on the basis of
academic achievement or in relation to political affiliation or family ties.
The changes mean that many of the students who join nursing today have
little real interest in nursing as such. The changes also help explain why
so many poor quality nurses are now graduated each year. No one can be a
good nurse without a special interest in nursing as a profession.

Lack of Cooperation between Ward and Training School Personnel

Students on the wards for practical experience are seldom given tuition or further instruction by ward sisters, staff nurses or doctors at the present time. That is, they are seldom given the kind of training on the wards that will help them become good nurses. If the training of nurses at Mulago is to be improved, hospital, ward and training school authorities will have to work in closer cooperation with each other than they now do.

Economic Situation in the Country

Spiralling upward as they have in recent years, costs in Uganda have had an indirect effect on the quality of nursing care given on the wards. Most of the nurses interviewed during this study have children to support and live three to four kilometres from the hospital. Daily round-trip matatu (van-taxi) fares for such distances come to roughly USh 200, meaning that monthly fares for the same services come to roughly USh 4000. But the salary of a staff nurse comes to only about USh 1300 a month!

Some nurses supplement their incomes through work of one or another kind or with the produce from the shambas (gardens) they or their people work. The walk to and from the hospital is clearly a necessary walk for many. In any case, matters of punctuality are often of secondary consideration under the conditions of life of many of Mulago's nurses, as are commitments to hospital routines, care in reporting procedures and pride in profession. A nurse who leaves her own children without food and drink at home can hardly be expected to look devotedly after other people's children on the ward.

Insecurity

The prevailing state of insecurity and lawlessness in Kampala has also had an impact on the morale and work of the nurses at Mulago. Robberies are commonplace in the areas in which they live, while murders are still far from uncommon. Nurses who spend a restless night in hiding can hardly be expected to do their best the next day on the wards.

Accomodation for Nurses

The majority of the nurses interviewed in this study, like most of the nurses at Mulago, fall into a nursing cadre in which they are not eligible for government housing. Most of them live in slum areas under very poor health conditions. Mulago does not provide lunches for its nurses, and many have no lunches to bring with them when they report for work.

CONCLUSION

Much can be done to improve the living and working conditions of the nurses at Mulago. More nurses with appropriate trainings are needed. More and better equipment must be made available. Salaries, travel and other allowances, housing and other benefits must be improved. Relationships among nurses, doctors, administrators, student nurses and other ward personnel are much less satisfactory than they should be. Problems of overcrowding must be solved for the advantage of patients as well as medical personnel. Nurses must be shown more courtesy and they must be given more chances to express themselves and participate in workshops, seminars and refresher courses than has been possible in recent years. If improvements are not made the problems in health care currently apparent will continue.

Paediatric Mortality in Mulago Hospital, June 1982 to June 1983

K. Wotton

Mulago Hospital in Kampala is Uganda's largest hospital. It is both the teaching hospital for medical undergraduate and postgraduate students and a medical referral centre. Concern in Makerere's Department of Paediatrics in early 1982 over the number of measles deaths among inpatients led to the examination of numbers and trends reported in this article.

The death register at Mulago records the name, ward and cause of death for each of the deceased. It does not record information concerning age at death. Attempts were made to obtain such data by cross-referencing names in the death register with information in ward medical records and admissions books.[1] This proved to be extraordinarily time consuming, however, and even with great diligence only about one-third of the relevant ages at death could be identified. The attempt was thus abandoned, with the result that the tabulations of paediatric deaths reported below are incomplete. For the period in question the deaths recorded represent almost all of the deaths on Mulago's paediatric wards, in the associated special care unit and in the labour suites. They do not include the deaths of paediatric patients on other wards--for example, the tuberculosis, cancer, surgery and orthopaedic wards. Our tabulations also omit the deaths of those children whose bodies bypassed the morgue because parents claimed them on the wards, or because in certain instances--as in the case of mwanamugimu, the nutrition ward--bodies were not routinely sent to the morgue.

Other difficulties were encountered in obtaining the denominator data necessary for use in comparing paediatric mortality at Mulago during the period under consideration and paediatric mortality in other hospitals and during other periods. The numbers of live births per month were not available from the labour suites or from medical records. Total paediatric admissions per month were available for February through April 1983 in the medical records department, but were highly suspect, differing by as much as 300 percent from the number of admissions recorded in ward admissions books. The number of admissions by diagnosis could not be determined. It was therefore decided to compare simply the number of measles deaths among children with the

---

[1] D. Okumu and A. Othieno, second and third year medical students at Makerere University, assisted me in the collection of the data reported here.

total number of paediatric deaths. Table 1 lists all paediatric deaths at
Mulago by cause of death for the period 1 June 1982 through May 1983. Table
2 gives monthly rates for the number of paediatric deaths from measles
alongside the total number of deaths over the same period.

TABLE 1: Mulago Paediatric Deaths by Cause, June 1982 to June 1983

Cause	Number	Percent
Perinatal and Neonatal Deaths		
Stillbirths	266	16.8
Premature	238	15.1
Neonatal tetanus	79	5.0
Congenital	10	0.6
Other	4	0.2
Postneonatal Deaths		
Measles	452	28.6
Pneumonia	200	12.7
Gastro and dehydration	81	5.1
Anaemia	62	3.9
Sickle Cell D.	4	0.2
Protein energy malnutrition	33	2.1
Pertussis	15	0.9
Tuberculosis	14	0.9
Meningitis and encephalitis	25	1.6
Sepsis	18	1.1
Malaria	15	0.9
Rabies	2	0.1
Polio	2	0.1
Other[a]	80	5.1
Total	1581	101.0

[a]Includes about 50 designated as CCF or Respiratory Failure without Eti-
ology.

Despite the incompleteness of the data, several significant conclusions can
be drawn from the tabulations. Firstly, in that measles is a preventable
condition, all such deaths must be regarded as unnecessary. The exceptionally high death rate from measles is undoubtedly due to complex interactions
between nutrition, immunity and dehydration. Nevertheless such death rates
denote primarily a failure of immunisation programmes and these must be
reactivated, reorganised and expanded as quickly as possible. No other
activity at present would result in such great gains for the health of
Uganda's children. Our evidence makes it clear that nearly half of all
postneonatal deaths at Mulago could be avoided if an effective immunisation
programme was in operation.

Secondly, even without knowing the totals for measles admissions to Mulago,
it seems clear that too many children are dying from measles while in the
hospital. Further information on number of days in hospital and complications in illness would obviously help clarify this conclusion. But there
can be little doubt that more adequate attention than is currently given in
the hospital to hydration, chest care, nutrition, medical management and

nursing care could result in a marked reduction in the number of measles deaths. Training programmes, staffing patterns and in-service needs will have to be thoroughly redefined and reorganised if care of a standard expected in a teaching hospital is to be accomplished.

TABLE 2:   Mulago Measles Deaths, June 1982 to June 1983

Month	Measles Deaths (N)	Measles Postneonatal Deaths (%)
June	31	35
July	43	40
August	31	34
September	43	51
October	19	40
November	9	26
December	29	55
January	18	38
February	34	52
March	65	56
April	69	55
May	61	52
Total	452	46

Thirdly, if paediatricians in Uganda are to be able to identify pressing paediatric problems and respond to them effectively and efficiently with the limited resources at hand, it is imperative that more accurate information be made available to them. If, for example, the ages at death of children who die from measles were known, the optimal age for measles immunisation could be objectively reassessed. Again, the reasons behind the apparently high numbers of deaths due to neonatal tetanus as a proportion of all neonatal deaths at Mulago (13%), and for perinatal and neonatal deaths as a proportion of infant mortality (38%), should be examined more closely than has been possible here or, more generally, at Mulago.

Records were once very carefully kept at Mulago. Suitable standards of care were formerly obtained. Effort is needed to improve both standards of record-keeping and clinical life.

Overall, the most pressing need is to reach more of Uganda's children through an immunisation programme while fortifying them nutritionally for their passage through the still perilous years of childhood.

Morbidity and Mortality in Selected
Uganda Hospitals, 1981–1982

D. J. Alnwick, M. R. Stirling and G. Kyeyune

INTRODUCTION

It is widely appreciated that most ill health and premature death in most
developing countries is attributable to a number of infectious and parasitic
diseases, the majority of which can be prevented or controlled through
appropriate, relatively low-cost health interventions. In Uganda there is
also a considerable body of opinion which holds that the health status of
Ugandans, and of children in particular, has deteriorated considerably over
the past decade as a consequence of the decline in both the quality and
coverage of community health services. For example the "Revised Recovery
Programme; 1982-1984" prepared by the Uganda Government (1982a: 81) states:

> Health standards have deteriorated over the past decade. Among the
> reasons for this are untreated water supplies, inadequate sanitation and
> poor nutrition. These deficiencies give rise to waterborne and water-
> related diseases and lower resistance to other diseases. Reduced immuni-
> sation programmes and falling standards of primary health care have
> compounded the problem.

While high levels of illness and death associated with a range of common
diseases are recognised, the magnitude of disease-specific morbidity and
mortality and changes over the past decade are not generally appreciated
given the virtual collapse of the health information system and regular
disease surveillance activities. For example, while the last Ministry of
Health annual statistical report was published in 1978, the Ministry considers that "statistical information collected since 1975 is grossly inadequate and unreliable" (Uganda, 1982b: 65).

In spite of the problems experienced some disease reporting from hospitals
has continued. However, no analysis of the available data has been undertaken since the mid-1970s.

This scarcity of reliable data on disease patterns and health facility
utilisation has presented as a major obstacle to the Ministry of Health and
the international donor community in establishing priorities for health
interventions and for monitoring the effectiveness of community health
programmes in reducing mortality and morbidity.

OBJECTIVES

As a first step in developing baseline data for health planning an examination of hospital reporting forms for 1981-82 was undertaken by UNICEF.

The objectives of the exercise were:

- to rank diseases in terms of their contribution to overall hospital admissions and hospital deaths.[1]

- to examine changes in the patterns of hospital admission and mortality occurring over the decade 1971-81.

- to promote interest in the importance of basic data for effective planning. It is hoped that this "rough and ready" exercise will help stimulate the reestablishment of a more thorough and ongoing health reporting system in Uganda.

METHOD

All outpatient (MF75) and inpatient (MF74) monthly returns which had been sent to the Ministry of Health Planning Unit from both government and voluntary hospitals, for the period July 1981-June 1982, were examined.

Diseases for study were selected on the basis of discussions with health staff and disease patterns in neighbouring countries. This list was subsequently compared to the hospital outpatient form and corresponded to eighteen classified respiratory, infectious and parasitic diseases or disease groups. For the hospital inpatient statistics it was decided to narrow further the range of disease categories considered to the nine commonest causes of hospital admission. While the number of diseases identified by this method represents only about 10 percent of the total number of diseases listed on the forms, the remaining diseases reported--for example, malignant neoplasms and circulatory disorders--were generally of such low levels as to be considered unimportant for the purposes of this exercise. The total returns for these diseases have been classified under the heading "other".

Only hospitals for which returns were available for at least eight of the twelve months, July 1981 to June 1982, were included in the study. In this way information from twenty-three Ugandan hospitals was selected (Table 1). Data for missing months were imputed by taking the average for the preceding and following month.

The results from this analysis were then compared with data presented in the 1970-71 medical services statistical records (Uganda, 1971).

LIMITATIONS OF THE STUDY

In interpreting these data three major considerations should be borne in mind. Firstly, the quality of the data must be of concern since the computa-

---

[1]It is only possible through hospital returns to obtain indicators of disease-specific fatality rather than mortality rates. While both fatality and mortality rates have the same numerator (the number of people dying of the disease during the stated period) the morbidity rate denominator is the

tion of disease-specific morbidity and mortality rates suspected of belonging to the identified disease groups requires accurate diagnosis in relation to the WHO International Classification of Diseases. This requires diagnostic and pathological support services which, in Uganda, are recognised to have deteriorated significantly over the past decade. Further, specific identification of vulnerable groups from the available data is not possible since there is no provision for disaggregation by age.

TABLE 1: Frequency of Reporting by Hospitals During the Period July 1981 to June 1982

	Number of Hospitals submitting the following Number of Reports			
	No Reports	1 to 3 Reports	4 to 7 Reports	8 to 12 Reports
Government hospitals (47)				
Outpatients	29	1	0	17
Inpatients	23	5	2	17
Voluntary hospitals (29)				
Outpatient	11	5	7	6
Inpatients	11	6	6	6

Secondly, caution must be exercised in comparing 1970-71 and 1981-82 data because of possible changes in the role of hospitals in the community which will effect the degree to which hospital records reflect community morbidity and mortality patterns.

Thirdly, the morbidity and mortality indicators presented here relate only to the hospitals for which data were available and may not be representative of the country as a whole.

RESULTS

The essential findings of the study are presented in Tables 2 and 3. Table 2 summarises outpatient attendances for eighteen selected diseases at government and voluntary hospitals, 1981-82 and 1970-71; and Table 3 presents a summary of the leading causes of admission and death in government and voluntary hospitals, 1981-82 and 1970-71.

The eighteen selected diseases accounted for only 32 percent of all outpatient attendances in 1981-82 compared to 46 percent in 1970-71. However, nine diseases accounted for 48 percent of all hospital admissions and 68 percent of all hospital deaths during 1981-82 compared to 35 percent and 47 percent respectively in 1970-71. Thus the proportion of people dying in hospital from the nine selected diseases has increased by 21 percent over the eleven years.

Looking to disease-specific outpatient attendance patterns during 1981-82 the most commonly treated cases were pneumonia and other respiratory dis-

---

total population within which the deaths occurred while case fatality is restricted to persons with the disease.

TABLE 2: Outpatient Attendances for Selected Diseases at Government and Voluntary Hospitals, 1981–82 and 1970–71

Disease	1981–82		1970–71	
	Cases	Percent of Total	Cases	Percent of Total
P & RI	190,995	12.1	805,543	18.1
Other fever	103,110	6.5	483,867	10.9
Malaria	72,891	4.6	264,093	5.9
Measles	36,692	2.3	68,384	1.5
Gastroenteritis	32,339	2.0	128,603	2.9
Hookworm	15,608	1.0	98,615	2.2
Ascariasis	12,659	.8	83,448	1.9
Anaemia	12,269	.8	23.650	.5
Whooping cough	10,445	.7	23,157	.5
Dysentery	9,600	.6	36,211	.8
Kwashiorkor	3,153	.2	21,681	.5
Tuberculosis	2,388	.2	6,143	.1
Vitamin deficiency	1,803	.1	9,033	.2
Schistosomiasis	1,669	.1	8,199	.2
Diptheria	828	.1	360	
Guinea worm	419		997	
Meningitis	331		643	
Poliomyelitis	1,279	.1	748	
Total above	508,478	32.2	2,063,375	46.3
Total all others	1,070,113	67.8	2,390,200	53.7
Grand total	1,578,591	100.0	4,453,575	100.0

TABLE 3: Leading Causes of Admission and Death in Government and Voluntary Hospitals (Inpatients), 1970–71 and 1981–82

Disease	Admissions (%)		Case Fatality Rate (%)		Proportion of Deaths (%)	
	1981	1970	1981	1970	1981	1970
Measles	12.4	5.3	9.5	4.3	25.6	5.4
Bronchial pneumonia	7.3	5.0	8.3	9.4	13.2	11.3
Malaria	9.8	9.1	2.5	3.0	5.2	6.6
Gastroenteritis	7.1	7.2	5.5	5.5	8.4	9.5
Tetanus	0.4	0.5	48.2	46.6	4.5	5.5
Anaemia	3.6	3.6	5.4	6.1	4.3	5.2
Dysentery	2.9	0.6	3.5	4.3	2.2	0.6
URTI	2.7	3.0	3.3	2.7	1.9	2.0
Pertussis	1.4	1.0	7.4	3.4	2.3	0.9
Total above	47.6	35.3	6.5	5.5	67.6	47.0
All other causes excluding maternity	52.4	64.7	2.8	3.4	32.4	53.0
Total	100.0	100.0	4.6	4.2	100.0	100.0

eases, unspecified fevers, malaria and injuries.[2]

As indicated in Annex 1, respiratory diseases accounted for 37.6 percent of the eighteen selected diseases; unspecified fevers, 20.3 percent; parasitic diseases, 20.3 percent; the immunisable diseases, 10.2 percent and gastro-enteritis/dysentery, 8.4 percent. Interestingly, nutritionally associated illnesses (kwashiorkor, anaemia, vitamin deficiency) accounted for just over 3 percent.

There has been no significant change in the ranking of the selected diseases since 1970-71 except in the category of immunisable diseases which have more than doubled. Though no significant increase in the proportion of children diagnosed with polio, tuberculosis, whooping cough and diptheria is evident, measles cases have increased from 3.3 percent to 7.2 percent of outpatients presenting in the selected categories (see Annex 1).

While the outpatients records indicate a general morbidity pattern, Table 3 suggests that a large proportion of inpatient admissions are concentrated among a small number of diseases. Measles, bronchial pneumonia, diarrhoeal diseases and malaria alone represent 39.5 percent of total hospital admissions and 54.6 percent of total hospital deaths. Most significantly, measles stands out as the primary cause of hospital admissions (12.4 percent) and death. Diarrhoeal diseases also rank highly accounting for 10 percent of admissions and 10.6 percent of deaths. In 1981-82, measles with a case fatality rate of 9.5 percent accounted for nearly 26 percent of hospital nonmaternity deaths as compared to 5.4 percent in 1970-71. The data suggest, however, that 1981-82 may have been an epidemic year for measles.

A simple ranking of disease-specific fatality rates indicated little significant change in the death rates associated with bronchial pneumonia, malaria, the diarrhoeal diseases, URTI and anaemia. However, it is notable that hospital deaths due to pertussis have more than doubled and dysentery fatality has more than quadrupled.

CONCLUSION

This study has confirmed the view that a relatively small number of infectious and parasitic diseases, representing approximately a third of reported hospital morbidity and over two-thirds of hospital deaths, are the greatest causes of morbidity and mortality in Ugandan hospitals. Further the study supports the contention that poor immunisation performance, the decline in environmental sanitation standards and deterioration of potable water supplies over the past decade have contributed significantly to the high morbidity and fatality rates associated with preventable diseases. This is particularly clear in the cases of measles and diarrhoeal diseases. However, prior to assuming that the prevalence or incidence of these diseases within the community have increased significantly, it is advisable to reflect on the degree to which hospital morbidity and mortality patterns represent the community as a whole. Even so, it is abundantly clear that much of the illness and death occurring and presenting in Ugandan hospitals can be reduced through the promotion of disease-prevention activities.

---

[2] Injuries are the third major cause of outpatient presentation and the second major cause of hospital admission in 1981-82.

REFERENCES

MacMahon, B. and T. Pugh (1970). Epidemiology: Principles and Methods. Little Brown, Boston.

Uganda, Republic of, Ministry of Health (1971). Medical Services Records. Government Printers, Entebbe.

Uganda, Republic of (1982a). Revised Recovery Programme: 1982-84. Government Printers, Entebbe.

Uganda, Republic of, Ministry of Health. 1982b. Plan of Action for Primary Health Care. Government Printers, Entebbe.

World Health Organization. 1981. Development of Indicators for Monitoring Progress Towards Health for All by the Year 2000. WHO, Geneva.

ANNEX 1

Outpatient Attendances for Selected Diseases at Government and Voluntary Hospitals, 1981-82 and 1970-71

Disease	1981-82		1970-71	
	Cases	%	Cases	%
P & RI	190,995	37.6	805,543	39.0
Other fever	103,110	20.3	483,867	23.5
Malaria	72,891	14.3	264,093	12.8
Measles	36,692	7.2	68,384	3.3
Gastroenteritis	32,339	6.4	128,603	6.2
Hookworm	15,608	3.1	98,615	4.8
Ascariasis	12,659	2.5	83,448	4.0
Anaemia	12,269	2.1	23,650	1.2
Whooping cough	10,445	2.1	23,157	1.1
Dysentery	9,600	2.0	36,211	1.8
Kwashiorkor	3,153	0.6	21,681	1.1
Tuberculosis	2,388	0.5	6,143	0.3
Vitamin deficiency	1,803	0.4	9,033	0.4
Schistosomiasis	1,669	0.2	8,199	0.4
Poliomylitis	1,279	0.2	748	0.0
Diptheria	828	0.2	360	0.0
Guinea worm	419	0.1	997	0.0
Meningitis	331	0.1	643	0.0
Total	508,478	100.0	2,063,375	100.0

ANNEX 2

Cause of Admission and Death by Selected Diseases in Government and Voluntary Hospitals, 1970–71 and 1981–82

Disease	Admissions		Deaths	
	1970	1981	1970	1981
Measles	20,678	14,081	887	1,341
Bronchial pneumonia	19,658	8,272	1,845	690
Malaria	35,798	11,110	1,088	274
Gastroenteritis	28,475	8,022	1,553	441
Tetanus	1,949	492	908	237
Anaemia	14,047	4,151	854	224
Dysentery	2,303	3,267	98	115
URTI	11,914	3,080	324	102
Pertussis	4,104	1,625	141	120
Total above	138,926	54,100	7,698	3,544
All other causes				
excluding maternity	254,074	59,318	8,706	1,694
Total	393,000	113,418	16,404	5,238

Evaluation of Government Rural Health Centres and UNICEF Essential Drug Input

F. M. Mburu

INTRODUCTION

In 1981 UNICEF began supplying 100 health centres with an essential drug kit on a quarterly basis. It was reasoned that the health centre was the main provider of services in Uganda and that curative services were essential to all other medical interventions. In March 1984 the programme was evaluated. The findings are reported here.

OBJECTIVES

The objectives of the study were:
- to determine the suitability of the forty-five drugs in the kits distributed;
- to establish the five or six major illnesses diagnosed by health centre staff;
- to determine if distribution was effective;
- to make recommendations on the programme.

METHODS OF COLLECTING INFORMATION

The methods used in collecting information were as follows:
- Mortality data were drawn from the Ministry of Health (MOH)/UNICEF study of hospital records for 1981-82.[1]
- Interviews were conducted with eleven district medical officers (DMOs) and fourteen health centre staff.[2]

---

[1]The mortality data are from twenty-eight reporting hospitals. They are not representative of all hospitals in Uganda. For further information here, see the article by Alnwick, Stirling and Kyeyune in this volume, Morbidity and Mortality in Uganda Hospitals, 1981-1982.
[2]Field visits were made to the following districts: Masaka, Mbarara, Kabale, Jinja, Tororo, Iganga, Soroti, Lira, Apac, Kumi and Mbale. These districts were not selected randomly but for convenience. However, because of their ready accessibility to Kampala, it is likely that the health situ-

- Health centre staff were requested to list the five or six major illnesses diagnosed in their area.
- DMOs and health centre staff were requested to write out a list of the fifteen most essential drugs.
- The author took an inventory of medicines at each health centre visited and noted stocks at four predetermined dates from inventory records.
- Staff at health centres were noted by qualification and number.
- Interviews were conducted with MOH and UNICEF personnel.
- Administrative secretaries and district treasurers were requested to provide budget figures (projected and actual expenditures) for collection and distribution of drug kits.[3]

The foregoing was completed over a two-month period in February and March 1984. A visit was also made to Tanzania as part of a Government of Uganda MOH and UNICEF mission to evaluate the Tanzania essential drugs programme.[4] I also drew upon my experience in Kenya and elsewhere in arriving at the recommendations included in this study.[5]

FINDINGS

Findings are reported in Tables 2 through 6. Table 1 gives information on mortality. In interviews and discussions with DMOs the following were noted:

- Drugs are in short supply. The UNICEF kits are often the only regular supply to reach the district.

- Some DMOs divide UNICEF kits into small kits and give an "equal" share to all health facilities in the district.

- Some DMOs borrow drugs from the kits for use in the district hospital.

- Some district hospitals refer patients to rural health centres when they are short of drugs.

- All DMOs lack transportation and cannot supervise their rural staff except when a crisis strikes.[6]

---

ation in the twenty-three districts not surveyed was worse than in the thirteen districts surveyed. The DMO Apac was on transfer to Lira when this study was conducted. The health centres visited were identified by DMOs, not selected randomly. Fifteen health centres were visited. Reliable information was received from fourteen on drug inventory, fifteen on most common diagnosis and thirteen on staffing.

[3]The figures reported were not verified and questions arise with respect to the disproportionately large expenditure reported in Kumi and the small expenditure reported in Lira. I attempted to question relevant district officials on their figures, and attempted to obtain proper records in Kampala from the Ministry of Local Government, but without success. Therefore the figures reported should be viewed with suitable caution.

[4]See AFYA/UNICEF, Tanzania (1983).

[5]See the Administrative Support Unit report of the Ministry of Health (Kenya, 1982).

[6]UNICEF provided nineteen districts with vehicles in 1980 but due to irregular maintenance, lack of tyres and spares, these are in general inop-

In interviews and discussions with members of rural health centre staffs, we noted:

- Many do not understand that diseases can be treated without pre-scribing medicines. Inadequate understandings of the uses of oral rehydration salts (ORS) is the best example.[7]

- Overdiagnosis often takes place resulting in overprescribing. Streptomycin is widely used for upper respiratory tract and gonoco-cal infections; aspirin is used for URTI, wounds, pneumonia and malaria.

- The "cure-all" drugs are antibiotics which tend to be overused at first, then underprescribed as they run short. This combination of practices was found to be universal and strictly enforced by health centre personnel despite the fact that antibiotics can produce resistant strains and seldom cure infections.

- Some health centre staff make patients swallow the prescribed medicine on the spot and return daily for treatment, regardless of how far they must walk and regardless of how long the treatment takes.

DISCUSSION

Comparison of Table 1 (mortality) with Table 2 (most commonly diagnosed illnesses) confirms the importance of measles and pertussis and hence the urgency of immunisation. Diarrhoeal diseases are the fifth-ranked diagnosis and compare to gastroenteritis and dysentery (from the mortality table) highlighting the importance of rehydration therapy. Malaria and acute respiratory tract infections are identified in both tables. While worms and venereal diseases are not identified in the Table 1 listing as they do not cause death, they are listed in Table 2. The catch-all category of "other" comprises 20 percent of diagnoses and accounts for 47.6 percent of mortali-ty. Further information here would be interesting but none was collected.

Table 3 lists thirty-four different drugs under subheadings for district medical officers and the collective list of the health centre staff. The figures here were derived by giving each DMO a blank paper on which he wrote his preferred list of fifteen most essential drugs; health centre staffs were requested to draw up a similar list on their own. The two preferred lists differ not so much in the type of drugs as in the frequency of prefer-ence. For example, more than 50 percent of the DMOs would order ORS while only 14 percent of the health centre staff would do so.

Comparisons between Table 2 (diagnosis) and Table 3 (preferred drugs) show a discrepency. Although anaemia and intestinal worms are listed as a leading health risk, the medicines to treat them--multivites, ferrous sulphate and mebendazole--do not appear to be "essential" to the health centre staff though the DMOs recognise their importance.

---

erable today.
[7]Continuing medical education, refresher courses and training material are all lacking. However, specialised training has begun in eastern Uganda, Mbale District, for immunisation and control of diarrhoeal diseases.

TABLE 1: Causes of Death by Disease in Government Hospitals, 1981

	Admissions[a]	Deaths[b]	Deaths as % of Admissions	Deaths as % Total Deaths
Measles	8900	760	8.5	28.5
B. pneumonia	4500	300	6.7	11.1
Malaria	6700	210	3.1	7.8
E. enteritis	3400	160	4.7	6.1
Tetanus	3200	140	4.4	5.4
Injuries	6800	140	2.1	5.3
Anaemia	1000	90	9.0	3.3
Dysentery	1400	70	5.0	2.8
URTI	1900	50	2.6	1.8
Pertussis	590	40	6.8	1.6
Total	35000	1960	5.6	54.4

*Source: Uganda (1983).
[a]Figures to the nearest 100, except for tetanus and pertussis which are to
to the nearest 10.
[b]Figures rounded to the nearest 10.

TABLE 2: Most Common Diagnosis in Health Centres

Problem	No. Reporting (Total 15)
Malaria	14
Acute respiratory infection	11
Measles	10
Intestinal worms	9
Diarrhoeal diseases	7
Pneumonia	6
URI/gonorrhoea	6
Whooping cough	3
Wounds	3
Others	14

We can conclude from the preferred list that the more expensive the drug
(and perhaps the most impressive to patients), the more likely it is to be
considered essential by health centre staff. Examples of such drugs are
tetracycline, ampicillin capsules, phenobarbitone and P.A.M.

The findings reported in Table 4 on availability of drugs in health centres
are important. Antibiotic capsules and injectables disappear from stocks at
a much faster rate than do others. However, in visits to local pharmacies
near each health centre, I found the drugs in short supply at the health
centres well stocked. It is thought that shortage of these items in the
public sector may be related to supply in the private sector. But there was
no easy way of identifying during the field visit whether or not the drugs
came from the health centre.

Whenever drugs run out in a health centre, attendance drops off. Patients
ask when the next delivery is expected and health centre staff naturally
give out the information. This results in clusters of attendance or "peaks"

when drugs are in stock, and corresponding "valleys" when supplies run out.
Also, when it is known that a health centre has drugs, patients often come
from as far as 30 kilometres away. This inflates the catchment area and puts
unrealistic demands on the limited drug supply, contributing to the shortage
of medicines.

TABLE 3: List of Drugs Recommended by DMOs and Health Centre Staff

Drug Item	DMOs % Listing (Total 11)	HC Staff % Listing (Total 14)
Chloroquine tabs	100	100
Chloroquine injection	81.8	85.6
Procaine penicillin fortified	100	100
Crystalline penicillin	90.9	92.9
Oral rehydration salts	54.5	14.3
Multivites	36.4	14.3
Mebendazole	90.9	50.0
Ferrous sulphates	63.4	28.6
Piperazine	27.3	28.6
Tetracycline caps	45.5	71.4
Tetracycline ointment	54.5	14.3
Phenobarbitone	27.3	50.0
Ampicillin syrup	45.5	28.6
Ampicillin caps	9.1	57.1
Adrenaline	18.2	21.4
Aspirin	90.9	100
Panadol	27.3	42.9
Sulphadimedine	81.8	85.7
Ergometrine	45.5	21.4
Ephedrine	18.2	21.4
Chloramphenicol	18.2	28.6
Streptomycin	36.4	28.6
INH	36.4	0
Pen. V	18.2	14.3
Whitfield ointment	18.2	0
P.A.M.	18.2	42.9
Mist expectorant	9.1	14.3
Magnasium trislicate	18.2	14.3
Probenaceid	0	7.1
Antiseptics	18.2	7.1
Dressing Solution	18.2	21.4
Anthisan	18.2	14.3
Metromodazole	18.2	0
Kaolin	18.2	28.6

The information of Table 4 can also be referred to in the redesign of the
contents and amount of medicine in the drug kits. Some drugs are under-
supplied, others are in excess.

The staffing pattern found at the thirteen health centres visited which were
able to provide reliable information has consequences for essential drug
management (Table 5). While the sample is small (there are 101 government
health centres in Uganda, and this sample of thirteen represents only 13

percent), the findings are interesting. The actual staffing pattern indicates nonuniformity: nursing aids were the largest cadre with between
three and eight aids; medical assistants were the clinical supervising
officers, though in six of the thirteen reporting health centres they were
not present, and nursing aids were found diagnosing and prescribing medicines. One DMO expressed a common dismay as follows: "People seem to be
hired because they need employment rather than because there is a job to be
done, but there is nothing I can do when they are posted to one of my
facilities."

TABLE 4: Availability of Essential Drugs as Identified by Health Centre Staff (14 HCs Surveyed)

	% With Stock During Selected Periods				
	Visit Day	Jan 84	Dec 83	Aug 83	Jun 83
Chloroquine tabs	35.7	64.3	28.6	28.6	14.3
Chloroquine injection	57.1	50	50	28.6	21.4
PPF	57.1	57.1	21.4	21.4	14.3
Crystalline penicillin	42.9	35.7	42.9	35.7	21.4
Aspirin	42.9	57.1	42.9	21.4	14.3
Tetracycline caps	50	64.3	21.4	14.3	14.3
Tetracycline syrup	0	0	0	0	0
Ampicillin caps	42.9	35.7	7.1	14.3	0
Ampicillin syrup	21.4	21.4	14.3	7.1	14.3
Sulphadimedine tabs	42.9	57.1	14.3	21.4	14.3
Ergometrine	42.9	28.6	42.9	28.6	28.6
Pen V	28.6	28.6	14.3	7.1	0
Ferrous sulphate	42.9	57.1	28.6	42.9	21.4
Chloramphenicol	0	0	0	0	0
Adrenaline	50.9	42.9	28.6	14.3	14.3
Streptomycin	28.6	14.3	14.3	7.1	0
Piperazine tabs	71.4	42.9	50	28.1	18.6
Mebendazole tab	14.3	21.4	0	14.3	7.1
Panadol	14.3	21.4	0	14.3	7.1
ORS	35.7	57.1	35.7	7.1	7.1
Hibitane	0	0	0	0	0
PAM	7.1	0	0	0	0
Triplopen	0	7.1	14.3	0	0
Kaolin	0	0	0	0	0
Phenobarbitone	21.4	35.7	14.7	0	0
Multivites	21.4	42.9	7.1	28.6	14.3
Tetracycline eye ointment	21.4	28.6	28.6	21.4	0

TABLE 5: Staffing Pattern in Thirteen Health Centres Reporting

	0	1	2	3	4	5+1	Total
Medical assistant		9	4				13
Enrolled nurse	2	8	2	1			13
Midwife		1	4	3	3	2	13
Nursing aid				1	3	9	13

The cost of collecting and distributing the essential drugs is reported in Table 6. This is especially relevant when we consider the interministerial arrangements and dichotomies between the Ministry of Health and Ministry of Local Government.

TABLE 6: Cost of Collecting and Distributing UNICEF Drug Kits, and debts to the Ministry of Health in Selected Districts

	Drug Budgeting ('000s of UShs)		Cost of (actual UShs)		Debt Owed MOH ('000s)
	Proposed	Actual	Collection	Distribution	
Masaka	2,300	1,500	45,000	30,000	NA
Mbarara	2,500	500	60,000	25,000	NA
Kabale	3,000	4,000[a]	150,000	30,000	4,000
Mpigi	NA	NA	40,000	NA	NA
Jinja	5,000	3,500	15,000	2,000	5,000
Iganga	5,000	4,500[b]	35,000	30,000	3,000
Tororo	4,000	6,000[c]	60,000	30,000	6,000
Mbale	3,000	1,200	45,000	12,000	6,000
Kumi	3,000	6,000	35,000	3,000	3,000
Soroti	3,500	2,500	80,000	35,000	10,000
Lira	1,500	45	100,000	55,000	6,000
Apach	NA	NA	100,000	10,000	2,000

[a]Of this amount 1.4 million went to reduce outstanding debts.
[b]Of this amount 3.2 million went towards the repayment of outstanding debts.
[c]Most of this went towards the repayment of debts.

The Ministry of Health is responsible for health policies, standards, manpower training and administration of all hospitals as well as Central Medical Stores, equipment and drugs.

The Ministry of Local Government is responsible for all aspects of all health facilities below hospitals; i.e. health centres, dispensary-maternity units, dispensaries, subdispensaries and aid posts. District medical officers are on secondment from the MOH to Local Government. In theory they are responsible to the MOH but in practice they are accountable to the local district administration. Local districts allocate budgets, develop and maintain health facilities and provide transportation.

Drug kits are delivered to the MOH Central Medical Stores. In 1981 and 1982 MOH distributed the kits and billed the Ministry of Local Government for transport costs. Local Government never paid; consequently the MOH discontinued deliveries and DMOs were advised over the public radio when a new consignment of drugs was available for collection. Thirty-three districts are expected to send separate vehicles to Entebbe to collect drug kits, a needlessly duplicative and expensive expectation. All but one of the districts visited collected their kits regularly. The one exception had not collected its kits for a year! Obviously the distribution of drug kits could be accomplished more effectively than it is.

The level of indebtedness shown in the last column of Table 6 indicates the magnitude of the problem inherent in this dichotomous system. UNICEF drug

kits cost between $1600 and 2000 per year per health centre, and there are
approximately three health centres per district yielding an annual cost per
district of between $4800 and 6000. This UNICEF input compared to actual
expenditures puts the essential drug programme into perspective, especially
when most actual expenditures went against debt repayment (see notes to
Table 6).

CONCLUSIONS AND RECOMMENDATIONS

The UNICEF essential drugs programme forms the backbone of the rural health
system. At the present time there is no solid indication that the Ministry
of Local Government can take over financial responsibility for the system in
1986 when the UNICEF programme is scheduled to end.

The proportion of budget allocations between hospitals and all other health
units, i.e. rural health centres, aid posts, etc., is a ratio of 3:1.
However, the daily attendance at the country's thirty-three district hospitals is estimated at 300 daily for a total of 2,613,600 visits per year.
Rural health centres number 101, and using a very conservative estimate of
100 patients per day, 2,666,400 visits per year can be estimated. Considering that there are an additional 644 rural health units in the country, it
is easy to conclude that the rural population which accounts for 91 percent
of the population is not getting a fair share of the health budget which
favours hospitals over rural units 3:1 in budget allotment.

The recommendations possible from this study are as follows for local admin-
istration:
- DMOs need transport to supervise staff.
- UNICEF drug kits should go regularly "intact" to health centres and
  should not be shared out.
- Health centres should have record books, keep better records and
  report monthly to the DMO.
- Minimal drug supplies should be sent to all rural units adjacent to
  UNICEF-assisted health centres to stabilise catchment populations.

Recommendations for Central Government include:
- Resource allocation favours hospitals over rural health centres yet
  serves fewer people. More equitable resource allocation should be
  considered.
- Coordination between the Ministry of Health and Ministry of Local
  Government with particular attention to budget preparation and
  allocation needs attention to minimise drug shortages.

Recommendations for Ministry of Health and Central Medical Stores include:
- UNICEF drug kits should be delivered immediately upon receipt
  directly to designated health centres under an annually negotiated
  budget allocation--either from MOH, Ministry of Local Government or
  UNICEF.

Recommendations for UNICEF include:
- The drug kit composition should be reconsidered to include only
  essential drugs for which rural staff are trained to administer.

Finally, recommendations for MOH and UNICEF include:
- Training of health personnel is absolutely essential for greater
  effectiveness in the management of essential drugs in diagnostic
  procedures, criteria for prescribing and management of records.

- The DMOs and other district and regional supervisory staff need reorientation and training in the importance of immunisation, oral rehydration therapy and personnel management.
- Staffing patterns need to be rationalised and adequately trained staff assigned to health centres.
- Regular continuing medical education should be instituted.

REFERENCES

AFYA/UNICEF (1983). Essential Drug Programme: Use and Storage of Essential Drugs: Handbook for Health Workers. Dar es Salaam, Tanzania.

Kenya, Republic of, Ministry of Health (1982). New Management System of Drug Supplies to Rural Health Facilities: Training Manual. Government Printers, Nairobi.

Uganda, Republic of, and UNICEF (1983). "Uganda Country Programme, 1983-86." Mimeographed, Kampala.

The Luwero Triangle: Emergency Operations in Luwero, Mubende and Mpigi Districts

Alastair Johnston

In early 1983 the Government of Uganda mobilised its security forces (UNLA) in a military operation against armed dissident groups who had become increasingly active in certain areas after the 1980 elections.[1] The operation commenced in areas of Luwero District flanking the Bombo road (which is the main road from Kampala to the north of the country). For a period of several months the road was effectively closed to all but military traffic.

The operation spread gradually northwards and westwards along both the Bombo and Hoima roads, eventually nearing the southern shores of Lake Kyoga in the north and Kiboga (Mubende District) in the west. From the outset an essential part of the strategy seemed to be the displacement of the civilian population into makeshift camps adjacent to temporary military posts, leaving only suspect groups and individuals in the rural hinterland.[2] The region in which such displacement of people has occurred is referred to as the "disturbed areas" (see Figure 1). It should be stressed that the military operation itself together with the resulting displacements was a dynamic process with continuous shifts in emphasis causing changes in circumstances for the local population. In some localities civilians gravitated to UNLA outposts for "protection"; in others they were forced into such outposts; in still others they were displaced by the fighting.

different forms of disruption have taken place in different locations within

---

*Editors' note: At the time this article was written in June 1984, "emergency operations" were still underway in the region under consideration. They were still underway when the article was presented for publication.

[1] These elections, which resulted in a victory for the party of President Milton Obote (Uganda Peoples Congress), were widely believed by his opponents to have been unfair.

[2] Controversy as to the nature of the camps has been continuous with the government insisting that people sought protection in UNLA outposts while the foreign press often accused UNLA forces of forcing civilians into the camps. The truth no doubt lies somewhere between the two perspectives. In illustration of the government perspective, see Uganda Times (9 July 1983). For an alternative perspective, see Righter (1983).

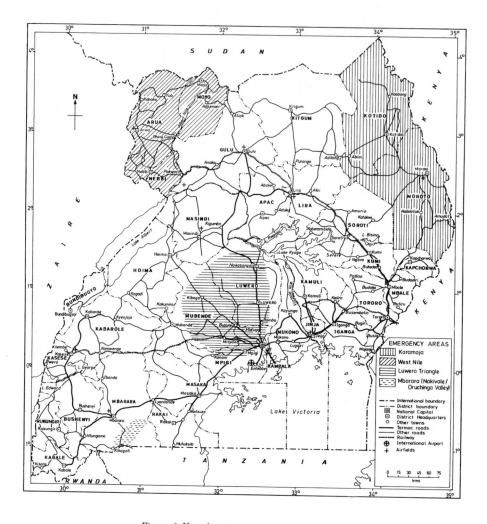

Figure 1 Uganda emergency areas, 1980–1984

the area at different times over the past fifteen months. In some places very few local people have been displaced. In other areas almost all the population was uprooted and restricted to makeshift camps.

After launching an international appeal in Spetember 1983 the Government of Uganda committed itself to a programme for the resettlement of the people in their home areas together with the restoration of normal government services.[3] Many of the camps have already been disbanded. However, at many of these "disbanded" camps a nucleus of people (sometimes numbering in the hundreds) remains, often because they do not originate in the surrounding areas and have no means for transporting themselves to their distant homes. In some cases new camps have been created (e.g. Nakitoma, Nabiswera and Nakazi) as the military operation continues in more distant locations. Recurring violent incidents even in areas long occupied by the UNLA serve to highlight the continuing tense security situation.[4] Figure 2 gives the locations of camps and other relief distribution centres in the "disturbed areas" of the Luwero, Mpigi and Mubende "triangle".

GEOGRAPHY AND DEMOGRAPHY

The affected parts of Luwero, Mpigi and Mubende Districts are estimated to cover an area of 22,000 square kilometres. In the southern parts of the affected area there is much luxuriant natural vegetation with fertile soils and a high annual rainfall. There are many low-lying swampy areas which drain eventually into the Kafu River or Lake Kyoga. On higher ground cultivation is very favourable, the typical pattern of agriculture being based on family small holdings (shambas). Such food crops as maize, matoke, beans, cassava, groundnuts and sweet potatoes are commonly grown. Cash crops such as coffee and cotton are important in this area. In particular the south of Luwero District is of strategic economic importance to Uganda because of its high actual and potential coffee production.

Further north the climate becomes drier and vegitation more sparse. Large ranching schemes were established to exploit the natural propensity of this area for cattle production. The population here is less dense than in the fertile south. In terms of ethnic origins the population in the southern areas is mainly Baganda (i.e the indigenous population of Buganda), with a sprinkling of people from other parts of Uganda and neighbouring countries. However, in the north there exists a significant minority of cattle-keeping peoples, especially the Bahima of Ankole and the Batutsi of Rwanda. Many of these people came to the area specifically to work on cattle-ranching schemes.

---

[3]For many months after the displacement of large numbers of people and the establishment of numerous camps, the Government of Uganda was reluctant to declare an emergency and request assistance. See The People (11 July 1983) and Hall (1983) for two perspectives. Perhaps the government's reluctance was due to definitions of the "camps" as the government repeatedly insisted that they were for the protection, not detainment, of the people. Whatever the reason, the international community and world press were relieved when the government finally admitted the emergency, appealed for assistance and set up a high level mechanism to deal with it (see Legum, 1983).

[4]See the report by Dash (1983) for a wider discussion of one perspective on insecurity in Uganda.

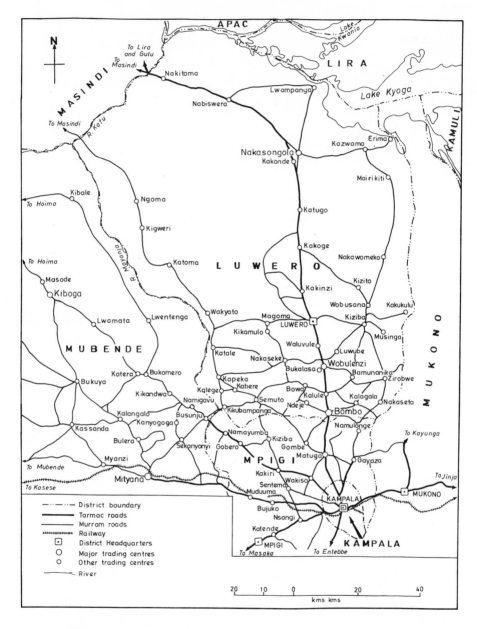

Figure 2 Locations of camps and other relief distribution centres in the Luwero, Mpigi and Mubende triangle

It is evident that over the past several years there has been a significant
depopulation of the disturbed areas. According to figures from the census
of 1980 the population is given as 750,000. The maximum figure for people
receiving relief over the last year has been about 150,000. Although there
are many people within the disturbed areas who were never displaced by the
military operation (e.g. most of those living in towns and trading centres
along the main roads), it would still appear that many of these three-
quarters of a million people are no longer present in the area, having
either died in the fighting and its aftermath, gone into hiding or fled the
area altogether.

PROBLEMS OF THE DISPLACED PEOPLE

The first camps to be visited in April and May 1983 revealed conditions
which proved to be typical. These camps were invariably next to military
garrisons at small trading centres, often at the junction of several bush
roads. Larger camps could contain anywhere between 2000 and 14,000 people.
The problems encountered among the displaced people can be summarised:

Shelters consisted mainly of looted and abandoned buildings at the trading
centres. In larger camps most habitations consisted of squat branch and
grass huts often crowded together in cramped conditions. In such an
environment there was a high risk of infections and disease due to the
overcrowded and insanitary conditions. There was often also a high risk of
fire.[5]

Many displaced people had lost many of their possessions including clothing,
blankets, cooking utensils, jerry cans and so on. Thus much hardship was
suffered including the effects of cold, weakness and disease by people
unable to clothe and warm themselves, or cook adequate quantities of food.

No provision was made by the authorities to secure adequate water supplies
or sanitary facilities when establishing the camps. Even in the area where
there was abundant water, the concentrations of people meant that long
queues were formed at the source. The source was often polluted by heavy
use. Many families had inadequate means of carrying and storing water. An
estimated 90 percent of the hand pumps in the area were broken forcing
people to use surface water, often from a small unprotected spring or swamp.

The displaced population foraged for food in nearby abandoned shambas.
Thus, as time passed and the land closest to the camps became exhausted,
people were forced to travel increasing distances in search of food.

All government medical services in the disturbed areas had collapsed. Most
rural dispensaries and subdispensaries had also been thoroughly looted. The
rural hospital at Nakaseke was a striking illustration of neglect--built
less than ten years before it was derelict, looted and overgrown at the time
when the relief operation commenced.

The combinations of factors mentioned above have grave implications for
nutritional status, morbidity and mortality rates, especially among children. In many camps the people were in great distress when first visited by
relief teams, lacking as they did the most basic amenities. During the many

---

[5]One such fire was filmed (and subsequently televised) by a British film
crew at Kapeka camp in January 1984.

thousands of consultations which have comprised the Red Cross Medical Relief Programme, the followqing diseases have proved to be the most prevalent: intestinal parasites, scabies, malaria, diarrhoea and gastroenteritis, measles, malnutrition,[6] tropical ulcers, eye disease, upper respiratory tract infections, tuberculosis, anaemia and sexually transmitted diseases.

THE RELIEF RESPONSE

Commencing with camps to the west of the Bombo road (e.g. Ndeje, Kapeka, Semuto) in April and May 1983, voluntary organisations, UN agencies and government workers concentrated emergency assistance to alleviate the severe problems outlined above. Uganda Red Cross commenced the distribution of food in some camps. As the number of accessible camps increased, UNICEF gave assistance by loaning trucks for food transportation, and Save the Children Fund (SCF) together with Oxfam established supplementary feeding centres in selected camps in June.

At the instigation of UNICEF regular weekly interagency meetings were commenced on 27 June 1983 for those agencies directly concerned in the relief effort. It is generally agreed that one positive aspect of the Luwero operation has been the high degree of cooperation and coordination among the agencies involved.

The Immediate Response

Through fora such as the interagency meeting, the roles of different agencies in the initial stages of the relief operation emerged. Especially with regard to essential supplies there was flexibility in the first six to eight months. For example, in the early stages the Uganda Red Cross Society/League of Red Cross Societies (URCS/LRCS) received much support in terms of additional vehicles, food and drugs from other organisations until it was able to build up its own capability.

The activities of the main international or voluntary organisations were as follows:

URCS/LRCS became the de facto lead agency, coordinating the main relief effort in terms of food distribution and medical care. Red Cross organised the distribution of certain non-food items such as clothing, blankets and cooking pots, and was assisted in this task by Oxfam and SCF. Red Cross also conducted registration of all displaced people receiving relief, which enabled them to trace relatives and reunite families, and provided support for all these activities in terms of supplies, logistics and personnel.

UNICEF coordinated and supported activities aimed at securing adequate safe water supplies, with the Government Water Development Department (WDD), Oxfam and SCF as implementing partners. These activities included borehole

---

[6]Nutritional statistics are not available. The ICRC, UNICEF and SCF decided to undertake a nutrition survey in December 1983 but had to abandon the attempt soon after when an attack was carried out against Red Cross personnel. Oxfam and SCF collected some arm circumferance measurements but never on a large enough basis for comparative analysis. Hundreds of the severely malnourished persons were brought to the nutrition unit at Mulago and to the Luwero Health Centre for treatment.

pump replacement, protection of springs and wells, water catchment systems
and the trucking of emergency water supplies to camps. Drugs, fuel and
incentive payments were provided for the Ministry of Health (MOH) relief
effort via the MOH Medical Task Force, Luwero Health Centre and Nakaseke
Hospital. Support in terms of emergency drugs was given to URCS, SCF and
Oxfam.

SCF and Oxfam worked jointly to establish supplementary feeding in the most
needy camps and therapeutic feeding in government health units (such as
Mulago Hospital, Luwero Health Centre and Lutete nutrition outreach clinic).
These organisations supplied additional nutrition and nursing personnel,
paediatric drugs and vehicles. Both Oxfam and SCF recruited water engineers
for implementation of the UNICEF-coordinated water programme. They also
assisted with occasional distribution of non-food relief items such as
plastic sheeting for emergency shelter, and later on, farming implements and
seeds.

World Food Programme (WFP) provided bulk food for Red Cross and SCF/Oxfam
programmes. This food was originally diverted from other WFP programmes.
Subsequently an agreement was reached and a separate allocation made for the
Luwero operation.

The Committee of German Emergency Doctors (CGED) reestablished medical
services (including surgical, paediatric and maternity) with help from MOH,
SCF and UNICEF in Nakaseke rural hospital in the heart of the disturbed
areas.

USAID supplied farm implements for distribution to returning displaced
people in the resettlement phase of the programme, through Red Cross.

The United Nations Food and Agriculture Organisation (FAO) provided seeds
for distribution during the resettlement phase.

Many other agencies such as CARE, the Mennonite Central Committee (MCC), the
Church of Uganda, Wnite Fathers, Lutheran World Federation (LWF) and WHO
contributed vehicles, personnel, relief goods, supplies and equipment at
various times.

The Relief Effort and the Government Response

The first estimate of numbers of people displaced came from the Ministry of
Rehabilitation in March 1983 when they requested assistance for 20,000
people in Luwero District. By the end of July 1983 URC had registered
45,300 people in twenty-one out of twenty-nine camps then known to exist.
The numbers of displaced people and the number of camps continued to rise
with 124,800 registered in thirty-seven camps by the end of 1983. The
numbers of beneficiaries were still rising until mid-March 1984 when registration figures reached 151,500. However, by this time many of the beneficiaries were no longer displaced people but rather people who had returned
to their homes in the disturbed areas. The food distributed to the displaced people averaged around 170 tons per week between November 1983 and
mid-January 1984. From February until the end of March the total gradually
increased to over 300 tons per week. After April, however, the picture
changed completely once more and the distribution of relief food in particular was severely cut back by order of the military authorities.

This is illustrative of the uncertainities under which all agencies have worked since the start of the relief effort. However, there have been a number of major changes in the relief operation of a more positive nature. In July 1983 the Government of Uganda asked ICRC to conduct a survey of conditions in the camps and the needs of the displaced people. After completing the survey and advising the government of its recommendations, ICRC was invited to join the relief operation. ICRC became operational at the end of October 1983, joining forces with URCS and LRCS.

Meanwhile, the government had underlined its intentions of assuring the welfare of the displaced citizens by making plans to coordinate relief, extend government services and eventually to encourage the people to return to their homes. The government launched an international appeal for assistance by publishing a memorandum on 16 September 1983 which also stated the government's intentions with regard to eventual resettlement. A Chief Relief Administrator was appointed to work through the Office of the Prime Minister as coordinator of all government and nongovernment organisation (NGO) relief and resettlement efforts. Regular fortnightly meetings were immediately established between the Government Relief Coordination Committee and the NGOs. The first of these joint meetings was held on 23 September. In addition to all NGOs, district commissioners from the three districts and representatives of all ministries concerned regularly attended and contributed to the meetings. Subcommittees on medical matters and relief distribution were established, and a Medical Relief Coordinator was appointed. The government reallocated some relief tasks by area. For example, the Italian voluntary agency Cooperation and Development for Uganda (C&D) took over the food distribution and medical care for 15,000 displaced people to the east of the Bombo road, while the Food Relief Department (FRD) became responsible for food distribution to a further 16,000 beneficiaries in Mpigi District.

CAMP DISBANDMENT

The first of the large camps to be disbanded was Ndeje in Luwero District, followed by Semuto and Kapeka towards the end of January 1984. In fact, disbandment did not mean that the camps were immediately evacuated, but rather that people were told to go home and start cultivating. In practice large numbers of people at each camp had no nearby home to go to, and so remained. Others who had dispersed to nearby abandoned shambas returned to receive food distributed and medical aid. Distributions of hoes, pangas, seeds and other relief goods were made to the people returning to their homes.

In many areas resettlement produced obvious benefits and the increase in cultivation was marked. In some areas, however, insecurity persisted and the benefits of disbandment for the local population were questionable. Red Cross became involved in moving families away from the area to their home areas. However, it was agreed that food distribution to returnees should continue at least until one cycle of crop production was complete.

CONCLUSION

The period of January through June 1984 has been one of continued instability in the disturbed areas despite public assurances by the government that the bandits have been beaten back, and despite the increasing and welcome involvement of the civilian authorities who have taken initiatives to disband many of the camps. Clearly the dissident groups are still active in

the area. In January eleven Red Cross medical team workers were kidnapped
in the Luwero, Mpigi and Mubende "triangle" by dissidents and it was nearly
two weeks before the last of them was released. During this time the relief
operation was suspended.

Meanwhile as a result of a military operation thousands of newly displaced
people from the Ngomo area were flooding into Nakitoma in the extreme north
of Luwero District. On 20 January, 1200 displaced people were reported to
be staying at the nearby small trading centre. By 9 February the figure was
reported as 8000. It continued rising to more than 10,000 until the site was
disbanded in April by the District Commissioner of Luwero and military
authorities. The site was unsuitable for such large numbers of people who
were completely dependent upon food brought in by Red Cross. Water was also
a very serious problem, and attempts made to make more water available could
not keep pace with the increasing population.

On 19 March the Bombo road was closed to relief vehicles for several weeks
by military authorities, affecting the life chances of some 50,000 people
who were thus left without food or medical care. Nakitoma in particular
suffered and it is suspected that many of the 700 children attending the
feeding centre there died of starvation. The camp was disbanded during this
time and many of the people who had sought assistance there set off on foot
towards the south. Some of them formed new camps at Nabiswera and Sisira.

Throughout April and May, despite continuing negotiations between the relief
agencies, the government and military authorities, there continued to be
severe restrictions imposed on the movement of relief vehicles to all relief
centres accessible from the Bombo road. In May similar restrictions were
put upon movements along the Hoima road.

The government policy which has now emerged seems to be to disband all
camps, to transfer all those who do not originate in the immediate vicinity
to temporary transit camps, to vett the people in transit camps before
transferring them to their home areas and to allow relief workers to visit
transit camps only.[7]

The UNICEF/WDD/Oxfam/SCF-assisted programmes for water and health have been
relatively less affected by restrictions than the food distribution and
medical/nutrition activities run by other organisations. Throughout the
period from January to June, except for the time of the kidnapping and a
short interruption in March, WDD and Oxfam teams have been allowed to move
along both the Bombo and the Hoima roads. Consequently considerable work
has been completed in terms of borehole pump replacement and protection of
springs and wells, despite the difficult working conditions due to
insecurity.

This success may be due to a number of factors: the universally beneficial
nature of the product (i.e. clean water), its inability to be "misused" or
to fall into the "wrong hands"; the full integration of government WDD
workers and vehicles in the water programme; and the generally good working
relations established between UNICEF and government ministries during the

---

[7]This policy has obviously resulted in increasing the suffering of people
hitherto benefitting from relief. It reveals the inherent contradiction
between the humanitarian concern espoused officially by the government, and
the often harsh and expedient measures implemented by military authorities
who view relief as aiding the cause of the guerillas.

postliberation years.

Given the current situation regarding relief and the reasons why it came
into being, it seems unlikely that the relief operation will ever resume on
the same scale as before restrictions were imposed. This lends even more
importance to the role that government agencies in the sphere of health
services and water supply must play in the improvement of conditions for all
those living in the disturbed areas. Specifically, it is increasingly
important that government rural health units previously abandoned and looted
become operational and that potentially available water sources are fully
exploited. Likewise, continued support for the MOH Task Force must be
encouraged now that Red Cross mobile medical teams are no longer operating
in many parts of the area.

REFERENCES

Dash, Leon. 1983. Brutality Marks Army's Conduct in Uganda. The Washing-
    ton Post. 29 November
Hall, Richard. 1983. Obote Warned to Protect Civilians. The Observer. 17
    July.
Legum, Colin. 1983. Uganda Moves to Aid Hungry Peasants after Routing
    Dissidents. Christian Science Monitor. 3 October.
Righter, Rosemary. 1983. Massacre in the Camp of Death. The Sunday Times.
    London, 5 June.
Uganda Times. 1983. No Internment Camps in Uganda--Obote. 9 July.

The West Nile Emergency

Cole P. Dodge

The famine in Karamoja has been the most severe and most widely reported emergency in the postliberation period in Uganda. West Nile and Mbarara, however, have also experienced emergency conditions during this period. The central focus of this article is the West Nile emergency that occurred between 1979 and 1982. Also considered briefly is the 1982-83 emergency in Mbarara.

WEST NILE

The origins of the West Nile emergency relate directly to the liberation war. In 1979 the military government of Idi Amin was driven from power by Tanzanian forces and the forces of the Uganda National Liberation Army (UNLA), and Amin and members of his forces retreated northward into West Nile, their home territory. While most of the defeated soldiers simply disposed of their guns and returned to their villages, retained their weapons and later faded into the "bush" of Koboko County or crossed into neighbouring territories in Zaire and Sudan.

Reports of occurrences in Uganda were in the world news during the liberation war and during the period of famine in Karamoja. The emergency situation that developed in West Nile, however, went largely unnoticed. It developed as the remnant band of Amin's soldiers attacked and displaced UNLA forces in Arua Town in October 1980. It developed further as UNLA forces recaptured Arua. A UN mission that visited West Nile in November 1980 estimated that between 230,000 and 300,000 people (some 50 to 60 percent of the population of West Nile District at the time) had become refugees as a consequence of the fighting. Most had fled into Zaire. Some 30,000 had fled into Sudan.

The second UN mission to West Nile was organised in February 1981 and involved personnel from the United Nations Development Programme (UNDP), the World Food Programme (WFP) and the Swedish Special Unit (SSU).[1] The mission

---

[1] I visited Arua District with the second UN visit and five more times during the next twenty-four months. Nutritional surveys were carried out in

107

reached Arua by the main Gulu-Pakwach-Nebbi-Bondo route late in the afternoon of 4 February. The town was deserted except for a heavy UNLA presence. The Arua and Maracha hospitals had been looted. Administrative services were paralysed. Some 40 percent of the buildings in the commercial district had been destroyed. Shops, offices, petrol stations and other facilities had been looted first by Amin's retreating forces, later by guerilla forces, then again by UNLA liberators. While some stranded civil servants were still around, they lacked entirely the resources with which to function. Typewriters, records, desks, chairs and vehicles had been lost, damaged or destroyed. No salaries had been paid for months.

The problem was not confined to Arua Town. Much violence took place in Rhino Camp and other towns of West Nile, and few of the small towns and hamlets to the north of the road between Arua and Rhino Camp had more than a few inhabitants after the period of conflict. The roads north of Maracha were unsafe and were not travelled. The triangle of territory with a point at Rhino Camp and emanating to the north on the one hand, and to the northwest on the other, remained in guerilla hands from late 1980 to mid-1984 (see Africa Now, 1983). The only hospital in West Nile operating at full capacity with surgical, X-ray and intensive care facilities late in 1980 was near Nebbi at Angal Mission, a two-hour drive from Arua over very rough roads.

RELIEF EFFORTS

German Emergency Doctors (GEDs) opened a small clinic at Maracha as soon as the fighting subsided, and later reopened the hospital itself. The Nebbi Hospital which had been looted was made marginally functional again in early 1981. The International Committee of the Red Cross (ICRC) was the only international agency with a presence in West Nile in early 1981. Later during the year Save the Children Fund (SCF) sent a medical team to Pakwach to assist in the rehabilitation of the health centre and rural services in the area, Medicins sans Frontieres (MSF) established a programme to rehabilitate Arua Hospital, and the SSU sent a relief team to West Nile to establish relief centres at Gulu, Pakwach, Nebbi, Arua, Moyo and Adjumani in facilitating the distribution of supplies and food. The Swedish Unit operated under the United Nations Relief Coordinating Unit established in Kampala in January 1981 by UNDP, UNICEF, the United Nations High Commission for Refugees (UNHCR) and the WFP. It also fielded a medical team and a water engineering team. The Irish voluntary agency CONCERN sent two nurses to Adjumani in 1981 to assist with relief, feeding and medical needs.

Guerilla activity increased in West Nile during the first half of 1981 with the killing of a prominent person in Rhino Camp and the seisure of the ferry at Larope. In late June guerilla forces were able to harass army outposts in Koboko County, then force demoralised UNLA forces who had neither been paid nor received rations regularly to retreat towards Arua. The Catholic mission at Ombachi, just three miles from Arua, was soon engulfed in fighting, and on 23 June eighty-two people were killed and fifty-three injured at the mission. Many of the persons who suffered casualities had come to the mission for refuge.

Ombachi mission, the West Nile headquarters of the Verona Fathers, was used

---

Arua District under UNICEF auspices in March 1981, November 1981, March 1982 and March-April 1983.

as a field base by the ICRC and the SSU during 1981. Agency personnel and missionaries were evacuated southward to Nebbi and Angal as intense fighting continued locally. UNHCR estimates in the wake of the guerilla push and subsequent UNLA counterattacks were that 180,000 people had fled across the Zaire and Sudan borders during this period.[2] Arua was again completely abandoned by all except for UNLA soldiers.

Due to problems of insecurity, the SCF team at the Pakwach Health Centre, the GEDs at Maracha Hospital, the team of French MSF doctors and nurses involved in the rehabilitation of Arua Hospital, the ICRC and the SSU all soon evacuated the Arua area. The Germans and French crossed the Zaire border with the refugees and quickly established medical and relief centres in conjunction with UNHCR to help meet the needs of refugees. SCF, SSU and ICRC retrenched to more secure areas within Uganda.

HEALTH IMPACT

UNHCR began surveying the problem of refugees in West Nile in November 1982 and estimated that 266,107 of the people of Arua County, and 45,329 of the people of Moyo County, were either internally displaced or had taken refuge in Zaire or Sudan (personal communication). While medical statistics are not available, a review of the findings possible during successive visits to medical institutions is meaningful, especially in combination with the nutrition data available.

Nutrition: February to June 1981

In February 1981, 650 preschool children up to approximately 5 years of age and below 115 centimetres in height, were anthropometrically screened. Twelve percent--or more than twice the number of children who would be expected--were found to be less than 75 percent of expected weight-for-height. All of the malnourished children were part of the population of displaced people.

From March through the time when they evacuated in late June 1981, the GEDs reported a malnutrition rate of 50 percent among young (including school-age) children who came to their clinic at Maracha. Kuluva Hospital ran a small nutrition ward during this period and fed up to ninety children a day. The areas in which malnutrition rates were highest were no doubt those for which no information was available.

Nutrition: Late 1981 to early 1982

The overall situation in southern Arua County did not begin to normalise until October-November 1981, when the Catholic Bishop of Arua returned from Warr where he had established temporary residence following evacuation in June. In the interim months the ICRC and SSU left Uganda as the government maintained that West Nile had been stabilised and there was no further need

---

[2]The border between Uganda and Zaire runs through the territories of the Lugbara and Kakwa tribes, and the border between Uganda and Sudan runs through the territories of the Madi and Kakwa tribes. Much population movement occurs across the borders involved. Whole villages and areas are abandoned for days, weeks and even months during periods of insecurity.

Cole P. Dodge

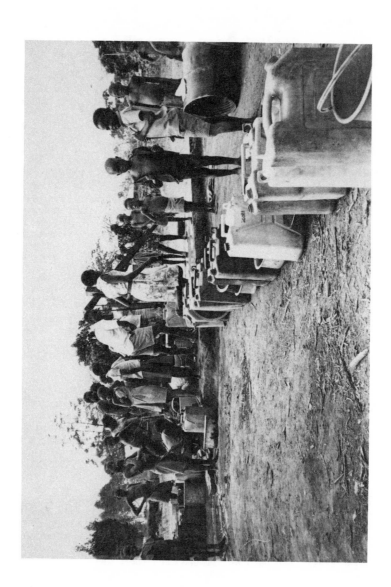

Figure 1 Queuing for water in West Nile, 1981
(Photograph courtesy of UNICEF/C P Dodge)

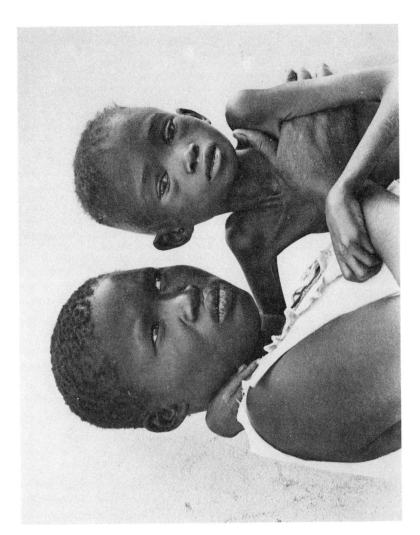

Figure 2 Mother with severely malnourished child in West Nile, 1982
(Photograph courtesy of UNICEF/C P Dodge)

for their involvements. The civilian population was only beginning to trickle back from places of refuge during this time, however, and there was much
need for continued relief effort in the area. The GEDs came back and
established a medical facility in conjunction with Kuluva Hospital, as
Maracha was still unsafe. The League of Red Cross Societies undertook the
rehabilitation of health units in Nebbi County.

By February 1982 the Catholic clinic at Ediofe near Arua Town was reopened,
and by late in 1982 the GEDs, who had begun to visit Maracha again earlier
in the year, reestablished their Maracha work. In June 1982 Arua Hospital
had twenty-two cases of "malnourished children", Kuluva Hospital had twenty-
eight, Maracha Clinic had forty and Ediofe had nine: most of these were
kwashiorkor cases, a few were cases of severe marasmus.

All of the hospitals of the area except for Arua Hospital established sup-
plemental feeding programmes during this period, on an outpatient basis, for
the treatment of children with kwashiorkor and marasmus who were not critical. Between 100 and 150 cases of kwashiorkor were being treated as outpatients at these medical facilities in June 1982. In order to assess the
extent of the problem and to check more carefully on treatment coverage, a
survey was conducted in three locations ten miles or more from an existing
feeding centre--and thus by expectation outside the catchment area of the
feeding centre--which were recently resettled by returning refugees and from
which most of the malnourished children seemed to come. Weight-for-height
was used in this screening, and 367 children were measured. No cases of
kwashiorkor were found, but 5.4 percent of the children measured were found
to be less than 80 percent of expected weight-for-height--a level generally
considered to approximate "normal" endemic malnutrition (Alnwick and Dodge,
1983).

TABLE 1: Arua Hospital Staff and Services

	November 1981	June 1982
Doctors	-	7
Medical assistants	2	8
Nurses	7	13
Paediatric services	-	Open
Maternity services	-	Open
Male/Female wards	-	Open
Surgical services	-	Minor Only
Electricity	-	Functioning
Water supply	-	Operational
Outpatients daily attendance	200	500+
X-ray	-	Parts ordered
Salaries	Arrears to April 1981	Paid

Arua Hospital

A comparison of conditions at Arua Hospital between November 1981 and June
1982 reveals great improvement in staffing and services (see Table 1).
Government determination to normalise the situation in Arua increased, and
the greatly improved security situation allowed medical staff to return. By
the middle of 1982, regular bus and air services had been reestablished,

the post office had been reopened, the White Rhino Hotel had been rehabilitated and most of the civil administration of the area was again functioning. The GEDs had reopened Maracha Hospital and the Church of Uganda had
posted a full-time medical superintendent to Kuluva Hospital.

The Uganda Red Cross Society, in conjunction with the District Relief
Committee, was responsible for food distribution. A flow of refugees was
returning to Uganda and boosting population levels back to normal in Vura,
Ayiva and southern Madi, Okolo, Maracha and Terego Counties. Koboko and
Aringa Counties, however, remained largely uninhabited and insecure.

UNHCR assigned a field officer to Arua in the fall of 1982. About this time
programmes for the resettlement of refugees and programmes to attract refugees back to Uganda from outside the country were also established (see
Table 2).

TABLE 2: Estimates of Population, Arua District by County

County	Census December 1980	March 1983	%
Ayivu	89,016	35,760	40
Koboko[a]	37,059	860	2
Maracha	86,304	85,420	99
Aringa	77,980	3,606	5
Madi Okollo	59,089	57,308	97
Torego	77,817	42,813	55
Vurra	45,018	42,061	93
Total	472,283	267,828	57

*Source: Figures for March 1983 were gathered in a visit to Arua District
from officials, missionaires, relief workers and the UNHCR.
[a]The population of Koboko County is largely Kakwa, Amin's tribe.

DISCUSSION

Health Facilities

The only consistent uninterrupted health service in the area west of the
Nile River in Uganda was Angal Mission Hospital in the southeast corner of
the region. Staffed throughout by Italians and Ugandans, the Angal Mission
Hospital was not affected either by the liberation retreat or by subsequent
guerilla conflicts.

Kuluva Hospital, situated about six miles southeast of Arua, never closed
but was without a doctor for several months in 1980 and 1981. It was
rehabilitated in part by GEDs in 1981 and restaffed by the Church of Uganda
in 1982.

Arua Hospital suffered the most, given its location and the difficulty staff
faced owing to the breakdown of all security considerations and all government services between 1980 and 1981.

Maracha Hospital was abandoned in 1980 by the Catholic mission in charge and reopened in 1981 by the GEDs.

Nutrition

While no quantitative population-based health indicators are available for
West Nile, the 1979-82 period saw an almost total breakdown of all services
in the area. The crisis was evident in the number of children treated in
hospitals for severe malnutrition. The number of children who could not
make it to hospitals was no doubt far greater than the number who could.

MBARARA

In September-October 1982 thousands of people of Rwandan ethnic origin were
"displaced" in southwestern Uganda. Communal disturbances in Mbarara, Rakai
and Bushenyi Districts were directed against such people in towns, villages
and rural homesteads, causing approximately 40,000 to flee across the border
into Rwanda. Approximately 27,000 people were crowded into the semi-arid
settlement sites at Nakivale and Orichinge in Uganda (Winter, 1983).

UNHCR coordinated relief inputs on both sides of the Uganda/Rwanda border.
The Church of Uganda, Catholic Church, Red Cross, SCF, Oxfam, WFP and UNICEF
provided direct relief assistance within Uganda. In his Christmas 1982
sermon the Church of Uganda Bishop of Kabale focused attention on the plight
of the 4000 people at the Merama Hill border post who had been stranded in
their attempt to flee Uganda. Within weeks of the establishment of the
encampment at Merama Hill, one-quarter of all of the children under five at
the camp were dead.

Because of political sensitivities and the magnitude of the problem that had
arisen, the district medical officer in Mbarara was unable to extend adequate services to the displaced people in the area in 1982. During late
October and early November the critically ill among the displaced were
refused admission at Mbarara Hospital and could find treatment only at a
school near their settlements. For a short time in 1982 army personnel at
the roadblock near the entrance to the settlements restricted the movements
of the people, maintaining that they were actually refugees and should be
confined to their camps.

Water and medical supplies were brought to the people of the settlements,
and district medical capacities were strengthened as quickly as possible
through the assistance of numerous international agencies. In late 1983 the
displaced people were moved to a new settlement site at Kyaka, 100 miles
north of Mbarara, under the supervision of the Ugandan Ministry of Culture
and Community Development and with the assistance of UNHCR.

CONCLUSION

The provision of health services cannot be separated from considerations of
local security. Government as well as mission medical facilities were badly
damaged in Arua District during repeated confrontations between insurgent
and UNLA forces. The destruction or severe damage of infrastructural supply,
distribution, transportation and administrative systems made it difficult to
reestablish services. Health services for the displaced people of the
Mbarara area could only be improved as the local security situation improved.

Under conditions as difficult as they were during the two emergency situations briefly reported here, the careful monitoring of developments, and the careful coordination of relief and development agency efforts, is problematic but necessary. Necessary also is improvement in the facilities of communication made available in an emergency area and improvements in the entire organisation of relief supplies delivery services.

REFERENCES

Africa Now. 1983. Uganda: The Forgotten West Nile. November.

Alnwick,D.J. and Cole P. Dodge. 1983. Nutrition Survey in West Nile. Kampala: UNICEF mimeographed report, March.

Arnhold,R. 1981. Nutrition Report to UNICEF on West Nile. Kampala: UNICEF mimeographed report, April.

Time. 1984. The Light that Failed. 16 January.

Winter,Roger. 1983. Uganda: Creating a Refugee Crisis. Newsletter: United States Committee for Refugees.

Water Supply, Sanitation and the Effect on the Health Care Delivery System

J. R. Hebert and S. Ssentamu

It is widely recognised that infectious diseases responsible for very high mortality, especially among children, are strongly associated with defects in sanitation and water supply (Sedgwick and MacNutt, 1910, and United Nations, 1980). In addition to its contribution to mortality, unhygienic environments contribute to increased morbidity. The magnitude of the effect is, however, very difficult to quantify (Blum and Feachem, 1983).

East Africa, in general, is an area traditionally poorly served with convenient and safe water supplies (White, Bradley and White, 1972). In comparison with either Kenya or Tanzania, however, Uganda has much better access to water resources and higher annual rainfall.

In comparison with other parts of the developing world, Uganda had a much higher proportion of people served by improved fecal disposal facilities (WHO, 1982). It was primarily during the period of the protectorate, 1893 to 1962, that sanitary conditions, as estimated by access to sanitary disposal facilities, improved.

Before 1893 and persisting through the early part of the protectorate the interest of the Euopean administrators was in preventing the spread of infectious diseases within the enclaves of the European community. These diseases were typically not waterborne or water washed and were therefore strictly not controlled by sanitation measures other than those aimed at removal of standing water (Feachem, McGarry and Mara, 1977).

It was in 1934-35 that rules were made governing sanitary waste disposal facilities in non-European, i.e. native, households. Rapid improvement continued through the 1940s and 1950s and by 1962, 80 to 90 percent of the homes had latrine facilities. During the early part of the postcolonial period sanitary conditions continued to improve. In contrast to sanitary waste disposal facilities, progress in provision of safe and convenient water supply was marked during the decade of the 1960s and into the early 1970s, due mainly to an aggressive campaign of installing wells.

The period beginning in about 1975 was one of sharp reversals in terms of water supply and sanitation. By 1983 only 30 percent of all existing homes had a functioning latrine (Batson, 1983). In a recent survey of borehole wells (Uganda/UNICEF, 1983), the primary source of safe drinking and cooking water nationwide, it was shown that only one-third of the 5180 existing boreholes were functioning in 1983 (see Table 1). Usually in places as water rich as the parts of Uganda near major lakes and riverways this would have implications only in terms of waterborne diseases. However, most surface water sources in Uganda present a very high risk of diseases such as schistosomiasis and dracunculiasis (Fontaine, 1984).

TABLE 1:   State of Boreholes as of 1983 by Region

		Total Number	Number Working	Percent Working
North		1675	654	39.0
West		574	129	22.5
East		1654	539	32.6
Central		468	127	27.1
	Total	4371	1449	33.2

The exact cost to human health of the loss of these water and sanitation facilities is estimable only in very rough terms. Loss of a safe and dependable water source may imply any or all of the following:

- that the people, mainly women, of the household responsible for water collection must divert extra energy into this activity (Isely, 1982);

- extra time spent collecting water deprives the collector from engaging in other useful labour such as farming;

- the family will use less water and will therefore suffer more from water-washed diseases such as scabies and yaws (Feachem, McGarry and Mara, 1977);

- substitution of an unsafe water supply for a safe one will result in increases in waterborne diseases such as amoebic dysentery and dracunculiasis.

The concern here will be on the effect of deficiencies in the water supply and sanitary facilities through these last two mechanisms.

Though it is recognised that these factors play an extremely important role in determining the overall burden of disease, quantifying effects is limited by a number of practical problems. One problem concerns estimates of prevalence or incidence density of disease in the population. Most of the diseases associated with defects in water supply and sanitation are very difficult to monitor with any degree of accuracy.

Retrospective data are invariably associated with the kind of differential reporting bias one encounters when using hospital, health centre or clinic records. In a country such as Uganda, where differential access to health facilities was exacerbated during the political troubles of the decade 1970 to 1979, this is an even more important problem than it otherwise might be. In other countries the bias is relatively uniform over time. Even mortality data, which are often used as objective estimators of health status of a

population, are heavily biased in that people who die in the health care
delivery system are often different from people who die without making such
contact; i.e. they simply die of a different constellation of diseases.

Disease prevalence or incidence rates from studies are often plagued by
recall bias as well as problems with objectively defining disease and willful misrepresentation of culturally sensitive information. In the case of
Uganda over the past decade and a half, the option of using data from field
studies simply does not exist. Hospital/clinic-based records, though
flawed, are the only information that can give a clue as to the distribution
of diseases in the population.

Hospital admissions and mortality data are available that give an indication
of the distribution and seriousness of diseases presenting to the medical
delivery system (UNICEF, 1983). Categorisation of diseases is not disaggre-
gated to a degree sufficient to enable identifying diseases so that proportional reduction due to various sanitary improvements could be estimated.
However, one can estimate that of total admissions 43.7 percent are for
diseases associated with defects in water supply and sanitation; i.e. waterborne, water-washed and water-related insect vector diseases. These same
diseases account for 30.7 percent of the deaths occurring in hospitals.
Because the diseases related to defects in sanitation disproportionately
afflict the dependent portion of the population, especially children, and
are therefore not perceived as serious, these hospital-based statistics are
probably biased toward lower than the real rates.

On the basis of both poor health facility access for the poorer segment of
the population who are at highest risk of sanitation-related diseases and
the assumption that sanitation-related diseases are the least likely to be
reported, the above figures may be viewed as the lower limit of the real
disease burden in the population. The percentage of total admissions attributable to these diseases may also conveniently be thought of as the lower
limit of the utilisation rate assuming that access to health facilities will
only improve, and as it does it will "reach" into portions of the population who are presently suffering a proportionately higher morbidity and
mortality burden due to these diseases.

The proportional decrease in sanitation-related disease mortality is not
easily estimable. However, we do have a historical perspective on the
upper and lower limits of disease-specific mortality corresponding to per-
turbations in the water supply and sanitary systems of the West. There we
see the mortality rates for diseases subsumed under the Ugandan Ministry of
Health list (UNICEF, 1983) dropped to about 10 percent of their former
levels once the populations were provided with safe and abundant water and
good excreta disposal facilities (Sedgwick and MacNutt, 1910).

In the European and North American countries of the early twentieth century,
as in the developing countries of today, accurate morbidity data on the
general population are very difficult to obtain. There is therefore no
suitable comparator for morbidity. Based on a series of assumptions that
are very well discussed elsewhere (Saunders and Warford, 1976), it is estimated that the total overall morbidity due to these sanitation-related
diseases could be decreased by about 60 percent if everyone were provided
with a safe and dependable water source.

In Uganda, where the water situation has deteriorated, but not completely,
one must invoke some sort of a model for increased disease burden and demand
for services due to the deterioration. The amount of health effect due to

Figure 1 Broken traditional Ugandan hand pump, a common sight in the
countryside in 1981
(Photograph courtesy of UNICEF/C P Dodge)

Figure 2 New hand pump, 1983
(Photograph courtesy of UNICEF)

given changes in a sanitary factor is probably not uniform over all values of the factor. That is, the relationship between sanitary inputs and health effects is not linear. It has been proposed that there is a threshold/satu-ration effect where at very low levels of the input, increases in the level have negligible effect; there is then an intermediary period where relative-ly large effects accrue per unit increase in input until a saturation point is reached beyond which increasing input has little effect (Shuval and associates, 1981: 243-248). In Uganda, where sanitation levels were once very good but have now become only average for the developing world, the input level is probably close to the midpoint between the asymptotes; i.e. between the lower threshold and the saturation point. At this midpoint on the curve a simplifying assumption of linearity is both useful and probably not too far from correct.

Rather than considering degrees of providing the service, information about which is not available in any event, we may view the UNICEF borehole and latrine data as simple predictors of dichotomous (maximal or minimal) out-come. That is, for all those persons who have safe water it is maximally safe in terms of health risk and is very dependable; for all those without safe water the source is minimally safe and very undependable. Likewise for latrines, those people with latrines would be at no risk for that proportion of disease attributable to latrine usage whereas those without latrines would experience maximal risk.

In the only study to quantify the relative health effects of latrine usage versus water quantity and water quality it was found that water supply characteristics were the much more powerful predictor; i.e. about four times more important over all ages of childhood (Hebert, 1984). Knowing that presently only 7 percent of the total population of the country has access to safe water (UNICEF, 1983), if all existing boreholes were made opera-tional, about 21 percent of the population could now be served. This takes into account neither the fact that projecting the progress of the 1960s would inflate this 21 percent figure nor that some people derive benefit from protected sources other than wells. The former probably more than compensates for the latter, and we may assume 21 percent as an underestimate of people who would have been served had the 1970s not been associated with political and social upheaval.

Saunders and Warford (1976) estimate that for all the sanitation-related diseases, 60 percent are prevented by safe water supply alone. Based on the above finding that latrines are about one-quarter as effective as water supplies in preventing disease, about 15 percent of the diseases are pre-vented by improved latrine facilities alone. Given that 60 percent of the latrine facilities were lost, this represents a net gain in the incidence of sanitation-related diseases of 3.9 percent for latrine lost access; 43.7 percent of diseases times 60 percent lost service times 15 percent effec-tiveness. Likewise, the decrease in access to safe and dependable water supply from the projected 21 percent to about 7 percent (67 percent lost) represents about a 3.7 percent increase in the incidence of these diseases due to loss of water facilities alone; 43.7 percent of diseases times 14 percent lost usage times 60 percent effectiveness. Therefore the total amount of increased demand at the health care delivery system can be calcu-lated to be 7.6 percent. In terms of the real disease burden in the popula-tion it must be noted that this is a very conservative estimate for the following reasons:

1. Hospital data are biased toward noninfectious nonsanitation-re-lated diseases which afflict mainly the productive portion of

the population, especially men.

2. Hospital admissions also respond to basic breakdowns in the
   sociopolitical infrastructure. That is, as wells and latrine
   facilities broke down in the 1970s, so too did the medical delivery system. The likelihood of disease, especially sanitation-
   related infectious disease, increased concurrently with the likelihood of not using curative medical facilities. To base estimates of disease burden on health care facilities usage with
   which it is negatively correlated leads to underestimation of
   real effect. For example, it is very unlikely that from 1980 to
   1981 the real rate of gastroenteritis in the country decreased.
   However, admissions data showed an 80 percent decrease during
   this period (UNICEF, 1983).

3. Breakdown of sanitary facilities is figured on the basis of the
   facility and not usage by the individuals at risk. Hospital
   utilisation is based on the individual. It is quite likely that
   the facilities which broke down had higher per capita usage than
   the ones which did not. Therefore, the proportion of facilities
   out of commission is lower than the proportion of people affected. Hence the estimate of increased demand is low.

4. Many diseases which are not strictly water related may, in fact,
   be exacerbated by faults in sanitation and water supply. For
   example, anaemia may be caused by malabsorption of iron which, in
   turn, may be caused by gastrointestinal disturbances due to
   waterborne disease.

It is clear that while the real increase in demand on health services is
probably at least slightly above the estimate of 7.6 percent, the potential
demand due specifically to sanitation-related diseases is probably much
higher. This is especially true for the paediatric portion of the population who are both at higher risk of these diseases and less likely to make
contact with the health care system as it breaks down.

REFERENCES

Batson, Michael St. Clair (1983). Low Cost Sanitation. Consultancy report to
   UNICEF-Uganda. Kampala, mimeographed.
Blum, D. and R. G. Feachem (1983). Measuring the Impact of Water Supply and
   Sanitation Investments on Diarrhoeal Diseases: Problems of Method-
   ology. International Journal of Epidemiology, 121: 357-365.
Feachem, R., M. McGarry and D. Mara (1977). Water Wastes and Health in Hot
   Climates. John Wiley and Sons, New York.
Fontaine, Robert (1984). Dracunculiasis Surveillance. Weekly Epidemio-
   logical Record (WHO, Geneva), 10: 9 March.
Hebert, J. R. (1984). Environmental Determinants of Nutritional Status of
   Children: Findings from Three Madras Communities. Unpublished doc-
   toral thesis, Harvard University.
Isely, R. B. (1982). Evaluating the Role of Health Education Strategies on
   the Prevention of Diarrhea and Dehydration. Journal of Tropical
   Pediatrics, 28: 253-261.
Saunders, R. J. and J. J. Warford (1976). Villlage Water Supply: Economics
   and Policy in the Developing World. Baltimore, Johns Hopkins Univer-
   sity Press.

Sedgwick, W. T. and A. B. MacNutt (1910). On the Mills-Reinck Phenomenon
    and Hazen's Theorem concerning the Decrease in Mortality from Dis-
    eases other than Typhoid Fever following the Purification of Public
    Water Supplies. Journal of Infectious Diseases, 7: 490-564.
Shuval, H. I., R. L. Tilden, B. H. Perry and R. N. Grasse (1981). Effect of
    Investments in Water Supply and Sanitation on Health Status: A
    Threshold Saturation Theory. Bulletin of the World Health Organisa-
    tion, 59: 243-248.
Uganda, Republic of, Ministry of Lands and Water Resources/ UNICEF (1983).
    Survey of Boreholes. Mimeographed, Kampala.
UNICEF (1983). UNICEF-Uganda Country Programme 1983-86. Mimeographed,
    Kampala.
United Nations, Report of the Secretary General (1980). International Drink-
    ing Water Supply and Sanitation Decade. Report number A/35/367, United
    Nations, New York.
White, G. F., D. J. Bradley and A. V. White (1972). Drawers of Water: Do-
    mestic Water Use in East Africa. University of Chicago Press.
WHO (1980). World Health Statistics. World Health Organisation, Geneva.

Section 3
Karamoja Considered

The 1980 Famine in Karamoja

D. J. Alnwick

The region of northeastern Uganda consists of the two present administrative districts of Kotido and Moroto. Because of its poorer land, less reliable rainfall and less developed infrastructure the people of the region have been less able than the rest of the country to cope with the disruption and economic chaos which the country has suffered since 1971. In 1980, almost unknown to the authorities in Kampala, a major famine developed in the region. This paper traces the history of Karamoja up to the present day with specific reference to the factors, within Karamoja and outside, which led to the tragic events of 1980.

Karamoja consists of 27,200 square kilometres of northeastern Uganda (14 percent of the total land area of the country) bordered in the east by the steep escarpment forming one edge of the Rift Valley which descends 2000 feet into the Turkana District of Kenya, in the west by the Labwor Hills and in the north by the Sudan. The population according to the 1981 Census (Provisional Results, 1983) was 350,000 or 2.8 percent of the total population of Uganda.

The region is now mainly populated by peoples speaking para-Nilotic languages, together with the Kalenjin-speaking Pokot or Suk, who inhabit the southeastern corner of Karamoja bordering Kenya, and a number of smaller Cushitic speaking groups largely confined to the mountainous areas. The major para-Nilotic groups comprise the Dodoth in the north, the Jie in the centre and the Bokora, Pian and Matheniko in the south. The para-Nilotic-speaking groups are closely related to the Turkana of Kenya, the Didinga of southern Sudan and the Ateso of neighbouring Soroti District.

Oral history indicates that prior to 1720 or so what is today Karamoja was sparsely populated by Cushitic-speaking peoples whose descendents are the present inhabitants of the mountainous areas, the Teuso, Ik and Tepeth (Lamphear, 1976). The main migration of agricultural para-Nilotic peoples from what is now southern Sudan occurred during the next eighty or so years. These people were the ancestors of most of the major modern groups in Karamoja as well as the Iteso of Soroti and Kumi Districts further south.

Oral history quoted by J. Lamphear (1976) suggests that the further expansion of the Karamojong to occupy something like their present-day

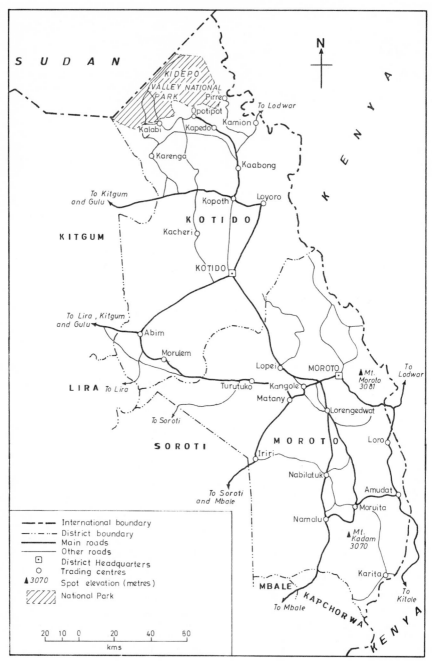

Figure 1 Karamoja region

territory was occurring during the period around 1840. These large migrations of people were fueled by the need for better land, more food and better grazing to feed an expanding population. Famines caused by crop failure or livestock disease spurred further exploration and settlement. The early migrations were rarely peaceful affairs, for the new lands usually had inhabitants who had to be subdued. Towards the end of the nineteenth century and into the twentieth, attempts to migrate met with even more opposition as the Karamojong came up against the agriculturalists of the more fertile areas around Sebei in the southeast, the Lwo-speaking Lango and Acholi in the east and the now-settled Iteso in the south.

The traditional political structure of the major groups is based around an age/clan system, with groups of elders being responsible for making decisions affecting the whole group rather that hereditary chiefs or kings as in the Bantu groups in Uganda.

AGRICULTURE AND LIVESTOCK

Some settled agriculture has been practised for as long as oral history is available along the central area of Karamoja where the permanent settlements are located. Women and young children stay in these settlements throughout the year whereas men stay only during the wet season when nearby grazing is abundant. Traditional staple crops are sorghum, finger millet and bulrush millet. Maize has become increasingly popular, especially in the southern and western areas having more reliable rainfall. Various types of beans are grown including grams and lab-lab. Cash crops formerly included cotton, kenaf and sorghum for commercial brewing.

Cultivation was done mainly by women using a pointed stick or, more recently, a hoe. Animal-drawn ploughs were never used in the past. The amount of land cultivated depended mainly on the availability of labour. Agricultural diversification is mainly hindered by the unreliability and erratic distribution of rain during the growing season rather than to low annual precipitation. N. Dyson-Hudson (1966) presents rainfall records and a note on agricultural conditions and their impact on the people of Karamoja for the years between 1924 and 1957. The mean annual rainfall during this period was 864 millimetres with a maximum of 1477 millimetres in 1937 and a minimum of 462 millimitres in 1924. In one year the rains might start "as expected" during late February and continue regularly throughout the growing season, ceasing before harvest time in July and August, and a good harvest would be reaped. During another year rains might not fall between February and May and the seedlings planted after the February rains would die and seed would have to be sown again, at least by those farmers who had stored enough seed. Then the rains might continue to be marginally adequate for the crop and a moderate harvest might be expected, but during harvest time heavy rains might fall with the result that much of the crop would be lost in the field or rot in the stores due to the conditions under which it was stored.

The keeping of cattle has for long been one of the key elements of the traditional economy of Karamoja. Like many pastoral peoples the peoples of Karamoja placed much greater faith in maximising the size of their herds than in the quality of individual animals. Cattle were mainly kept as a form of wealth, because of their importance in arranging marriages, for the milk and blood they yielded and as an insurance to exchange for grain in very bad years. Cattle were rarely killed for consumption except on special occasions.

The Karamoja people's cattle have for long been seen by outsiders as a major way of bringing the region into the modern economy. A major buying campaign took place in 1940 to feed the British Army fighting in East Africa in the scond world war (Barber, 1968: 211). A large modern meat-canning factory was built in Soroti, to the south of Karamoja, in the early 1970s in an attempt to establish a domestic and an export market for canned Karamoja meat. The factory suffered from the outset from a lack of cattle due to the reluctance of the pastoralists to destock. The last can of beef was produced in 1976. In 1981 the factory's large warehouses again served the Karamojong, this time as a UNICEF/World Food Programme (WFP) store and operations base for famine relief.[1]

Animal health has been a major constraint in the marketing of Karamoja's cattle. Rinderpest and contagious bovine pleuropneumonia have frequently been enzootic in the region necessitating quarantine restrictions on the movement of cattle. The major quarantine station was at Iriri, on the border of Karamoja and Soroti District. All cattle being moved to the south were required to be held in quarantine stations for several weeks to prevent the spread of disease to the rest of Uganda's herds.

Karamoja has few other identified natural resources. Semiprecious stones have been found in the rock of the mountains and some gold has been mined in the north. Recently panning for gold by small prospectors has started again in the area around Kaabong

ADMINISTRATION

The colonial military administration established in Karamoja District in 1910 gave way to a civil administration in 1921. The immediate effect of the colonial presence was to sanction the status quo by freezing the peoples of Karamoja in the positions they occupied at the beginning of the twentieth century and imposing fixed boundaries to stop all further migration and expansion. An uneasy peace was imposed by colonial troops and by 1921 intertribal fighting had been more or less completely suppressed. Colonial policy for the next thirty years continued to be based on maintaining peace and the status quo, and discouraged development. According to J. Barber (1968: 208-210), "The development of Karamoja District had to be related to what Uganda could afford, and this, in turn, had to be related to the overall interests of the protectorate and not the particular interests of one district. The question remained: Was it worthwhile to divert resources to this remote district when the other, more established districts were crying out for development? The answer in 1923 and in the quarter of a century which followed was: No, other than the resources necessary to keep the district quiet. . . . It was obvious that had the decision been for development, heavy expenditure would have been involved in building up veterinary services and marketing facilities for the cattle industry. Also there was the very real fear that an active development policy would have met continuing resistance from the pastoral tribes so that additional security forces would have been required. As it was, by easing back, the government controlled the district with a small police force of thirty men."

The quality of what might be called benign neglect of the 1920s began to be

---

[1] For a detailed description of the problems of marketing Karamoja's cattle see Randall Baker (1976).

challenged in the 1950s and 1960s as the British began to consider an
independent Uganda and Karamoja was seen as something of an embarrassment.
To quote Barber again (1968: 215), "The problems of the past were as clear
as ever--the absence of a strong indigenous administrative structure, the
continuing intertribal enmity and the absence of economic and social
development. Added to these was the new problem of rapidly increasing human
and stock populations."

The years immediately prior to independence saw a relaxation of the attempt
by the authorities to keep Karamoja and its inhabitants separate from the
rest of Uganda and the rest of the world, a policy that led M. Cisternino
(1979) to call the area a "human zoo". Missions expanded their activities,
schools, health centres and a hospital were built, and an agricultural
training institute established near Moroto.

Some of these belated development efforts actually made worse a number of
Karamoja's problems.

ENVIRONMENTAL DETERIORATION

Many changes occurred to the vegetation of Karamoja over the sixty years or
so prior to 1964. I. Langdale-Brown and associates (1964) quote the
accounts of local chiefs, elders and Western visitors as evidence that most
of Karamoja was much more extensively grass covered in the 1920s than in
1964. The erosion caused a change in the nature of the vegetation from
savanna to steppe to bushland and dry thicket. The erosion was attributed
mainly to overgrazing by cattle. Prior to 1900 or so inhabitants of
Karamoja subsisted largely by hunting and gathering with minimal disruption
to the environment. The Karamojong and the Suk also relied much less on
cattle in the past. The accounts of elders and chiefs are that life was
formerly much more dependent on the collection of wild fruits and seeds in
the dry season and cultivation of grain on a small scale. Cattle and small
stock were kept in small numbers only.

Between 1920 and 1950 various outside pressures greatly reduced the amount
of grazing land available to the Karamojong. Important among these was the
administrative agreement between Kenya and Uganda that resulted in the
transfer of about 2000 square miles of land to Kenya, the loss of use of the
extensive grazing of Usuku country in northern Soroti District, and the
creation of Kidepo National Park in the north and other game and forest
reserves. The concentration of stock caused by restriction of grazing land
was exacerbated by the indiscriminate development of valley tanks and dams
for cattle watering. The extra water available encouraged grazing far
beyond the capacity of vegetation and accelerated erosion, and by 1954 the
need for stock limitation and the serious state of erosion resulting from
vegetation changes due to overstocking were widely recognised (Langdale-
Brown and associates, 1964). However, the disastrous effects of the initial
dam construction programme were not recognised in time to prevent a larger
dam construction programme which began in 1955. Further uncontrolled stock
increase led to trespass of cattle into neighbouring districts and fighting
and increased raiding between groups.

By 1964 it was possible to conclude that the cattle population of the
district was close to the maximum possible and would decrease rapidly if
practices at the time continued (Langdale-Brown and associates, 1964).

There has been a long history of groups in Karamoja having access to the

most up-to-date weapons of the day. Marshall Tomas (1966: 43), referring to
the period around 1920, states that ". . . a group of Abyssinian hunters
established themselves by the Kaabong River. They lived in harmony with the
Dodoth, trading bullets for grain and rifles for oxen."

During the 1950s and 1960s the peace which had prevailed for the previous
thirty years came to an end and fighting restarted, both among the peoples
of Karamoja and between them and the Turkana (see Barber, 1968: 43).

KARAMOJA DURING THE PERIOD 1961-1980

In 1961 the commission set up to report on the best form of government for
an independent Uganda noted the vivid contrast between the people of
Karamoja and those of the rest of the country, and it was suggested to the
commission that Karamoja District should be treated as a special area that
should remain under British control for a period after the remainder of the
country obtained independence. This suggestion was however rejected by the
commission as impractical, and the commission concluded that "future
independent Uganda must face her own problems, of which Karamoja will be
one" (Barber, 1968: 214).

Karamoja had indeed a number of its own problems. The human and cattle
populations continued to grow, the quality of grazing land continued to
deteriorate, and the amount of raiding and insecurity continued to increase.
Access to firearms dramatically changed the balance of power between the
rival groups in the region. Following the resumption of large-scale
fighting in the 1950s and 1960s the warring factions of Karamoja had no
difficulty in finding willing suppliers of modern weaponry. Immediately to
the north of Karamoja the southern Sudan was engaged in a bitter civil war,
to the west in the newly independent Congo, now Zaire, another civil war was
raging, and a little further away Ethiopia was fighting Somalia. Arms
supplied to the various sides in these conflicts by outside powers easily
found their way down to Karamoja where they could be bartered for cattle. A
further boost to the supply of sophisticated arms and ammunition came when
remnants of Idi Amin's army fled northwards through Karamoja after being
driven from Kampala by Ugandan exiles and Tanzanian troops.

The Amin government had little real interest in Karamoja, but regarded its
sparsely clad inhabitants as an embarrassment. Various attempts were made,
with little effect, to force the essentially naked Karamojong men to wear
trousers. President Amin also had the idea of resettling people from the
densely populated areas of Western Uganda in Karamoja, but nothing came of
this (Baker, 1976). The marketing of cattle from Karamoja declined during
the latter half of the 1970s in line with the general collapse of most
sectors of the modern economy during this period.

A summary of the agricultural, livestock and food supply situation for the
years 1964-80 has been made from the District Agricultural Reports for these
years for Moroto and Kotido Districts (see Annex 1). Famine relief food was
distributed in parts of these districts during nearly half of these sixteen
years. The precarious nature of life in Karamoja during so-called normal
times can be seen from these notes.

THE START OF THE 1980 FAMINE

The widespread insecurity in Karamoja in the latter half of 1979 and early

1980 resulted in many family groups planting far less than in a normal year because people feared to cultivate far from the safety of their relatively well-protected dwellings. Many families may also have had seed from the previous harvest stolen or destroyed. Erratic rainfall in some parts of the district in 1980 resulted in low yields from the already reduced cultivated areas, although some parts of the district, notably Labwor County in the West, had a relatively normal rainfall both in terms of quantity and distribution over the growing season. General insecurity and the rapidly changing balance of power between rival groups also resulted in the herds of some groups being taken away to remote corners of the region in an attempt to avoid them being taken. Many families lost all of their cattle and wealth in raids. The settled population, consisting mainly of women, children and old people, no longer had access to milk or blood from the herds. More importantly, insecurity within the area and within the country as a whole resulted in a more or less complete breakdown of trade and commerce. Families who received a poor harvest, either due to climatic conditions or because of the small area planted, could not trade cattle for grain. Many families no longer had access to cattle, either because the cattle had been taken by rival groups or because the cattle had been hidden in distant and secret grazing areas. Even families with cattle to sell could not find a trader willing to take the risk of transporting cattle out of Karamoja because of the high risk that he would be attacked and lose not only the cattle he was transporting but his life as well. For similar reasons virtually no grain from outside the region was brought in and families who still had money could find little grain to buy at any price. Another reason for the absence of grain in the markets of Karamoja in 1980 was the attempt by the Kampala authorities to control producer and consumer prices at an artificially low level in an attempt to curb inflation. This acted as a strong disincentive for producers to grow any more than they needed for their own subsistence. Shortly after the fall of the Amin Government currency notes were demonetised and new notes issued. In 1980 Karamoja had only one bank, at Moroto, and the few Karamojong who had some cash savings were probably unaware of the procedures for changing money and found their savings worthless.

The cumulative effect of all of these factors was that many families started running out of food from the 1979 harvest, early in 1980. In turn, little planting took place in the new year for a number of reasons. Some people were too weak to work, and many families had consumed their stores of seed during the previous year. Poor and late rains prevented land preparation.[2] By May 1980 the situation became critical and people began to starve. The July/August harvest was poor because of insufficient planting due to lack of seeds and insecurity, and poor rains. The poor harvest was made worse because starving people ate immature maize and sorghum crops straight from the fields. By August 1980 there was a famine in many parts of Karamoja.

The poor rains and insecurity also reduced the amount of wild food which could be obtained by gathering. Poor rains reduced the growth of wild plants and berries and insecurity prevented people travelling far in search of what wild food there was. Wild fruits and berries have always provided a source of food for the Karamojong during hard times.[3]

---

[2]The tradition is to wait for the rains to soften the ground before cultivation is started.

[3]J. Wilson (1962) has made a list of forty fruits and seeds, ten flowers, leaves and shoots and several types of wood and resin that are or were consumed in Karamoja during periods when other foods were in short supply.

To the north in Karamoja, in the first few months of 1980, an epidemic of cholera started to claim the lives of many people already debilitated by hunger.

INTERNATIONAL RELIEF

By June 1980 people were coming to the (mainly Catholic) missions in the area in ever-increasing numbers. Many of the missions had small stores of food which they used to feed destitute people during "normal times" and to pay for services rendered to the mission such as the gathering of firewood. The mission staff quickly realised that alone they would not be able to cope with the rapidly increasing numbers of desperate, starving people turning up at their gates. In July 1980 the Verona Fathers in Karamoja made an appeal to the World Food Programme (WFP) in Rome for immediate assistance. About the same time Western news media, including television crews, began to take an interest in the situation in Karamoja, and pictures of dead and dying children outside mission stations began to appear on the European television networks.

A survey carried out in southern Karamoja in November 1980 (Biellik and Henderson, 1981,) estimated that the infant mortality rate for the previous twelve months was 600 per 1000 live births compared with a rate of 139 per 1000 quoted in the 1969 Census. A similar survey carried out in Dodoth in the north of Karamoja in February 1981 (Alnwick, 1981) confirmed that around one-half of all young children had died during the previous year. The nutritional status of the survivors at the time of this survey had, however, markedly improved. Five percent of children were less than 80 percent of their expected weight-for-height compared to 18 percent of children found to be in this category in a survey carried out four months earlier (Save the Children Fund, 1980).

Clear evidence of the severity of the famine was still easy to find in the first months of 1981. Skeletons and skulls abounded and could be seen around most settlements. In February 1981 it was still possible to visit deserted dwellings in Kathile near Kaabong in the south of Karamoja and find the shrivelled remains of the former inhabitants lying on the floor.

Partly through the efforts of WFP and partly due to the media coverage a number of European voluntary agencies prepared to send teams to Karamoja. Among the first to arrive was a team of medical students from the London-based Save the Children Fund (SCF). SCF had had a long history of involvement in Uganda from pre-Amin days and had staff familiar with the country. SCF had also been responsible for establishing a nutrition rehabilitation unit at Mbale to the south of Karamoja. SCF's initial involvement was in establishing centres to rehabilitate malnourished children.

Another British charity, Oxfam, was also quickly on the scene. Oxfam had also had previous involvement in Uganda, including experience in assisting with the provision of food for famine relief in 1984 and with the supply of seed in southern Karamoja in 1971 (District Agricultural Report, Moroto, 1971). Oxfam's main initial involvement was to assist the WFP establish an infrastructure to distribute relief food.

In September 1980 the French Medecins Sans Frontieres came to Uganda to assist mainly with the medical aspects of the Karamoja relief operation, and about the same time Agence International Contre Le Faim, also based in

Paris, fielded staff and vehicles to help with the distribution of relief food.

Christian Aid of the United Kingdom provided medical doctors and nurses to assist in the reestablishment of health services under the auspices of the Church of Uganda. The League of Red Cross Societies, working closely with what remained of the Uganda Red Cross Society, fielded personnel to assist with relief food distribution.

In October 1980 other European agencies had become actively involved in relief operations. The Irish agency Concern started to operate feeding programmes for malnourished children and assisted with relief food distribution, the Swiss agency Terre des Hommes and the German-based Order of Malta worked in child feeding and medical care. Logistical support to voluntary agencies was provided by the French-based Aviation Sans Frontieres and the Swiss-based Helimission who provided light aircraft and helicopters to transport staff and supplies. Oxfam also had access to a light aircraft flown by the coordinator of the Oxfam relief programme.

During the early stages of voluntary agency involvement in Karamoja there was little coordination. Agencies located themselves where they identified the greatest need and where there was some infrastructure to enable them to establish a base. For most agencies this meant a mission.

By October 1980 the Government of Uganda had changed three times in little over a year. The plight of 300,000 starving people in a remote corner of the country with little economic or political importance was not high on the list of priorities on the governing Military Commission in Kampala. The voluntary agencies had a virtual carte blanche to go where they liked and do what they liked with negligible interference, or indeed interest, from the country's government.

Agency staff, vehicles and equipment could be taken into and out of Karamoja through the unmanned Amudat border post with Kenya without even stopping. Immigration, customs and other formalities were nonexistant. Agencies could work directly with the missions, or what remained of local government staff, to establish their relief programmes. Health centre buildings were taken over, new buildings erected, and in at least one case a new airstrip was constructed completely unbeknown to the authorities in Kampala.

As the number of agencies involved in the relief effort became greater towards the end of 1980 the need for coordination of the overall effort became increasingly clear. Some of the agencies which were already operating resented the intrusion of new arrivals onto what they saw as their own "turf". Each wanted to be clearly responsible for one particular area of Karamoja or at least for one particular type of operation in that area such as child feeding. Cooperation between agencies offering the same kind of services was unusual. In a number of places tempers flared and agency (and to an extent national) pride was hurt when the teams from one agency arrived at a place they had picked out for themselves only to find another agency had already arrived and was getting on with the job. Government was clearly unable to coordinate the relief effort and many of the agencies turned towards the United Nations for help. Two UN agencies, WFP and UNICEF, had encouraged and, to an extent, facilitated the involvement of the voluntary agencies by the provision of vehicles and the supply of relief food, equipment and drugs. Neither, however, was in a position to coordinate the overall effort in late 1980. In fact, neither UN agency had a single staff member stationed in Karamoja until January 1981. In late 1980

Figure 2   Karamojong woman, 1982
(Photograph courtesy of UNICEF/A Vollan)

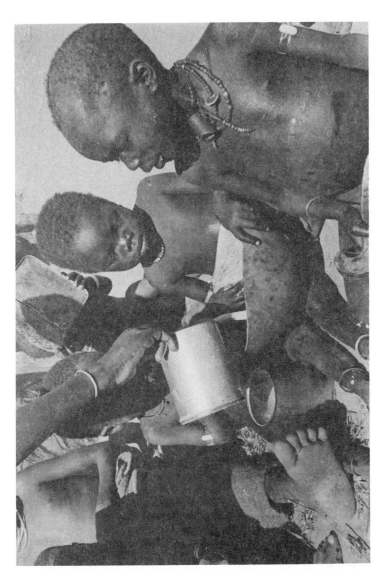

Figure 3 Feeding children in Karamoja, 1981
(Photograph courtesy of UNIECF/A Vollan)

Figure 4 Organised feeding in Kabong, Karamoja, 1981
(Photograph courtesy of UNICEF/A Vollan)

Figure 5 "Food for work" project in Karamoja, 1981
(Photograph courtesy of UNICEF/D Allan)

and during the first three months of 1981 the distribution of relief food
was coordinated by the Church of Uganda in Moroto with the assistance of
staff seconded by the Lutheran World Federation. Trucks were obtained from
the Uganda Cooperative Transport Union and the United Nations High
Commission for Refugees (UNHCR), the first UN agency to assist with the
internal distribution of relief food. Poor maintenance facilities, shortage
of fuel and spare parts and unmaintained roads made the distribution of
relief food a difficult undertaking.

Initial famine relief efforts fell into two broad categories, the rehabilitation of malnourished children and the distribution of uncooked food
directly to families. These two types of activities proved to be closely
interdependent. The supervised feeding of malnourished children became
impossible if needy families had no food of their own because the feeding
centres became swamped with desperate, hungry adults. There was also, of
course, little point in discharging a child who had gained weight from a
feeding centre if it was known that the child would receive no food at home
and return to the feeding centre in his original malnourished condition
within a week or so.

Towards the end of 1980 the rehabilitation of malnourished children was
rationalised throughout Karamoja. Criteria for the admission of children
for intensive nutritional rehabilitation and supplementary feeding were
agreed to by all of the agencies involved and a common reporting procedure
established.   Children's nutritional status was assessed using the weight-
for-height chart making possible an objective measure of their thinness.

Data on the number of children being admitted to the twenty child feeding
centres that had been established throughout Karamoja by the beginning of
1981 provided a useful guide to the adequacy of the quantities of food
being distributed to the general population.

The total quantity of relief food distributed increased from just over 1000
tons in October 1980 to a maximum of 2940 tons in March 1981. The bulk of
the food distributed consisted of whole maize, rice, maize meal, dried skim
milk powder, edible oil and beans. It was impossible to know exactly how
much food was needed. The 1980 Census was undertaken at a time when the
famine was starting, a cholera epidemic was present in parts of the region,
most of the administrative staff had deserted their posts because of
disease, insecurity and lack of food, and petrol and vehicles were virtually
unobtainable. Not surprisingly the 1980 census figures were widely regarded
as being inaccurate, and the 1969 figures hopelessly out of date. The
number of people who still had cattle was unknown, and the amount of wild
fruits and leaves consumed impossible to estimate with any certainty. An
attempt to use all of the available data to calculate food requirements
needed to meet the shortfall in the month of June 1981 resulted in an
estimate of 3500 tons of grain per month for the whole of Karamoja (Biellik
and Henderson, 1981).

As soon as sufficient food flowed into Karamoja to feed the most desperately
needy people, worries started to arise about the way the food was being
distributed. The missions, voluntary agencies and UN staff all expressed
fears about the danger of creating a dependency on free food handouts.
Various food-for-work schemes were devised in an attempt to get people who
were able and fit to work for the food they needed. The level of organisation necessary to devise useful projects and get people to work
productively on them was generally underestimated by all concerned and in
many cases food-for-work projects turned out to be little different from

free food handouts.

In 1981 the harvest was again poor in many parts of Karamoja and relief food was again needed on a large scale. 1982 and 1983 were relatively good years, and surpluses of grain were produced in the agriculturally better areas in the south and west. All general distribution of relief food ceased and the only relief food going into Karamoja was used for feeding a relatively small number of malnourished children and in small, well-organised food-for-work projects. In early 1984, however, the rains were again very poor, and the number of children reporting to feeding centres again increased. Clearly the problems of the peoples of Karamoja are not yet over.

REFERENCES

Alnwick, D. J. (1981). Nutritional Status of Young Children in Dodoth County, Karamoja, Uganda. Mimeographed, UNICEF, Uganda.

Alnwick, D. J. (1981). Towards a Food Aid Policy for Karamoja. Mimeographed, UNICEF, Uganda.

Baker, Randall (1976). Cattle Marketing in Karamoja. Occasional Paper, University of East Anglia.

Barber, J. (1968). Imperial Frontier. East African Publishing House, Nairobi.

Biellik, Robin J. and Peggy L. Henderson (1981). Mortality, Nutritional Status, and Diet During the Famine in Karamoja, Uganda, 1980. The Lancet, 12 December: 1330-1333.

Cisternino, Mario (1979). Karamoja: The Human Zoo: The History of Planning for Karamoja with Some Tentative Counterplanning. PhD thesis, University of Swansea.

Dyson-Hudson, N. (1966). Karamojong Politics. Oxford University Press.

Lamphear, J. (1976). The Traditional History of the Jie of Uganda. Clarendon Press, Oxford.

Langdale-Brown, I., H. A. Osmaston and J. G. Wilson (1964). The Vegetation of Uganda and Its Bearing on Land Use. Government of Uganda.

Save the Children Fund (1980). Nutritional Survey in Dodoth. Unpublished, December.

Thomas, Marshall (1966) Warrior Herdsmen. Secker and Warberg, London.

Wilson, J. G. (1962). The Vegetation of Karamoja District. No. 5, Series 2, Memoirs of the Research Division, Department of Agriculture, Uganda Protectorate.

ANNEX 1

Summary of Agricultural Situation and Other Problems, 1964-80, as Abstracted from District Agricultural Reports

1964

Rain started in April and tailed off in May. Heavy rain later. Late planting.

Reports of famine in Pian County. Oxfam provided food. Maize issued to Labwor people against future payment from cotton sales.

1965

Dry from mid-May to October. Harvest only 20 percent of normal.

Widespread famine affecting all counties except Labwor. Effects of drought not immediate as cattle and goats sold to buy food. As from October one packet of posho (ground maize) given to each adult. Expenditure on famine relief up to 31 December was USh 1,035,689.

1966

Dry from May until mid-July. Famine conditions grew worse and 80,000 people affected. Large-scale famine relief given in all areas from January to end of August. Further small outbreak of famine occurred in December. Food distribution started in December for Dodoth and Tepes near Moroto.

Armed raids by Turkana and Jie against Pian, Dodoth and Bokora.

1967

Weather most favourable for many years. By end of August all relief measures ceased. Good harvest.

1968

630 millimetres of rain during year. Prolonged dry spell following early cessaton of rains. Late planting widespread. Bulk of crop planted in May and June. Central shoot fly attacks on sorghum. Distribution of relief posho started in September in Jie and in December in Bokora and Jie. Labwor crops fail.

Cattle raiding in Jie by Turkana. Byelaw making planting of at least one acre of cassava compulsory throughout the district. Influx of Didinga refugees.

1969

550 millimetres annual rainfall. Very unusual rain pattern. April and May dry. All areas on famine relief except Labwor, Karenga, Iriri and Namalu. Dressed seed eaten in the few areas where crops germinated. Yields poor. Movement westward for grazing expected to affect food availability in Labwor.

Constant raids by Turkana on Dodoth, Jie and also Upe.

1970

645 millimetres annual rainfall. Food from harvest available from June onwards. By end of August the whole district self-supporting. Ample rainfall both in quantity and distribution. Early planting, dry harvest period, some farmers obtained second crop harvested in November and December.

Less cattle raiding. People more settled than before. Oxfam provided seed.

1971

760 millimetres annual rainfall. Rains late but adequate. Famine relief from May to mid-August in south. Good early crop harvests. Famine relief posho until September in North.

Raids responsible for food shortage. Oxfam provided seed.

1972

Rains started late in May and finished in July with severe dry spell between. Poor harvests. Many farmers relied on last year's harvest.

1973

Famine relief posho given out in Kaabong, Loyoro, Kopoth and Jie from January to August. Good harvests in North. Upe and Matheniko had very poor harvests. Raiding reported around Moroto. In South, famine relief operations started in July and ended in mid-September.

1974

Weather not as good as 1973. Jie, Nyakwae, Loyoro in North and Karita and Lorengedwat in South affected by drought which set in when sorghum was flowering. Good harvests only in Central Karamoja. Rest of district had to buy posho in shops.

Central shoot fly affected yields of sorghum in North. People in South started to feel the "heat of famine" by April. Famine relief slow in coming. Even Nakapiripirit and Namalu needed relief.

1975

Most parts of central Karamoja received appreciable harvests, but not enough to last until 1976 harvest. Famine relief from March to August.

1976

Weather not as good as 1975. Rains started in March and continued in June and July. Drought from early September. Crops planted late (for example in Dodoth and in parts of South Karamoja) failed. No serious food shortages because food still stored from 1975.

Cattle raiding and insecurity, particularly in Upe County.

1977

Some families (for example in Lokopo Subcounty) experienced food shortages early in the year. Good weather, and no food shortages after harvest.

Rains started early in March and reached a maximum in April-May. Good rains also in September-November except in North Karamoja.

Some sorghum damage by central shoot fly. Satisfactory yields from ratoon crop.

1978

1977 harvest lasted until June. In the North unfavourable weather resulted in poor crops, even during harvest. Yields were so low many farmers depended on imported foodstuff. Price of food rose due to high demand. Rains started in February and March. April and May were dry, June and July rainy, but the growing crops had already been affected. Crops planted in July failed due to drought after July.

Continuous cattle raids in North. Cattle not brought from the nawies (cattle camps) due to insecurity.

Lack of rotation and increasing tendency to sorghum monoculture increased resulting in greater pest attack on the crop.

Outbreak of CBPP in goats and later in cattle. Exceptionally large raids at Kacheri. Thousands of cattle stolen.

Bad food shortages reported in October. Cheap beans and posho suggested as alternative to "free famine relief". Outmigration as far as Teso by people seeking to work for food. Influx of people from Upe to Pian.

1979

(Report for North only.) Rains late and of short duration, finishing mid-May. Second rains insufficient. Crops withering at flowering stage. No inputs of seed from the Department of Agriculture. Karamoja seed project could not meet alarmingly high demand for seed. Insecurity during planting season reduced areas planted. Harvests very poor. Some farmers harvested absolutely nothing. Reports of outmigration. 160 deaths due to famine reported in Dodoth County, 213 in Jie County. Labwor County conditions not bad. International Red Cross and UNICEF approached by Department of Agriculture for relief food. Relief food arrived in August.

1980

(Report for North only.) Rains started late in March and stopped in June. Total crop failure. Starvation common. Seed arrived June-July, but much eaten. Total deaths recorded by Department of Agriculture: Dodoth County 2915, Labwor County 1745, Jie County 753.

Mortality, Nutritional Status and Diet During the Famine in Karamoja, Uganda, 1980

Robin J. Biellik and Peggy L. Henderson

Summary

Drought and the cattle raiding associated with a breakdown of civil order caused a famine in Karamoja, Uganda, during 1980. In November-December 1980, a study of mortality, nutritional status and dietary conditions was undertaken in south Karamoja.[1] Of 309 randomly selected children ⩽110 centimetres in height, 4.8 percent had acute malnutrition (<80 percent reference median weight-for-height). Interviews in 150 randomly selected households revealed that the crude mortality rate and the infant mortality rate during the previous year were increased almost fivefold and tenfold, respectively, above 1969 census data. Food supplied by the World Food Program was eaten the previous day by only half the families which were not self-sufficient in food. Relief officials' hopes that the 1981 cereal harvest might end the dependence on international aid were tempered by reports of further drought. Agricultural yield and food supplies should thus be monitored to assess the need for more international aid.

INTRODUCTION

The Karamoja District, in the northeastern corner of Uganda, has so far had three major famines this century, the last being in 1980. The region is mainly a plateau about 4000 feet above sea level, interrupted by occasional clusters of mountains of up to 10,000 feet above the plateau. The vegetation consists largely of thorn scrub and ephemeral grasses in the east, and a denser cover of grasses and scattered small trees in the west. The inhabitants are mainly seminomadic. Their economy has traditionally depended on cattle-herding and, to a lesser extent, on sedentary (non-nomadic) agriculture. Where crops are grown, they usually consist of finger millet, sorghum or maize.

*Editors' note: This article was first published in Lancet, ii (12 December 1981): 1330-1333.
[1] We thank CONCERN, 1 Upper Camden Street, Dublin 2, Ireland, for its support, and the members of its field team in Uganda for their help.

Erratic rainfall (Dyson-Hudson, 1966; Deshler, 1975), epidemics of rinder-pest and pleuropneumonia amongst the herds, and sporadic locust plagues, create a harsh environment in Karamoja, although there is great diversity between areas in the district in any given year. When rain is scarce or falls at the wrong time, the dependence on cattle becomes more absolute. Between 1919 and 1958, about 45 percent of crop yields were good to ex-cellent, 30 percent were just sufficient to avert hunger, and 25 percent were total failures. When poor grain crops follow animal loss, then there is famine. The 1980 famine was also preceded by drought starting in late 1979 and by animal loss; however, it was not disease but a breakdown of law and order following the ousting of President Idi Amin Dada by Tanzanian troops early in 1979 that was largely responsible for the animal loss. There was cattle raiding and theft of grain and clothing between tribes. Conditions were made worse by the looting of military, police and other government stores, including Ministry of Health dispensaries; by collapse of the local market systems; and by the nationwide disruption of transporta-tion. Some areas were deserted as people moved to be closer to religious missions for protection and, where available, for food and medical services. By July thousands of deaths had occurred in the district (Robinson and associates, 1980).

International agencies began to help. The Food and Agriculture Organisation (FAO) sent missions to Uganda in August 1979, and March 1980 (FAO, 1979 and 1980), to assess needs; the UN Disaster Relief Organisation headed a multi-agency mission in October 1980, which had urgent instructions to formulate recommendations for a comprehensive relief operation; and the UN Secretary-General launched a worldwide appeal for the means with which to implement it (UN Secretary-General, 1980). The response was general food supplies from the World Food Program (WFP); supplementary food for vulnerable groups from UN Children's Fund (UNICEF); medical supplies and equipment from UNICEF and some private voluntary agencies; potable water supply mainly through UNICEF; and manpower from British, Irish and French private voluntary agencies to put into operation various aspects of relief plans. Unfortunately, the help available did not reach a large proportion of the people. For example, the WFP food-for-work (FFW) ration (Table 1) was not fully distributed because of logistic difficulties in the supply system; and although feeding centres were set up in all county headquarters and several subcountry headquarters to provide vulnerable groups with on-the-spot feeding with UNICEF food supplies (high-protein biscuits, maize-meal, dried skimmed milk, oil and a "protein source" when available), the method of distributing the food was not standardised--there was wide variation between the voluntary agencies in qualifying criteria for aid and in methods of assessing for such criteria, in meal size and frequency of feeding, and in community surveillance.

TABLE 1: World Food Daily Program Food-For-Work Ration, Karamoja District, October 1980

Item	Daily Ration (g)[a]
Maize	300
Dried skimmed milk	75
Vegetable oil	75
"Protein" (beans, dried fish, &c, when available)	100

[a]Total caloric value: 2480 kcal.

Our study of mortality, nutritional status and dietary conditions was conducted to provide baseline community data which would permit the periodic evaluation of the effectiveness of the relief operation. Mortality rates should show the impact of the famine; data on nutritional status should indicate the condition of the nutritionally most vulnerable group--infants and young children; and knowledge of dietary conditions should help in the prediction of nutritional trends and in the evaluation of the extent of coverage by the general food distribution programme.

Resources made it possible to survey only one of the eight counties of Karamoja. Kadam, with a population of 23,794 (approximately 8 percent of the district population)(Kabera, 1980), was selected since conditions there are representative of conditions in the three counties usually designated as south Karamoja (see accompanying figure). Although the findings may not be strictly representative of conditions in north Karamoja, they can be accepted as being illustrative of the general profile of the famine throughout the district. The data for the study were collected between 15 November and 5 December 1980.

METHODS

A sampling frame was constructed by mapping the location and size of fenced settlements throughout Kadam. The population was divided into seventy-five clusters from which fifteen were selected by the use of standard sampling procedures (Abrahamson, 1974). In each cluster, mortality and dietary data were collected by interview of heads of ten households, and nutritional status data were collected of twenty children who were 110 centimetres or under in height. A pilot survey revealed an average of about 0.7 eligible children per household. Houses in a settlement were numbered consecutively in a clockwise direction. When all the houses in a settlement had been numbered, numbering continued in the same manner in the next settlement (identified by going clockwise). Kitchens and storehouses were ignored. Anthropometric data were collected on all eligible children in consecutive households until twenty had been assessed (all eligible children in the last household were assessed even if the sample of twenty was thereby exceeded). Household interviews were conducted in one household in three until ten had been interviewed.

The household interview schedule was designed, pilot-tested and refined. For population structure and mortality data, four age-groups were defined according to the most practical methods available in the absence of reliable age data. Births and deaths are not generally registered, and birthdays have very little social significance. Infants under 1 year of age were identified by the use of a simple local-events calendar. Children 110 centimetres or less in height were chosen because they are likely to be prepubescent and in a well-nourished population are aged up to approximately 5 years. Although this kind of cut-off clearly means that some older, stunted children are included, its use has practical advantages in crises (Graitcer, 1981). Older children were distinguished from adults by the use of the common local definition of the age of maturity; by this definition adults were approximately 18 years of age and over.

A persons's residence was defined as the place where an individual slept the previous night (care was taken to assign polygamous males to only one household); residents were classed by sex and age-group. Mortality data were classed by sex, age-group and cause of death of each household resident who died in the previous year (defined using the local-events calendar). It

Karamoja District (northeast Uganda) and its counties.

is recognised that cause of death represented family members' perceptions and cannot be clinically verified. Causes were put into three categories: starvation, disease (including accidents and "old age") and violence (homicide associated with cattle-raiding).

Denominators for calculating age-specific mortality rates were constructed by combining current population numbers with deaths during the previous year, since the mid-year population was unknown. During a proportion of the household interviews, data on migration in and out of the community were collected; these variables were found to be virtually equal in magnitude and were therefore ignored in the analyses.

Nutritional status was classed according to weight and height relative to those of a reference child. Weight-for-height is the most reliable indicator of nutritional status in crises for three reasons. Weight is very sensitive to acute changes in food intake, whilst height remains relatively constant; in prepubescent children the index is virtually independent of age, sex and race; and low weight-for-height has been shown to be a valid predictor of subsequent morbidity and mortality (Graitcer, 1981). A value of less than 80 percent reference median weight-for-height was taken to indicate moderate acute malnutrition, and less than 70 percent reference median weight-for-height to indicate severe acute malnutrition (National Center for Health Statistics, 1977; de Ville de Goyet, Seaman and Geijer, 1978).

Weight was taken to the nearest 100 grammes on a suspended "Salter" spring balance. For children up to approximately 85 centimetres tall, supine length was measured, and for those taller than that, standing height was measured to the nearest 0.5 centimetre by the use of standard procedures on a locally constructed stadiometer/infantometer. Oedema was present if pressure applied to the dorsal surface of the feet and to the backs of the hands for three seconds produced pitting. All measurements were made by one investigator. A bilingual Karamojong assistant was trained as guide and interpreter and to assist with anthropometric measurements. The weight and height measurements were analysed by the use of the PCTL9Z computer sub-routine available from the Center for Disease Control and the SPSS8 statistical package.

Data on dietary conditions were obtained by enquiring very carefully into the main source of the food eaten the previous day. The sources were put into five exclusive categories: family cereal harvest; food purchased or exchanged with relatives or friends; food from relief agencies; wild weeds, fruits or seeds collected in the bush; or no food taken all day.

Interviewers ignored empty households and went on to the next occupied house in the sequence, but enquiries were consistently made regarding the nature and whereabouts of the occupants. Children said to be <110 centimeters in height who were absent on the first visit were followed up at home, in institutions and elsewhere in the community. If the child remained absent on repeat visits, the investigator satisfied himself that the child was unobtainable before abandoning the search. Only three allegedly eligible children remained missing throughout the survey.

RESULTS

The population structure and socioeconomic status of the residents of the 150 households surveyed are presented in Table 2. Ninety-one percent of the homes were of traditional thatched construction. In 81 percent of homes, most of the adults wore traditional clothing of cotton or hide or went naked. None of the heads of households reported currently owning cattle, a finding in keeping with the absence of cattle observed throughout the county; however, since there was the possibility that respondents might be evasive in their answers to what has now become a sensitive issue (it being unmanly not to own cattle, yet dangerous to be still having some), the interpreter took into account the general expression and language of the respondents and others present to try to identify any frank cases of incorrect or evasive answers. A small proportion of houses were occupied by persons not likely for cultural and economic reeasons to own cattle (unmarried teenagers, newly-wed couples, elderly widows), and most of the other householders reported their cattle stolen by raiders.

Age-specific mortality rates and mortality by cause of death are presented in Tables 3 and 4, respectively. The method of calculating denominators for

TABLE 2: Population Structure by Age and Socioeconomic Indicators of Survey Sample,[a] South Karamoja District, December 1980

Variable	%
Age-group	
<1 year	2.7
1-4 years	19.8
5-17 years	31.2
≥18 years	46.2
Socioeconomic indicators	
Traditional housing	91
Traditional dress	81
Reported cattle ownership	0

[a]666 residents in 150 households; average 4.4 residents per household.

the age-specific mortality rate gives a moderately accurate estimate of the infant mortality rate--the rate of 607/1000 live-births shows a fourfold to fivefold increase in infant mortality compared with the 1969 general census finding of 139/1000 live-births (Langlands, 1974). The crude death rate of 212/1000 was 9 to 10 times higher than the rate of 23/1000 in 1969 (Langlands, 1974). Mortality was greater for males than for females ($p < 0.01$), although no significant sex-specific differences in cause of death were found. This excess mortality was clearly associated with the famine, since 78 percent of reported deaths were attributed directly to starvation.

TABLE 3: Mortality Rates by Age

	Reported Deaths	
Age-group	Number	Rate/1000
<1 year	28	607
1-4 years	58	305
5-17 years	43	171
≥18 years	50	140
All ages	179	212

TABLE 4: Causes of Death

Cause	Number	%
Starvation	139	78
Disease[a]	36	20
Violence[b]	4	2
All causes	179	100

[a]Includes accidents and "old age".
[b]Includes only homicide associated with cattle-raiding.

The nutritional status of children is presented in Table 5. The 309 children had a mean percentage median weight-for-height of 92.8 percent, SD 8.9 percent. Moderate and severe acute malnutrition was detected in 4.8 percent of the children assessed, and the distribution of weight-for-height was characteristically skewed towards moderate to extreme thinness. Not one case of oedema was discovered, which confirms the observations of other investigators (Hall, 1969) that kwashiorkor is much less common than marasmus in the areas of primary millet and sorghum cultivation in the north and east of Uganda. The prevalence of malnutrition was higher amongst female than amongst male children, although the difference was not statistically significant. The two cases of severe malnutrition were female. Infants <1 year had a nutritional status similar to that of the reference population, probably because of the protection afforded by adequate breast-feeding. Children over 1 year often had the large bellies and skinny limbs characteristic of famine conditions. Palpation showed that the swollen bellies were unlikely to be due to helminthic infestation; some were definitely the result of swollen spleens associated with malarial infection.

TABLE 5: Distribution of Nutritional Status of 309 Children ≮110 Cm in Height, by Median Weight-for-Height: South Karamoja District, December 1980

% of Standard[a]	Distribution (%)
≥ 120	1.3
110-119	3.6
100-109	11.7
90-99	41.4
80-89	37.2
70-79[b]	4.2
< 70[c]	0.6
Total	100

[a]Reference standard: National Center for Health Statistics, 1977.
[b]Moderate acute malnutrition
[c]Severe acute malnutrition.

A summary of the responses to the dietary recall questions is presented in Table 6. Informal observations inside a large proportion of the households visited indicated that WFP relief food was not reaching all beneficiaries. Six of the fifteen clusters had never received food aid, and in 30 percent of the households surveyed in the nine clusters which had received food aid, the rations had run out. Overall, relief agencies were the principal source of food in only 42 percent of households.

TABLE 6: Sources of Food

Main Source	% Households
Family cereal harvest	11
Food purchased or exchanged with relatives or friends	7
Relief food[a]	42
Wild weeds, fruits or seeds collected in the bush	26
No food all day	15

[a]Supplied by World Food Program, FAO, Rome.

Eighteen percent of households still had sufficient grain reserves or cash
with which to buy food, but those resources were not enough to last until
the next crop harvest. Fully 41 percent of the population surveyed were
subsisting on wild weeds, fruits and seeds collected in the bush, or had
consumed no food all day. Under the arid conditions prevailing the quantity
of woody fruits and seeds available to those with the strength to collect
them was of little nutritional significance; it could only temporarily stave
off the worst physical effects of hunger. It is therefore no exaggeration
to state that at the time of the study severe nutritional deprivation was a
daily reality for over 40 percent of the population in south Karamoja.
International food assistance was the only significant protection against
starvation available to the Karamojong.

DISCUSSION

The 1980 famine in south Karamoja that followed drought and civil chaos
resulted in extremely high mortality rates; 21 percent of the population
died in the twelve months up to December 1980, mostly from starvation. Such
a mortality rate is similar to that associated with other recent famines. A
similar type of interview survey amongst soup-kitchen beneficiaries showed
that the mortality rate during the 1974 famine in Bengal was 123/1000
(Alamgir, 1980). The infant mortality rate of 607/1000 in south Karamoja was
not substantially different from the rate, obtained by an identical method,
of 615/1000 amongst the infants of Issa nomads during the Ethiopian famine
in 1974 (Seaman, Holt and Rivers, 1978). The mortality rate of 305/1000
amongst Karamojong children aged 1-4 years was practically identical with
that found amongst Issa children in 1974 (Seaman, Holt and Rivers, 1978),
but much higher than the 166/1000 rate reported for children 0-4 years in
the Niger in 1974, the highest figure reliably reported for that age-group
during the Sahel famine (Hogan and associates, 1977). Despite high mortality under famine conditions in Karamoja, moderate and severe acute malnutrition (that is, wasting due to nutritional deprivation) was not as widespread
as expected. In 1963 when there was no famine, the prevalence of clinically
frank kwashiorkor and marasmus amongst a nonrandom sample of 1047 Karamojong
children aged 0-5 years was 1.1 percent (Jelliffe and associates, 1964;
Rutishauser, 1971). During a period of "widespread shortage of food, due to
drought" in 1966, a similar survey amongst 298 children aged 0-3 years gave
a prevalence of 1.3 percent (Rutishauser, 1971; Rutishauser and Whitehead,
1969). Although our finding of a 4.8 percent prevalence of acute malnutrition was considerably greater than that found in Karamoja by previous investigators, it seemed low when compared with the results of anthropometric
surveys which used similar criteria of undernourishment in other famines
(Table 7). A possible explanation for this discrepancy is that the
Karamojong children surveyed were survivors of the famine. If most of the
malnourished children have died, the point prevalence of malnutrition
measured one to two months after the stabilisation of the feeding programmes
serves only as a limited guide to the extent of the disease at the height of
the famine (Bengoa, 1970).

Since the dietary conditions in south Karamoja at the time of the study can
most accurately be described as being of marginal sufficiency, children
remained thin and were at risk of rapid deterioration in nutritional status
if any disruption were to occur in the international relief operation. Only
18 percent of families were temporarily self-sufficient where food was
concerned. The other 82 percent needed food aid in order to survive, although only about half had received an adequate quantity during the latest
WFP general food distribution. However, shortly after the circulation of

TABLE 7: **Prevalence Rates of Acute Malnutrition in Recent African Drought-Related Famines**

Location	Year	Prevalence of Malnutrition[a]
Ethiopia	1974	15.9
Chad	1974	22.5
	1975	12.1
Mali	1974	10.7
	1975	6.2
Mauritania	1974	9.9
	1975	7.7
Upper Volta	1974	9.1
	1975	9.2
Zaire	1978	8.7
Uganda	1980	4.8

*Source: The data for Ethiopia are from Seaman, Holt and Rivers (1978). For Chad, Mali, Mauritania and Upper Volta they are from Hogan and associates (1977). For Zaire they are from Nkamany and associates (1980).
[a]Percentage of children <80 percent reference median weight-for-height.

the interim report of the present study, food supply logistics improved greatly and distribution was extended to parts of the county which had not formerly received food.

The prognosis for the future in Karamoja is not encouraging. In these last months before the next cereal harvest, the entire population of Karamoja will become dependent on WFP food aid for survival. It seems unlikely that cattle will resume their former significance in the economy in the south of the district for some years to come; greater dependence on cereal grains will be inevitable. Despite the Karamojong farmers' early problems in the procurement and distribution of agricultural tools and fresh seed grain, substantial fields were planted in 1981. Relief officials had hoped that food aid operations could be suspended by August 1981, after the crops had been harvested. The rains were heavy in March, but lack of rain from April to June, inclusive, caused the reported loss of the maize crop and threatens the more drought-resistant sorghum crop (UPI, 1981).

Under these circumstances, therefore, it is essential that the FAO continue to monitor closely the condition of agriculture and food supplies in Uganda in general and in Karamoja District in particular, in order to assess the need for a further international appeal for food assistance through the 1981-82 agricultural cycle.

REFERENCES

Abrahamson, J. H. (1974). Survey Methods in Community Medicine. Churchill-Livingstone, London.
Alamgir, M. (1980). Famine in South Asia: Political Economy of Mass Starvation. Oelgeschlager, Gunn and Hain, Cambridge (Mass.).
Bengoa, J. M. (1970). Recent Trends in the Public Health Aspects of Protein-Calorie Malnutrition. WHO Chronicle, 24: 522-28.
Deshler, W. (1975). Drought and Food Shortage in North Karamoja, Uganda,

1916 to the mid-1950s. Presented at the 18th annual meeting of the African Studies Association, 19 October-1 November, San Francisco.

de Ville de Goyot, C., J. Seaman and U. Geijer (1978). The Management of Nurtritional Emergencies in Large Populations. WHO, Geneva.

Dyson-Hudson, N. (1966). Karamojong Politics. Clarendon Press, Oxford.

Food and Agriculture Organisation (1979). Republic of Uganda: Report of the FAO Emergency Assistance Mission. Office for Special Relief Operations rep. no. W/N3264. FAO, Rome.

Food and Agriculture Organisation (1980). Republic of Uganda: FAO/WFP/USAID Emergency Mission. Office for Special Relief Operations rep. no. W/N7320. FAO, Rome.

Graitcer, P. L. (1981). A Manual for the Basic Assessment of Nutritional Status in Potential Crisis Situations (Second Edition). Center for Disease Control, Atlanta.

Hall, S. A. (1969). Nutrition and Infection. East African Medical Journal, 46: 58-63.

Hogan, R. C., S. P. Broske, J. P. Davis and associates (1977). Sahel Nutrition Surveys, 1974 and 1975. Disasters, 1: 117-24.

Jelliffe, D. B., F. J. Bennett, E. F. P. Jelliffe and R. H. R. White (1964). Ecology of Childhood Disease in the Karamojong of Uganda. Arch. Environmental Health, 9: 25-36.

Kabera, J. B. (1980). Demarcation of Constituencies, 1980 (map). Makerere University Department of Geography, Kampala.

Langlands, B. W. (1974). Atlas of Population Census, 1969, in Uganda. Occasional paper 48, Makerere University Department of Geography, Kampala.

National Center for Health Statistics (1977). Growth Curves for Children, Birth-18 Years. Vital and Health Statistics, Series 11, no. 165. NCHS, Rockville (Maryland).

Nkamany, K., R. Glass, J. Schamper and associates (1980). The Consequences of the Drought in Bas-Zaire, 1978. Disasters, 4: 55-64.

Robinson, S., A. Streetly, M. Farrant, S. MacSweeney and A. McCracken (1980). Famine Relief in Karamoja, Uganda. Lancet, ii: 849-51.

Rutishauser, I. H. E. (1971). Statistics of Malnutrition in Early Childhood (with reference to Uganda). Journal of Tropical Pediatrics, 17: 11-16.

Rutishauser, I. H. E. and R. G. Whitehead (1969). Field Evaluation of two Biochemical Tests which may reflect Nutritional Status in three Areas of Uganda. British Journal of Nutrition, 23: 1-13.

Seaman, J., J. Holt and J. Rivers (1978). The Effects of Drought on Human Nutrition in an Ethiopian Province. International Journal of Epidemiology, 7: 31-40.

United Nations Secretary-General (31 October 1980). Special Economic and Disaster Relief Assistance: Assistance to the Drought-Striken Areas in Uganda. UN General Assembly rep. no. A/35/562. UN, New York.

United Press International (2 July 1981). Drought Threatens Ugandans' Crops. Houston Post.

Famine and Food Relief in Karamoja

Mario Cisternino

The Dodoth, Jie, Karamojong and Pokot peoples of Karamoja are seminomadic and remain almost as socially and administratively independent of each other today as they were during the years of colonial domination. Smaller tribal groups, inhabitants of the area before the larger seminomadic tribes moved in, act as cushions between any two of the latter and complement them in agricultural and trade activities.

Cattle management among the pastoralist seminomads is still organised traditionally and is aimed at subsistance rather than trade, numbers rather than the quality of stock. Herdsmen move their cattle westward during dry seasons, back toward their homesteads during rainy seasons. Herdsmen from among the Turkana of Kenya occasionally join their herds with Karamoja herds in seasonal migration.

Cattle raiding among the different Karamoja groups at one time served in redistributing wealth, identifying allegiances and restocking herds. With the introduction of modern weapons, older raiding patterns gave way and raiding now often occurs indiscriminately and involves great loss of life.[1] Many machine guns (perhaps 2000) were stolen from army barracks in Moroto in 1979 when Amin's army fled before the advancing Tanzanians. Guns and bullets have been acquired more recently through trade with Ugandan militiamen and soldiers--often with the help of local or Somali middlemen--and in the ambush of soldiers and policemen. Meanwhile, bands of young men among the Karamojong today frequently raid cattle or rob travellers and suppliers. Guns have given them a certain freedom from older restraints, and young men often act now without the consent and knowledge of tribal leaders. Plunder is traded for whatever it will bring in market centres.

Colonial and more recent governments in Uganda have encouraged agricultural

---

[1] The Jie tribe, for example, which counts some 25,000 persons, during 1981 lost not less than 1000 young men in gun battles. The best armed among the Karamoja tribes are the Jie and the Matheniko (a subtribe among the Karamojong). The least armed are the Dodoth. During 1979-81 the Dodoth, illequipped to defend their stock from better armed raiders, lost practically all of their cattle.

development in Karamoja. Such projects, however, have often been encouraged without the slightest knowledge of the fragile ecological balances of the area and have often been far more detrimental than effective, especially in reference to the introduction of cash crops such as cotton.

The peoples of Karamoja in the years before independence lived as if in a "human zoo".[2] Administration within the region was organised under leaders imposed by the British and was often restrictive and unfortunate. But within such outlines tribal elders exercised their own authority and rough balances in access to grazing land, water resources and the cultivation of crops existed between the different tribes and their environment.

Population changes and changes in raiding patterns basically challenged the earlier patterns of social life that occurred within and between the tribal groups of Karamoja. Combined with other factors--for example, the expulsion of the Indian middlemen from the region (as from the country) under Amin's dictate, the deterioration of national and international trade relation- ships during the 1970s and the failure of the rains between 1978 and 1981-- population and raiding pattern changes contributed to the circumstances behind the terrible 1980-82 famine in the area. Between 1957 and 1980 Karamoja's human population doubled. By 1980 only about half the cattle present in the country in 1957 remained.

The purpose of this article is to examine some of the socioeconomic conse- quences of the relief programmes introduced by outsiders in response to the famine. Suggestions concerning development possibilities in the region are given in conclusion.

RELIEF AID AND EMERGENCY ASSISTANCE

Government organisations within Uganda were unable to respond to the Karamoja crisis as it grew. Most of the foodstuffs that flowed into the area as a result came from foreign sources. The total quantity of food- stuffs entering Karamoja per month peaked early in 1981 at approximately ·3000 tons.

The distribution of aid in Karamoja during 1980 and into 1981 was coordi- nated primarily by the United Nations World Food Programme (WFP).[3] Unable to use local government structures in the distribution process--because they had collapsed or because they had become hopelessly corrupt, the WFP used the services of various independent voluntary agencies and numerous church organisations to assist in the transportation, storage and distribution of supplies during the emergency. Through the channels that opened up, the supplies brought into Karamoja reached down and into the village level quickly and deaths from outright starvation were soon put to an end. Within a few months, in turn, levels of malnutrition among children and old people,

---

[2]See my "Karamoja: The Human Zoo" (1979, mimeographed) for a thorough examination of the background and characteristics of the Karamoja region and its people in Uganda.

[3]Coordination was facilitated through monthly meetings held in Kampala and in Moroto and Kotido in Karamoja. The meetings at first involved aid agency personnel only. Later government personnel also attended. The meetings in Karamoja were eventually chaired by regional government authori- ties; in Kampala they were chaired under the authority of the Ministry of Rehabilitation when it was established.

the most susceptible groups during periods of famine, were effectively reduced.   The method of distribution after September 1981 shifted from general food supply to distribution through food-for-work schemes and distribution to targeted groups, in particular to malnourished children through schools and health centres.

The food-for-work schemes introduced were devised to help the people get back to some kind of work and normalcy. Unfortunately, in this they were not particularly successful.   The work proposed was considered necessary by the government and had to do with modern sector schemes--for example, road building, reforestation and the construction of schools; in general, it was alien to the interests of the tribals themselves. Furthermore, in that planning and supervision were in nontribal hands, the execution of the work did little if anything in teaching the tribals new skills and confidence.

Food-for-work schemes were ended in Karamoja in August 1982 as new crops ripened after good rains. The schemes brought some understanding to the people of Karamoja about the interests of outsiders in their welfare. Together with other dimensions of the general relief effort, in reality they no doubt also brought the influences and structures of the outside world closer in upon the people of Karamoja. But overall they did little in providing the people with a broader chance for survival in the face of another period of famine.

Motivations of Donors

Agencies of many kinds responded to the need for assistance in Karamoja. Some came in focusing on the needs of children, others with interests only in the poor, one with interests only in the construction of schools and another interested only in the sick. Some agencies sent people in for two or three months, others for longer periods of time. Some were interested in working only in affiliation with the central government. Others were uninterested in Ugandan or regional affiliations of any kind.

Agency differences were sometimes confusing to the people in need of help. Differences often resulted in problems in the coordination of efforts. Yet all of the agencies came in with at least a strong expression of humanitarian interest. People all over the world had watched on television as the people of Karamoja died of starvation and cholera. Humanitarian responses under the conditions were inescapable.

But other reasons for participation in the distribution of aid also occurred. For example:

- once the logistics of supply in Karamoja were established, United Nations relief agencies had to keep going, whateverhappened, for the region had become another dumping ground for the excess food produced in donor countries;

- Ugandan administrators became more and more complacent with, or at least less and less concerned about, the problems of the people of Karamoja as outsiders rushed in with their own programmes and supplies;

- international, national and local traders gained profits in the transport and supply of commodities for relief agencies and local people during the emergency;

- missionaries in places experienced an increase in the number of baptisms as their parishes became involved in food distribution.

Now the supply process in Karamoja during the famine was never easy. Armed bandits operated along the roads and assaults on lorry drivers and civil servants, particularly during the last few months of relief supply, became almost daily occurrences. Most of the personnel of the relief agencies had to leave Karamoja before the deadline they had set for themselves (August 1982) in order to secure their lives. Government structures for all prac- tical purposes were nonoperative except for during those times when the repression of local raiding was attempted with the participation of soldiers and militiamen from neighbouring tribes.[4] Poorly paid but armed soldiers often took advantage of the situations in which they found themselves.

Nevertheless, important as were humanitarian motivations in the provision of relief supplies to Karamoja during the famine years, other motivations were also simultaneously important.

Effects on Social Structure

Some of the efforts of aid agency personnel were badly misdirected. Others were simply unfortunate in the circumstances. Much relief food was brewed into beer or exchanged for beer. The longer food relief lasted the more it fostered a certain passivity, or beggar's mentality, among some sectors of the population. Emergency relief efforts were far more common than attempts to involve the people in locally meaningful developmental schemes. Between 1976 and 1979 several thousand Karamojong had migrated to nearby districts to become petty traders, cultivators or common labourers. Many poorer mi- grants lived on the edges of the townships of Mbale and Soroti. Food relief drew many migrants back into areas in Karamoja where there was no chance for them to survive once food relief was suspended. One American relief organisation attracted several thousand migrants back from regions south of Karamoja into a resettlement scheme, and even built huts for some of them, in the face of the fact that once outside supervision was withdrawn the new settlers would be unable to remain on their own.

In general, while aid offerings affected the welfare of a great number of people in Karamoja, related influences hardly penetrated thoroughly the core structures of local life. Scattered elders were consulted in the develop- ment of food-for-work schemes, particularly in the definition of procedures to be followed in the distribution of food. But such involvements had little positive or negative influence on the roles of the elders. Herders continued to tend their herds. Wives and weaker males came into touch with relief agents; strongermales and elders, in general, received food only indirectly. The tribals were now as before referred to as "natives" by representatives of the government, while the Karamojong referred to a civil servant or an aid agency representative either as an "aryan" (stranger) or an "emoit" (enemy).[5] A few of the tribals who could speak at least a smattering of English were called upon to act as spokesmen for aid repre- sentatives or managers in various projects. Several gained at least a measure of wealth and power in the process. By and large, the local people, like the civil servants of the area, were not involved in any organised sense in the overall relief process. In short, necessary as was the emer-

---

[4]Raiding between tribes continued throughout the period of relief food distribution. Attempts at the repression of raiding were often brutal.

gency provided by outside agencies in cutting short the terrible starvation under way, little was done during this period to strengthen the authority of local leaders or to build more effective linkages between the people of Karamoja and the more widespread social networks of the country. As a result, local organisational resiliency was weakened during the famine in relation to the aid process iself, whereas it might have been strengthened.

Effects on Economic Patterns

The sector of the local economy most directly undermined by food aid had to do with the internal marketing of foodstuffs. Both 1982 and 1983 were good years agriculturally, but it was impossible for farmers to market sorghum and maize in the townships of Moroto, Kotido and Kaabong during this period. This was the case for these townships had been centres for the distribution of relief food (food-for-work food and food provided for distribution through schools and health centres), food stolen from relief agencies had become locally available at very low prices and regional farmers (particularly farmers from Namalu, Iriri, Labwor and Karenga) could not sell their own produce at profit to local traders.

The situation cannot be so easily described, of course. The purchasers of excess food in most of Karamoja are not the tribals themselves, but civil servants who live in towns and trading centres and officials associated with schools and health centres. Money among the people is used almost exclusively in the purchase of cloth, soap, salt and other items not commonly produced in the villages, and barter is commonly used in the procurement of necessary food.[6] Again, agricultural activity in Karamoja expanded in 1982 and 1983, especially in some of the drier areas, as intertribal raiding subsided, contacts with the outside world continued to expand, and pastoralist traditions were eroded.

Yet the impact of the aid poured into Karamoja was significant along the lines indicated. While in the period May through July 1982 one kilogramme of maize produced in Namalu could not be sold in Moroto at USh 30, it could fetch USh 60 in Mbale. Local marketing patterns were short circuited as food relief was introduced.

Another side effect of the entire relief process had to do with the introduction of ready-made tools from the outside for use in food-for-work and other schemes. The tools brought in were of better quality than those made locally and could be brought in in numbers thought appropriate. In the process, the capacity of local iron and wood workers to support themselves in the production of tools was undermined.

Education

In 1979 only some 3 percent of the children of Karamoja attended school.

---

[5]Similar as was the labelling used by the Karamojong for civil servants and aid personnel, during 1980-82 foreign aid personnel were never directly threatened with violence, while civil servants were repeatedly threatened. Many civil servants in Karamoja were killed during this difficult period; many fled the area.

[6]Food purchased by the people with cash, in fact, is commonly used in the preparation of beer.

Famine and war had reduced the already low attendance rates of the preceding years. In 1983 the number of school-age children attending school came to roughly 30 percent.

Attendance rates in 1983 varied by region. They were lower among the Matheniko and Jie--where herds were larger and more children were needed to tend them--higher among the Dodoth, Bokora, Pian and Labwor with their smaller herds. The fact that food aid was still given through schools after it was no longer given in food-for-work and other schemes helps explain changes in school attendance rates. So does the reduction in size of many of the herds of livestock.

But whatever the reasons, changes in patterns of attendance at school have given church, government and other outsiders in Karamoja a wedge into local patterns of life that they had not had earlier. The people of Karamoja are not yet fully aware of the possible consequences of the new penetration. Local schools are very poorly equipped and the kind of education they enable will hardly prepare local youngsters for the new world into which they will have to step. Nevertheless, changes in patterns of school attendance are indicative of changing times, and the consequences of the changes themselves will be very significant in the long run.

SURVIVAL AND DEVELOPMENT

Most of the Karamoja people have never been outside their own tribal boundaries. In the past they responded to natural and other disasters by shrinking into tribal cohesion, then taking on the challenges they faced as best they could. And so they responded again when confronted by drought and famine conditions at the end of the 1970s.

This time, however, their conditions of life had changed. Their population had more than doubled in the past twenty-five years. Modern weapons had transformed older patterns in cattle raiding. Traditional patterns in leadership and social organisation had lost their resiliency. Only the responses of aid agencies in other parts of the world cut short the famine that stalked them.

Unfortunately, the responses that occurred did not basically alter the capacities of the local people to respond effectively either to similar crises in the future or to what will no doubt continue to be the further encroachments of the outside world. During the famine, as before, administrators, relief agents and civil servants did things for the people in relation to their own definitions of the situation, not with the people in utilisation of local understandings and local organisational strengths.

Many of the Karamoja people do not yet understand the changes that are upon them. Bewildered by the violent disruptions in local life that have occurred in recent years, others are aware that new understandings and relationships among different tribes, and between themselves and outsiders, will have to be introduced if further tragedies are to be avoided. In general, at least the following points should be kept in mind as the future of the people of Karamoja is considered. Firstly, unchecked raiding, particularly unchecked raiding by a heavily armed tribe against a lightly armed tribe, must be prevented, and the restocking of cattle should be encouraged as reasonable.

Secondly, spontaneous migration out of Karamoja should not be hindered.

Such migration has long occurred. From 1960 onwards it has occurred in substantial numbers among families deprived of cattle into the newly developed agricultural areas around Nakapiripirit, Namalu and Iriri in south-central Karamoja, and into the more settled territories around Labwor and Karenga.

Thirdly, traditional tribal leaders should be recognised as such by outsiders and held responsible for the administration of their own people. Their authority should not be subverted.

Fourthly, the introduction of cash crops that sell only in outside markets, and the further introduction of consumer goods from outside sources, should be very carefully monitored. The older planning mentality geared to export marketing and the wholesale importation of goods from the outside must be recognised as exploitative.

Fifthly, development projects should be introduced at the boundaries of the territories of the seminomadic groups. Such groups already have "brother clans" agriculturally, rather than pastorally, organised. Agricultural development schemes and appropriate level industrial developments (say in tanning, iron works and the preparation of milk by-products, resins and gums) at such locations would help in the absorption of displaced people from among the seminomadic groups.

In short, even as the Karamoja people continue to be further absorbed into regional and national patterns of life, their own patterns must be safeguarded.

REFERENCE

Cisternino, Mario. 1979. Karamoja: The Human Zoo: The History of Planning for Karamoja with Some Tentative Counterplanning. PhD thesis, University of Swansea.

Resettlement in Karamoja

J. G. Wilson

The Karamoja Rehabilitation Scheme (see Evan-Jones, 1963), which was drawing to a close in 1958, was perhaps the last great throw of colonial effort in Karamoja.[1] It came into being in recognition of the serious and ongoing deterioration that was occurring in the Karamoja environment, and was an attempt to turn the situation around.

Ironically, the problems of Karamoja in the late 1950s were in large measure the result of colonial emphases. Pandering to the needs of the pastoralists in the area, administrators continued to develop open grazing lands. This worked well enough for awhile but eventually caught up with them as they ran out of unexploited lands. Spillovers of cattle into neighbouring territories in turn increased the chances for strife between the members of different tribes.

Secondly, in that pastoralism was identified by colonial administrators as the ultimate way of life for the Karamojong, no alternative ways of life were opened up. As a result, even while other groups with pastoral backgrounds in Uganda were becoming familiar with introductions in material culture, possibilities in agriculture and new styles of life, the Karamojong were encouraged to cling to old ways of living, fighting and raiding, and to spurn modern dress. Thus to enter Karamoja circa 1953 was to enter an area in which time had virtually stopped a thousand years in the past, an area in which, for example, men inevitably carried spears and wore magnificent headdresses, and perhaps beads and bangles, but were otherwise naked.

Thirdly, cattle numbers continued to grow as a result of the territorial stability and advantages enabled under Pax Brittanica. Epidemic cattle diseases such as rinderpest were controlled in the postwar years. Equally

---

[1] The Karamoja Rehabilitation Scheme was begun largely as the result of my preliminary work during 1953-54 on the eradication and control of thornbush (see Wilson, 1959 and 1962). Some 600,000 pounds of Protectorate funds were spent under the scheme but little was achieved other than the construction of the "watershed road"--because it passed for part of its length along the ridge thatcomprises the Kyoga/Turkwell watershed--that linked Moroto and Mbale and opened up the Namalu area of southern Karamoja.

importantly, the earthen dam construction programme launched in the area by
the colonial government in 1946 and continued for the next twenty years
opened up hitherto waterless areas to large numbers of cattle. The problem
was that such developments, in conjunction with changes of the kind already
identified, led to uncontrolled numbers of cattle grazing on relatively
fragile grasslands, the deterioration of grassland into bushland and, eventually, severe soil erosion.[2]

In short, at the end of the 1950s the Karamojong lived relatively well off
of swollen herds of livestock even while their living situation had become
more and more precarious.[3]   Internecine struggles had become increasingly
common. Some two-thirds of Karamoja District, which then measured slightly
more than 12,000 square miles and had once been largely grass covered, was
now bush covered. The context remained anachronistically, and so it appeared that it might remain with all of its problems.

Events, however, soon radically altered the lives of the Karamojong forever.
In 1959 a raiding party of Turkana from neighbouring Kenya, with firearms,
attacked three settlements of the Dodoth tribe in northern Karamoja and
wiped out every inhabitant. Successive raids followed, and the Dodoth, who
could offer very little resistance with their spears, were forced to migrate
westwards and concentrate around places like Loyoro, Koputh and Kaabong.[4]
In 1960 a British police officer was killed in an engagement with Turkana
raiders near a place called Nakiloro north of Moroto Mountain.

The Special Force branch of the Uganda Police kept raiding reasonably well
in check until General Amin's advent in 1971, when it was disbanded. Between 1971 and 1979 Amin's forces took up the task of keeping order in the
area and brushed several times with Turkana and other raiders. But they
fared badly in each such encounter and towards the end of the 1970s lost
much of their will and reason to fight as Amin's government folded. As a
result the peoples of Karamoja found themselves unprotected both from each
other and from outsiders. This, together with the fact that spear fighting
had become obsolete as the use of guns had become more and more common,
meant that herds could now be scattered or stolen overnight, and frequently
they were. Confronted as never before by hardships as a result of such
developments, many of the Karamojong turned, as best they could, to cultivation in order to survive.

Amin's advent resulted in other adverse changes for the Karamojong as well.
In April 1971, just three months after his accession and in the attempt to
rush the Karamojong into the twentieth century, Amin decreed, among other
things, that the Karamojong should be forced to wear clothes and give up old
practices such as the carrying of spears. Such decrees were never fully
implemented, of course, but they did have an important effect upon the
people, particularly in their dealings with outsiders. Such regulations
undermined the significance of local status symbols and insignia, and they

---

[2]In my "Vegetation of Karamoja District" (1962), I examine the consequences for the surrounding vegetetion of the construction of Lokiporangitome
Dam. The dam stands out clearly amidst grassland in aerial photographs taken
in 1946. By 1956 the grassland around the dam had become bushland.
    [3]Agricultural activity expanded in Karamoja during the 1950s through the
increasing adoption of ox-drawn ploughs. But the livestock of the people
now, as before, carried them through the years of bad harvests. The 1959
veterinary census in Karamoja counted nearly a million cattle.
    [4]Thomas (1981) chronicles much of the story here.

undermined tribal morale. More generally, some of the older bonds that had
once linked together groups such as the Bokora, Matheniko and Pian gave way
to rivalries as new allegiances were encouraged.

A spin-off of the clothes-wearing edict might be termed the "charcoal revolution". Desperately seeking ways and means of scratching together the
money needed to buy cloth, the cowed Karamoja populace settled on the making
of charcoal for which there was demand among the civilian and uniformed
employees of Moroto. Thousands of individuals first felled all of the
beautiful trees around Moroto township, then the trees on the peripheral
lower slopes of Moroto Mountain, then the trees on the plain around extending westwards to Kangole.

The tree and bush felling that occurred around Moroto was repeated elsewhere
in Karamoja. It resulted in tragic denudation in many places. Interestingly, however, it simultaneously solved the perennial problem of bush en-
croachment with dramatic suddenness. In combination with the tremendous
fall in livestock numbers that occurred during the 1970s--because of uncontrolled raiding, the inability to gain medicines for the control of cattle
diseases and so on--bush felling enabled grass to spring up again and a
return to the original savanna.[5]

Another event that altered irrevocably the outlines of social and cultural
life in Karamoja occurred at the very end of the Amin period. When Amin's
forces left Moroto prior to the arrival of the Tanzanian-dominated liberation forces, they left the doors of the fully stocked armoury wide open.

The Matheniko group of the Karamojong, in whose territory Moroto is sited--
and who, like other Karimojong, over the years had been manufacturing
homemade guns--were not slow in coming forward. They organised women and
children as bearers and quickly plundered the armoury of usable weapons and
ammunition.[6] Thus, when the liberation forces arrived they had to watch
their step and not intrude exploitatively in the deceptively old-fashioned
setting.[7] The warring traditions of the people were alive, and in a new
way. Firearms had become the recognised weapons of warfare; spears had
become relics of the past.

The change in weapons was dramatic and resulted in horrifying carnage between 1980 and 1982. In fact, so many men, women and children were needlessly slaughtered in massacres of whole villages and settlements during
this period, say for a hundred or so cattle, that the leaders of different
warring tribes finally met in order call a halt to the killing.[8]

Other tragedies that have hit the Karamojong in recent years include the
epidemic of cholera in 1979 which killed thousands of people, especially in
Dodoth County, and the 1980 famine which killed thousands more. Overall,
changes and upheavals in Karamoja have entirely altered local patterns of

---

[5]In particular, the maps showing the vegetation of the district which I
drew up circa 1961 (see Wilson, 1962) were no longer applicable in 1980.
    [6]Persons present at the time speak of columns of bearers lined up in
front of the armoury over a three-day period, and of some individuals bringing pack donkeys to hasten the operation.
    [7]Before they did learn how to step appropriately, two commanding officers
of the liberation forces had been killed in local action.
    [8]This halt is still in general effect at the time of this writing (Janu-
ary 1984). It is unclear, however, whether or not it will last.

life. The Karamojong have travelled far along the pathways of change.

THE NEED FOR RESETTLEMENT

Karamoja

Karamoja is the driest corner of Uganda and is oriented roughly north-south,
measuring approximately 200 miles in length by fifty miles in breadth. The
people of Karamoja are predominantly of Nilotic origin and may be grouped
culturally and linguistically as Karamojong. They are closely related to the
Teso of Uganda, the Turkana of Kenya and the Topossa of southern Sudan.

Most of the Karamojong are settled in the drier eastern and central parts of
their region. Hill ranges such as those around Labwor and Napore are settled by small agriculturally oriented tribes with ethnic and cultural characteristics different from those of the Karamojong. The western stretches
of Karamoja are largely unsettled.

Average annual rainfall in Karamoja's eastern areas seldom exceeds twelve
inches. It climbs to twenty-two inches in the settled area near Loyoro to
perhaps twenty-eight inches at Kangole in the central belt. In the western-
most parts of the district rainfall averages range between thirty-five and
fifty-five inches.

The figures for average rainfall in even the driest parts of Karamoja may
not appear to be particularly low to some readers. When considered in
relation to other factors, however, the precariousness of local agricultural
balances becomes clear. Firstly, the rains occasionally do not come at all.
Secondly, the growing season is very short. In most years rains come in
April and May, then again in July and August, and the growing season is
effectively confined to these four months.[9] Thirdly, the dry season is long
and severe. It begins with the gradual drying of vegetation in September,
intensifies through October and November with the advent of seasonal desic-
cating winds that bring leaf fall and total withering to grasses. The dry
season has been the customary season of transhumance with the bulk of the
cattle moved to the western parts of the district as grazing becomes problematic in the settled eastern and central parts.

Vegetation in Karamoja roughly follows rainfall patterns. The western third
of the district is largely grass or tree savanna and has the highest grazing
potential; thornbushes are more common towards the east. With reduced
grazing and the common practice again of dry season grass burning--a practice increasingly possible again as grassland has reemerged--the threat
that bushland would replace grassland in much of central Karamoja has subsided.

The soils of Karamoja are closely linked with the topography of the region.
This is gently undulating in general, interrupted here and there by isolated
hill and mountain ranges. The common soil of the ridge tops and upper
slopes is usually reddish-brown and texturally a sandy clay or clay loam.
This red soil in the eastern and central parts of Karamoja is often
shallow, slightly acidic or basic in reaction and low in plant nutrients
such as nitrogen and phosphorus. Towards the west it tends to be deeper and

---

[9]In practice over most of the region cultivation is carried out only in
April and May.

slightly more fertile, and in some instances lateritic.

The common soil of the lower slopes and the lowest elevations of the vast Karamoja plain are black calcareous clays of very stiff texture that extend to a depth of six to twenty feet. These clays are more difficult to cultivate by hand than the red soils but are slightly more fertile and in some areas have been cultivated continuously for twenty-five or more years.

The few rivers and streams of Karamoja extend for very short distances and are mainly ephemeral or of flash-flood type. They are important as sources of subsurface water, however, and their flood plains are commonly usable as highly productive farm land.

Resettlement

Some people have argued recently that after all the trauma the Karamojong have been through they should be encouraged to remain in the east and central areas of Karamoja and gradually reacquire cattle.

Those who argue along such lines are uninformed about the past of the Karamojong and the grave environmental situation that existed when the livestock population in the region was at its zenith. They are blind to the serious security problems that emerged as automatic weapons replaced spears in cattle raiding and intertribal warfare, and blind to the continued potential for loss of life and destruction that would exist should the Karamojong be encouraged to return to older patterns of life even while the world around them had made such reversion impossible.

In relation to such considerations, very extensive experience among the Karamojong and thorough understandings of regional rainfall, vegetation, soil and drainage patterns, my own conclusion is that the case for resettlement in the more productive western areas of Karimoja of those who have been deprived of livestock has become unarguable.[10] The reasons for this include at least the following. Firstly, the majority of the Karamojong do not now possess cattle. As a result the only avenue of support open to them is farming. The problem is that farming in the eastern and central areas of the region, where most of the people currently live, is far less reasonable than it is towards the west. Farmers in the west would face far less liklihood of total crop failure during droughts and would be able to grow more crops. Deprived of cattle in their old settlement areas, many of the Karamojong today are forced to try to scratch out a living growing almost only their common varieties of sorghum. Cassava, sweet potatoes and maize, in addition to sorghum, can be grown in the west both for food and for sale.

Secondly, how would the poor and stockless Karamojong keep themselves and their families while they were reacquiring cattle? Would they be charges of the government or, once more, of international famine relief?

---

[10]My experience in Karamoja covers some thirty-two years. In my early years in the region I conducted soil/vegetation and land use surveys for the government. Later I had a number of years of experience as Agricultural Officer of the region both under colonial administration and in the immediate postindependence period. After retirement I spent a further period in the area as a retired individual. I am now manager of the Kapedo Resettlement Project in Dodoth County in the northern part of the district.

Thirdly, what good would there be in the reacquisition of cattle by the populace as a whole, given the conflicts over raiding that emerged in the past, dramatic increases in population in recent years and the problem of overgrazing that would soon reemerge?

Fourthly, many of the Karamojong are today, as it were, in a state of shock. Many, men as well as women, have become completely disillusioned with armed conflict and want to settle down in peace however this is to be achieved.

Surely the answer to the current problems of the Karamojong is to move out of the past and wake up to the fact that perhaps 3000 square miles of agricultural land not at present utilised are available for exploitation. The people of Pian County in southern Karamoja, after losing nearly all of their livestock over the 1970s, and after experiencing the famine of 1980, have needed no prompting in resettlement. They are currently moving en masse to a place known as Namalu in order to build new homes and create a new way of life for themselves. The scene would be repeated among other groups should they be given opportunity and encouragement.

IMPLEMENTATION

Considerations

The principal consideration in planning resettlement in Karamoja would have to do with the choice of suitable land. Logically preference would be for unoccupied land, and there is no shortage of this. But there would also be scope for siting a project adjacent to an existing settlment. Certainly plenty of unoccupied land can be found around Iriri, for example, and further into the Napak mountain area. What the matter boils down to is the need for a preliminary survey to locate suitable land.

The most important survey consideration must be the availability of water. A borehole supply would be the most desireable, but if this was not possible a supply from tanks or wells would have to suffice. There are a number of tanks in western Karamoja around which the nuclei of resettlement projects could be founded. Wells potentially proliferate along west-exiting river systems such as the Kapeta and the Lokichar systems.

Another survey consideration would obviously be type of soil. Balance here between heavy black clays and light soils would be effective. So, of course, would be considerations of soil quality and crop potentials.

Overall, the agricultural productivity potential of the western parts of Karamoja could help solve the chronic problem of recurring famine among poorly based subsistence farmers now living in other parts of the region. In the long run the opening of new lands could also prove productive in growing wheat and other crops for sale. The potential is one that could in time even extend to plantation crops such as mangoes, citrus and sugar cane.

Kapedo

A brief account of our experiences in establishing (in 1981) and running a resettlement project at Kapedo is relevant here.[11] This project success-

---

[11] This project is supported by Oxfam, UK.

fully pioneered an approach suited to the Karamoja people and their environment. Its implications might well be helpful in the establishment of other resettlement projects.

The soils of the Kapedo area are the usual black clay and lighter red soils, plus extensive stretches of productive alluvial soil along the course of the Nalakas River. The area was unsettled prior to the initiation of our project.

One of our first considerations was to encourage settlers to rely on their own efforts, and in this we proceeded consistently. The settlers worked their land and constructed their own earthen dam by hand. They organised their own communal work projects. We felt that they should learn their new "trade" the hard way and made no attempt to make things unreasonably easy for them through free or subsidised tractor cultivation and so on.

We encouraged the settlers to plant their staple crops (sorghum and millet) during the early rains (April-May), bullrush millet during the later rains (July-August). From the beginning of the project we also encouraged the introduction of groundnuts, cassava and beans and were glad to note no reluctance whatsoever on the part of the settlers to cultivate these additional crops. In fact, in the planting season of 1983 the demand for groundnut seed and cassava sticks already exceeded supply.

The settlers who entered the Kapedo project in 1981 and 1982 no longer needed supplementary feeding by the end of 1983.[12] Most of the 1600 who had come by the end of 1983 had come voluntarily. Almost all of them had walked in with only their pathetically few belongings, some from places as far as fifty miles away.

Perhaps success comes from not putting one's sights too high, by not attempting too much at one time. Certainly in our simple approach we seem to have found a formula that could be applied in the resettlement of Karamojong in other suitable places in Karamoja. But more than that we have in fact established our settlers as "hoe farmers" and now look forward not only to extending their settlement area but also to upgrading local farming to include a wider variety of crops. In 1983 we introduced sunflower seeds which were widely planted. We introduced wheat without fertiliser on a trial basis in both 1982 and 1983 and found it yielding at more than 1400 pounds per acre, a yield as good as can be expected from farms in the Kenya highlands with fertiliser applied. We shall now see what local market exists for whole wheat. If prices are good we shall encourage settlers to grow it while we further explore the possibility of marketing it more widely in Uganda.

Another crop that has shown great promise is maize. Planted on the alluvial soils of Kapedo the variety known as Kawanda Composite has yielded up to 3000 pounds of grain per acre. We are convinced yields would be greater if seeds were planted in lines, not simply broadcast as they were.

Bananas for cooking as well as market have also shown promise. A one-acre plot we developed in 1983 showed growth throughout the dry season and yielded fair-sized bunches just a year after planting.

---

[12]Food supplies for the sustenance of the new settlers at Kapedo have been obtained since the project's inception from the World Food Programme in cooperation with the Uganda Ministry of Rehabilitation.

Varieties in cropping possibilities give our Kapedo farmers choices they can follow as they wish. The extension of the settlement is possible along the alluvial deposits which follow the river course from Kapedo for thirty miles or more. The exploitation of soils around Kapedo would be greatly aided by ox or donkey cultivation, should increased security allow its establishment to spread. Surely thousands of acres of fertile land in western Karamoja await cultivation by persons similar to those who have moved to Kapedo.

CONCLUSION

The Karamojong in the last thirty years have experienced tremendous changes in their environment and way of life. Most of them have been deprived of cattle and most of them remain settled in the relatively unproductive eastern and central parts of their territory.

Accordingly, there is a need for their resettlement, and the most reasonable parts of the region for resettlement lie towards the west. Settlers can start off as subsistence farmers, later grow cash crops as well. Such a projected change has begun to the south around Namalu, and in the north around Kapedo. So far, however, only a small proportion of the populace has been resettled. There remains considerable need for the establishment of new resettlement projects and the expansion of existing projects.

REFERENCES

Evan-Jones, P. (1963). Report on Karamoja Rehabilitation Scheme, 1955-1960. Mimeographed, Uganda Administrative Office, Kampala.
Thomas, E. M. (1981). Warrier Herdsmen. W. E. Norton, London.
Wilson, J. G. (1959). Soils of Karamoja District. Research Division, Department of Agriculture, Kawanda Research Station.
Wilson, J. G. (1962). The Vegetation of Karamoja District. Research Division, Department of Agriculture, Kawanda Research Station.

The Karamoja Health Service: A Proposed Revolution

P. S. V. Cox

It is very easy to put the blame for the breakdown of health services on poor security--which is a fact; poor facilities--which is less tenable; lack of drugs--which is self-evident; and the difficulty of distribution of what little there is. However, this analysis would not give the whole story or even the most important part of the story.

In a recent visit to Karamoja I found the main reasons for the decline in the health services include lack of morale among the staff, total ignorance of a community approach, and complete incomprehension of the fact that a great deal can be achieved without complex drugs and modern equipment by the rank-and-file staff. Senior staff have not yet had sufficient time to rectify this situation and have so far been given no encouragement to branch out with innovative alternatives.

THE COMMUNITY APPROACH

Health services eventually boil down to one individual proffering advice to another. This advice may be good or bad, appropriate or inappropriate to the situation, comprehensible or incomprehensible, didactic or reasoned and so on--but if the professional adviser is demoralised, not taught how to function in the circumstances in which he is placed and completely preoccupied with his own problems, it is very unlikely that he will be able to discharge his function effectively.

I was able to visit most of the hospitals and several health centres in Karamoja, and also two dispensaries, both of them run by young men who had almost no drugs in stock. I asked each of these men the question: "What would you advise a woman to do if she brought an infant with gastroenteritis into your dispensary now?" Both gave similar answers: "I have no medicines in stock," and one went on to say that the child would probably need a chloroquin injection as malaria was a common cause of diarrhoea. When I looked at his register I noted that a case of epilepsy had been given penicillin, and that his total allocation of penicillin for the month had been used up in two days.

I next asked the men if they knew about oral rehydration and that a spoonful of salt and some sugar in water was the most modern and up-to-date form of treatment for gastroenteritis. They did not.

I asked if they thought it would be worthwhile to weigh the children brought in and advise mothers on feeding methods even if they found themselves without drugs on hand. Both answered that such reactions would probably be very difficult to accomplish.

Surely part of the answer to any breakdown in health services is to make the best uses of the facilities available until better facilities and supplies become available. It is reasonable, too, to be trebly careful about how precious drugs are used when there is a shortage. To this end criteria must be drawn up and rigidly enforced if the small supplies of drugs available are to be used to best advantage.

There is only one answer to the current situation: Every person from top to bottom has to be retrained. We are now playing a different ball game. New criteria apply. We cannot forget what we have learned, of course, but new knowledge and new techniques must be added—either permanently, as with the techniques of ORS, or temporarily, as with perhaps over-stringent rules for giving penicillin.

The new education programme must start with medical officers and senior nursing officers educating medical assistants and nurses, and particularly the juniors in charge of dispensaries and clinics. It must work on the ripple principle and reach out beyond medical professionals to the community. Every person instructed must be enthused with the idea of passing the message on to someone else.

The principles to be taught are:

- In the absence of drugs we still have a valuable and perhaps essential part to play in any community. We have knowledge that can save lives. We have simple skills that can prevent diseases. We have advice to give that does not require drugs or equipment—only common sense, motivation and enthusiasm.

- Perhaps the crisis in which we find ourselves is the spur to a far more rational and useful approach than the penny-in-the-slot mentality we have so far been taught. We are used to thinking that when a patient presents with a problem we diagnose the problem and give the necessary treatment. By this approach we inevitably give the impression that every problem has a remedy and that all we need to do is inject patients or give them tablets to ingest for their conditions to be cured. There is no doubt that such responses work in some cases, at least temporarily. Malaria is cured by chloroquin (though this situation may well not pertain in two or three years' time), pneumonia needs penicillin, headache needs aspirin and so on. We cannot apply such responses alone, however, for we have not got sufficient supplies of the proper medicaments. We have to think of other strategies.

- If small supplies of drugs are to be utilised fairly and to best advantage it is vital to spell out priorities and insist that every dose of anitbiotic is to be backed up by a history or justification. Thus, for example, for a chloroquin injection we should stipulate that the patient have a fever of perhaps 38° (or more), be vomiting (unable to swallow a tablet) and, if in hospital, have

a positive slide; for diarrhoea ORS should be encouraged, unless
the diarrhoea occurs with blood in which case chloramphenicol and
sulpha drugs might be allowed; and for a penicillin injection, the
diagnosis of an approved selection of conditions might be expected,
including, for example:
>   coughing blood (acute)
>   meningitis (neck stiffness, headache and fever)
>   bronchitis (chronic cough)
>   sore throat with fever
>   ulcer or boil with large glands.

Listings of medications and ailments such as this should be prepared separately for each health unit and reflect local disease
patterns and the average number of cases seen locally. In fact a
centre's allocation of drugs should be based on an "average" requirement worked out in reference to attendance figures. If certain
drugs are not to be given they should not be supplied. Clear-cut
sets of rules should be worked out for referrals from dispensaries
to health centres and from health centres to hospitals.

- The working of the proposed scheme in general would depend very
much on good communication. Communication could be facilitated with
a control radio in Moroto, sets in the health centres for communication with Moroto and small sets in the dispensaries for communication with the health centres. The capital cost of small radios
would be possible through the assistance of an aid agency. With
regular reporting times identified for each unit, guidelines on
decisions and options could be given easily to set users.

- If drugs run out there must be alternative employment encouragement
for the attendant to visit a **manyatta**, carry out a census and
weigh and measure the under-fives and report on results. The
attendant could also make sure each mother knows the simple reme-
dies for diarrhoea—and has on hand the small plastic measure for
salt and sugar—and find out how many people have been vaccinated.
Such work would best be carried out with teams comprising a minimum
of one health assistant and one curative worker.

FACILITIES

The spread of health centres and dispensaries is probably reasonable for the
area and was started in the 1950s by Dr. Mitford Barbiton and Dr. Robert
Karrach. Since, the 1950s health centre and dispensary buildings have been
improved and added to. It is now necessary to use such fixed points in the
education of the people of surrounding communities, and the further spread
of health delivery points should be made only in relation to community
involvement.

Minor structural repairs and redecoration would improve buildings as well as
attitudes among staff members, particularly if staff members were involved
in the upkeep of the buildings. The construction of nutrition gardens round
each unit should be encouraged.

Health centres in Karamoja were originally designed for standard treatment
and were excellent in their day. But we are now in a new situation and the
use of the centres must be rethought. Perhaps they should now be considerd
more as bases for outreach than as centres to which the sick must come.

MOBILE UNITS

The sort of community work envisaged depends on visitation and supervision. Unless this is undertaken and made possible people on the periphery will be unable to cope with the new tasks and philosophy encouraged. If people are to refer patients the means for referral must be made accessible. Mobile work is never an effective way of bringing curative medicine to an area. For community work, education and morale boosting, on the other hand, mobile work is without equal (see Cox, 1969).

TRAINING

In my brief visit to Karamoja in September 1983 I found great willingness on the part of men to send members of cattle camps--even (vicariously) local midwives-- for training in health and medical understandings and practices. Such opportunities should be seized. The award of simple first aid or midwifery packs, with colour-coded contents for use by illiterates, might be offered as incentives to encourage participation. In any case, health concerns can lead to dialogues with hitherto intransigent and vastly influential members of tribes on far-reaching issues of politics, security and cooperation.

KARAMOJA

Even in the 1950s Karamoja was held to be different from the rest of Uganda. Today differences are still apparent, though the general crisis in the country during recent years has seen a levelling of services and security throughout the country (see Cox, 1974).

The big problem in providing health service in Karamoja is quite simply distance and isolation. Whereas in other parts of the country a dispensary attendant can be expected to walk out and visit houses in his area, in Karamoja the "walk" would perhaps be ten miles there and ten miles back. Then too, security is a problem. If work is done within communities, however, the problem of security is not insurmountable. The community itself would be involved and provide protection for the workers.

STAFF

All health services consist of curative and preventive services, each supporting the other. At present the staff members expect to do curative work but find the methods they know impossible to apply because they have no supplies. Doctors are few and far between and tend to concentrate on the curative side of medicine, using what means they have to do the work they feel most competent to perform. Meanwhile, the majority of doctors in Uganda go to great lengths to avoid posting to Karamoja.

It is essential to have a team at each centre with at least one member concentrating full time on curative work--if this is neglected or of low standard, preventive efforts will also be discredited--at least one other concentrating with satisfaction on work in the community. Staff members should be directly under the supervision of the DMO of the district, and the whole programme should be coordinated by one RMO with power and responsibility to post and train staff, and coordinate activities in the whole of Karamoja. Enrolled nurses should be upgraded to "community nurses" and ungraded staff should be given repeated refresher courses on site or in Moroto. A permanent tutor should be assigned to the RMO to help in the design and conduct of refresher courses.

CONCLUSION

The health crisis in Karamoja is in line with the crisis in the rest of the country, excepting for the proliferation of international aid introduced as a result of the famine in 1980. This aid will not last forever. It is thus vital to act quickly to get a new and imaginative health service off the ground before international agencies withdraw.

Necessary facilities and staff are available. What is needed is encouragement and retraining for the staff, and strict resource allocation. Finally, community participation is essential.

REFERENCES

Cox, P. S. V. (1969). The Value of Mobile Medicine. East African Medical Journal, 46: 1-5.
Cox, P. S. V. (1974). Planning for the Future in a Nomadic Community. In C. Anderson and W. L. Kilama (Eds.), Parasitoses of Man and Animals in Africa. East African Literature Bureau, Nairobi.

The Relief Operation in Karamoja: What Was Learned and What Needs Improvement

Melissa Wells

Before my 1980-82 experience in Uganda I shared the commonly held misconception that emergencies occur in what we might call "assignable lots". In other words, depending on the nature of the emergency--be it an epidemic, a drought or a population displacement--action can be taken under the mandate of the appropriate agency. Uganda taught me that this simply is not the case. While WHO will respond to an epidemic and UNHCR to refugees crossing international boundaries, what happens to people internally displaced who are starving? Unfortunately there is no recognised international agency mandated to assist in complex emergencies such as the emergencies in Karamoja and West Nile in the 1979-81 period.

Was the Karamoja disaster a drought? An epidemic? A war zone? An economic disaster? Was it man made? We certainly had large displacements of people but they didn't cross any international borders. Clear only was the fact that the Karamoja disaster was a "complex disaster".

This paper addresses the difficulties experienced in mounting relief operations from the perspective of United Nations' agencies against the background of the disaster in Karamoja between 1979 and 1981.

LOGISTICS

Most disasters or emergency situations are first and foremost logistics crises. Many of the people I worked with in Uganda had participated in the major disaster relief operations of the previous decade. One of the recurring themes was that time and again the same problem arose in every disaster situation: logistics.

The same mistakes are repeated over and over again. Yet there does not seem to be any point within the UN system where an effort is being made to address this question. By logistics, I refer to communications, transportation and distribution.

Our reference essentially is to two elements: one is personnel, the other is equipment. We will first consider personnel.

In Uganda we ran two distinct relief operations: the Karamoja relief operation and the relief operation mounted for West Nile Province. For the
relief operation in West Nile we were very fortunate to have a team from the
Special Swedish Unit (SSU) for disaster relief, following the request of the
Government to the Swedish Government. The Swedish team was in West Nile
from the start of relief activities and stayed for six months. It included
medical and engineering skills, but in particular, came to manage the logistics of the entire operation. The unit immediately installed a radio communications network. They managed the fleet of trucks used in the operation.
They maintained the trucks in running order, kept careful records on fuel
used and on mileage, and managed the transport and distribution of all
supplies for the relief operation, not just those channeled via the UN.

The smoothness, efficiency and cost-effectiveness of the relief operation
in West Nile were simply remarkable. Unfortunately I cannot say the same
thing for the relief operation in Karamoja. There were several phases of
logistics management in the Karamoja operation and it was fraught with
problems which were overcome only towards the end of the crisis. In this I
am not criticising any agency. If there is any blame, it lies in the fact
that we had no one to turn to, to give us what we needed in terms of
logistics management. The SSU was committed somewhere else at the time, and
within the UN system there was no one who could respond to the need. So we
did the best we could. The lesson to be learned from our Uganda experience,
however, is that in a relief operation it is absolutely vital to have one
unit with direct operational responsibility for the management of logistics.

The existence of a unit with such a responsibility is first and foremost in
the best interests of those who need the help and are suffering, because it
makes for the more efficient delivery of relief supplies. But such a unit
is also in the best interest of the government of the country experiencing
the disaster. For example, a complaint frequently heard is that during a
relief operation too many makes of vehicles are ordered. Quite often it
doesn't matter which manufacturer you choose, but what you want to avoid is
too many varieties of vehicles because this introduces problems of maintenance, spare parts and so forth. With a professional and integrated approach from the beginning, one is in a better position to say to donors, "We
need 'x' number of tyres of such-and-such size, and we need the following
spare parts. . ." in order to get existing in-country transport mobilised
quickly while waiting for new vehicles to arrive. But all this is possible
only with a professional assessment on the spot at the beginning of the
operation.

I have referred to the Swedish unit that came and worked with us. A number
of other countries have already instituted, or else are considering the
institution of similar units that can operate in disaster situations. This
indicates that some thinking is going on along these lines. But the question as to whether or not a solution should be found within the UN system
also needs to be raised. For each agency that works in emergency situations
to develop its own logistics unit would create duplication and would not be
in the best interests of maximising response capabilities. Yet with some
imagination and innovation a solution to the logistics problem might be devised. Let me describe an idea that was considered in Uganda.

We conceptualised the creation of a "strike force" of reservists based
within the UN system, among the various agencies. The volunteers or reservists who would make up this force would have experience and specific
skills: telecommunications, transport management, supply--the various
skills required for a successful logistics management operation.

As an alternative solution to the logistics needs, a valid case can be made for an emergency logistics unit to be set up within the World Food Programme. Certainly of all the UN agencies, it is the WFP that is most intensively involved in transport problems. Food requirements of varying magnitudes are needed in almost all disaster situations. The WFP is recognised as the coordinating agency responsible for moving "multilateral" food. It is also frequently used by bilateral donors to coordinate their particular relief shipments to a disaster area. Moving all this food around to reach emergency areas is not a simple task. It is the responsibility of the WFP to deliver the food to the border of the recipient country. In the case of land-locked countries the food is delivered to the border and not simply to the nearest port. But in any event, the transport of the food to the border of the recipient country is at the expense of WFP. In certain exceptional cases, WFP is permitted to pay 50 percent of the cost of internal distribution of that food.

In the case of Uganda, we qualified for that 50 percent subsidy. But the difficulty was that immediately after the war the government was not in a position to come up with its share of 50 percent. So the UN system had to organise the transport and find the money to pay for it. It is precisely in circumstances such as these that a valid argument can be made for WFP responding quickly on its own by instituting its own logistical support unit.

The other aspect of logistics is equipment. It is one thing to pre-position medical supplies (this is already being done), and the pre-positioning of food has been tried, though this is more complicated because of limited shelf life, warehousing problems and so on. The problem is that the pre-positioning of vehicles and equipment for logistics is too costly to be considered seriously. One category of equipment which I believe should be an exception, however, is radios. It is feasible to stockpile a readily accessible supply of radios that could be available for immediate dispatch to a disaster area. Radios could be made available for a limited period of time for the emergency. They would then be returned and could be reused. They obviously don't take the kind of beating that vehicles and other equipment take, and are reusable. The acquisition of other items used for logistical support--vehicles, tyres, spare parts, fuel, tarpaulins or whatever--should be determined by the logistics team referred to above.

ASSESSMENT

Joint assessment missions involve several agencies within the UN. They go to emergency areas in order to assess requirements for food, medical supplies, shelter and other needs. There is no need to comment on them here. This aspect of the UN system is already rather well organised.

What is not organised, and what needs to be addressed, is that when a joint assessment mission goes and lists the requirements, at the same time (in fact as part of that mission, ideally) there should be people who can make a professional assessment of the type of terrain on which the relief operation will be carried out and who can assess what is required in terms of logistical support. When part of that assessment mission goes back and starts mobilising relief supplies, there should be a team left behind to begin working with the government on how to distribute supplies efficiently.

PROCUREMENT AND PROCEDURES

However they are made available, once funds are allocated the delegation of spending authority must be increased and it must go right down to the field level.

Now this obviously presents problems of accountability and control. But if agencies looked into their emergency procedures, systems could be devised whereby delegation to disburse at the field level could be implemented swiftly as required and we could enhance our relief effectiveness. Financial regulations and rules imposed on the system have a long chain of responsibility including auditors and budgetary committees right back to member governments. So the problem of greater spending flexibility in an emergency is not simply one for UN agencies.

In one instance during our relief work in Uganda, a UN agency received a donation of a very substantial investment for transport equipment: approximately three-quarters of a million dollars, targeted specifically for the relief operations in Karamoja. The contribution specified that a consultant would be sent to Uganda to assess our transport requirements. Then the donor made available consultants to be there when the equipment arrived in order to get it running. I regret that much valuable time was lost--quite literally months, when it should have been weeks--because we were required to follow certain agency purchasing procedures. I am sure such procedures exist for very sound, valid reasons. But we found them totally inadequate in the emergency situation we found. It is essential that procedures such as these be reviewed in order to establish how we can reconcile accountability and other important safeguards with quick purchase and delivery which are absolutely essential in an emergency.

PERSONNEL

Any review of administrative procedures in cases of emergency should not be confined solely to procurement. There is also a great need for more flexibility in hiring. Were it not for the fact that staff from several of the voluntary agencies working in Uganda were assigned to UN agency offices on a full-time basis, I doubt whether we could have coped. Procedures for hiring locally qualified people were cumbersome. The recruitment process via headquarters did not produce results. This is of course the glory of the voluntary agencies, the NGOs (nongovernment organisations)--their flexibility, their ability to move quickly. They don't get tied up in bureaucratic procedures. They are quite truly the first line of action in an emergency operation. Agencies in the UN system cannot equal the type of operational flexibility that the NGOs have. The nature of the UN agencies is different. But we must introduce greater flexibility into our emergency procedures in order to interact better with voluntary agencies. This difference in administrative procedure between UN agencies and NGOs is a continuing source of frustration at the field level.

One way of introducing more flexibility into the hiring process during emergencies could be to institutionalise what became an excellent ad hoc arrangement that we worked out with voluntary agencies in Uganda. I am not suggesting that the UN count on voluntary agencies assigning personnel regularly to UN field offices. Rather, we should encourage voluntary agencies to recruit for us. In other words, if they found qualified people, and we agreed that they were qualified, we could then hire them on a short-term basis. It is important that something be worked out in this area.

INFORMATION

A relief operation usually involves several UN agencies and it is important, should there be press interest in the emergency, to give a complete picture of relief activities. The need in Uganda for the UN to speak with one voice on relief activities--to the outside world, the press, and probably most importantly, to the inside team--was very evident.

Some agencies are more gifted than others in presenting their cases to the outside world and informing their publics, and this is an issue of some sensitivity within the UN system. But there are other concerns far more important than agency sensitivities. Quite apart from external information there is a vital need to keep all components of a team working on a dis-aster--UN and voluntary agencies alike--adequately informed.

The information that must be passed on (in a regular flow) to the whole team must include information on how the disaster is going to be cleared up. In other words, what is the resource picture? How are supplies to get from A to B? What are the missing resources? Such information is available to a limited number of people directly involved in the coordinating aspect of the operation. They simply must make it a point to keep everybody else informed to the extent possible.

Information is an essential aspect not only of teamwork but of morale build-ing when working in difficult circumstances. Nothing short of a profes-sional information officer should be considered to deal with both "external" and "internal" information flows.

DISCUSSION

Relief operations, once they get going, carry a momentum of their own which can greatly benefit the development of that area. When I visited Karamoja in the late spring of 1981, I saw an area that quite literally had been a living hell only one year before. The seeds had been planted, the early rains had been good, the crops were coming up, the violence had largely subsided, people had been fed and there were medical facilities providing services. Then I was struck by the misfortune of some of the people living further away, around Kampala, desperately poor, who had not known the impact of international emergency assistance. The point is, a relief operaton generates a momentum that must not be lost but carried on into development.

It is essential, therefore, that coordination take place within the total development picture of the country. A relief operation does not lead a life of its own. It has its impact on the country; it has repercussions far beyond the area in which it is directly working.

Finally, there is the real need for an effort to be made to eliminate bureaucratic obstacles--a more polite term would be technical obstacles. All those who have worked in emergency situations are familiar with the bureaucratic "roadblocks" encountered when it comes to border clearances, visas or trans-shipment of supplies. There is a whole tangled web of administrative procedure that needs to be eased if a relief operation is to take place effectively.

It would be a great help to all future people stricken by disaster, as well as to the many generous men and women who go to their assistance, if an international convention could be drawn up and agreed to set standards for the movement of relief supplies and personnel in emergency areas.

The Uganda emergency experience has taught us to look at the complexity of disaster situations and has compelled a new look at the ways in which responses to such situations are made.

Preparedness for Disaster Operations

Karl-Eric Knutsson

The purpose of this article is to give a brief and hopefully concrete description of the background factors significant in the emergence of the 1979-81 emergency situation in Karamoja, an overview of the emergency situation itself and a few suggestions concerning appropriate responses to such situations by international aid and development agencies. To anticipate my conclusions, preparedness by international agencies for disaster operations must be improved.

BACKGROUND

Uganda

The situation in Uganda in 1980 was at best chaotic. The liberation war had removed one of the most oppressive regimes experienced in Africa. The period following the overthrow of the Amin regime was unfortunately characterised by continued destablilisation and anarchy. The destruction of infrastructure, continuing security problems, sky-rocketing inflation and the direction of the major part of political and intellectual energy into faction- and ethnic-based strategies for future control (although indeed important) was not conducive to a national concentration of will and resources for the solution of fundamental problems of basic needs and social security.

In Karamoja the extreme destructive results of this situation could be easily seen.

Karamoja

It is not my intention here to provide any detailed description of Karamojong society.[1] I shall only make some--surely oversimplified--comments on

---

[1]For further readings on Karamoja I recommend Dyson-Hudson (1958, 1959 and 1966), Gulliver (1952) and Turpin (1948).

the type of society, culture and production system that was overwhelmed by
the set of new events that generated the catastrophic situation of 1980. I
dare to do this because I feel strongly that each "emergency" situation must
be analysed and approached in a "context-specific" way. Although lessons
learned in one relief operation ought to be utilised in another, the catastrophe in Karamoja could not have been dealt with in the same way as the
catastrophe in Kampuchea in the late 1970s.

The following brief statements, in turn, concern the ecological adaptation
of the pastoral mode of production of the Karamojong, local political organization (so essential for access to existing channels for distribution of
available resources) and the "traditional defence" systems worked out a-
gainst the major threats to the survival of the Karamojong.

Most pastoral societies in the arid and semi-arid zones of Africa live on
the very margin of the ecological potential. A sophisticated knowledge of
geographical, climatological and ecological factors is a must for the maintenance of production, and thus survival. Like their pastoral colleagues in
other areas, the Karamojong have therefore developed a remarkable expertise
in these fields. A combination of mobile cattle management and dry agriculture close to homesteads is the dominant pattern. Minor droughts which
quite regularly hit each third year, major droughts that seem to return once
each decade, the threats of cattle epidemics and prolonged periods of climatic change at least once in a generation, are considered in the survival
strategy. One result of such considerations is that the Karamojong like
other pastoralists in East and West Africa tend to maintain fairly large
herds of livestock with a special sexual and age composition.[2]

The Karamojong are divided into clans and other subgroupings. They live in
clusters of "villages" near water. During times of insecurity these villages tend to grow to increase protection. Around the settlements subsistence agriculture, mainly by women, is practised.

The present administrative and local political organisation does not reflect
the Karamojong way of decision-making. There are no "chiefs". Each village
or cluster is represented by a "spokesman" who derives any influence from
his ability to convince his co-residents who may accept or reject his interpretation of a situation and his advice. This must be borne in mind when
channels for the distribution of food are considered.

On this structure a colonial system was superimposed in the form of district
commissioners, county and subcounty chiefs, and so-called "parish" chiefs
never heard of and never understood by the Karamojong. The selection of
these officials was artificial and led to the formation of an alien elite
which was not hesitant to abuse the power bestowed upon them.

Against the hazards created by the environment and by the lack of a centralised political system guaranteeing social and economic security (cattle
raiding has always been endemic), the Karamojong have designed their own
defence systems. The first of these has a redistributive quality and can be
described as a desire to maintain relatively equal access to cattle--the
main food supplier in terms of meat, milk and blood. Raiding in its traditional forms did not upset the system, for raiding with traditional weapons
amounted to a kind of circulation of stock.

---

[2]See Hjort and Dahl (1978) for information about pastoralists in East and
West Africa.

The other system of defence against food shortages was developed during the protectorate and early independence periods. If food shortages occurred the Karamojong demand for food invited entrepreneurs to transport and sell food and cattle at high prices (which the fairly rich Karamojong and civil servants could afford) in the area.

The Emergency Situation

The emergency situation of severe food shortages that reached a peak in April to August 1980 (the preharvest period) has often been explained by the onslaught of a severe drought. This is not correct, and in fact a number of causative factors were involved. During the chaotic period of the so-called liberation war a weapons store in Karamoja was looted. As a result modern weapons and ammunition got into the hands of people in the general region. This transformed the whole pattern of traditional raiding and social security/insecurity. Those in possession of the weapons could now raid everbody and vast numbers of cattle were rapidly concentrated in the hands of a few cattle "barons". This in its turn broke down the defence system of cattle distribution and left approximately 80-90 percent of the Karamojong without access to their main supply of food.

Secondly, this created a security problem preventing the flow of commercial food into the area. The result was that the second defence system broke down.

Thirdly, looting deprived the people of the absolute minimum of health services. In the biggest town of Moroto, for example, a hospital with 150 beds was completely empty, without medical staff and supplies but with lots of children and adults outside suffering from severe malnutrition and diseases. Other health centres were similarly looted and personnel nonexistent after several raiding episodes.

Fourthly, and I am convinced only as a fourth factor, the drought hit. Because of the breakdown of the previously mentioned systems, it created unprecedented effects.

THE RELIEF OPERATION

Early Responses

The first, and to my mind very convincing, reports of a severe emergency situation were reported in November 1979 by members of the Verona Fathers in Karamoja. UNICEF convened a meeting in late 1979 to review the situation but according to their own reports "did not take the reports very seriously." Early in 1980 UNDP and WFP initiated action by surveying the area and negotiating for food supplies. UNHCR was also put on alert. Unfortunately the procurement of supplies by exchanging 10,000 tons of WFP wheat for Kenya maize met with difficulties because of unforeseen Kenya shortages. In early spring 1980 some small quantities of maize were delivered, but by then it was already too late and the logistics backup was deficient.

Voluntary agencies moved in, desperately uncoordinated, without a conceptual framework appropriate to the Karamoja situation and without any experience in how to deal with local authorities, not to mention the local people.

In July 1980 UNICEF found out that what it had been possible to know eight
months earlier about the proportions of the disaster in Karamoja was in fact
true. The explanation for the delay was in part the evacuation of all UN
staff from Uganda at some time during 1980 due to security problems. The
delay was also due to the general impression that UNDP and WFP were in full
control of the situation, and staff inadequacies.

The way things were sorted out eventually, however:

- UNDP became the lead organisation in the coordination of the entire
  relief effort.

- The whole operation was nationally placed under the National Relief
  Commission with representatives from various ministries and with
  four subcommittees dealing, among other things, with supplies,
  transportation, health, social welfare and water. On the district
  and local level government involvement was designed to be through
  district committees chaired by district commissioners.

- UNICEF had the responsibility to coordinate all child intervention
  projects.

- WFP was responsible for food supplies and general food distribution.

- UNHCR stretched its mandate to assist both in supply and transportation (until it withdrew in early 1981).

- Voluntary organisations had the operational responsibility for
  child-feeding centres and food distribution.

UNICEF's Involvement

While operating within the overall relief structure established by the
United Nations system and the Government of Uganda, UNICEF was given the
role of "coordinator" for the Vulnerable Group Feeding Programme which was
conceived by UNICEF following the serious deterioration of conditions affecting women and children in Karamoja. UNICEF geared its participation in the
relief effort in Karamoja for an initial period of two years.

Two main factors dominated UNICEF's approach as it eventually developed to
devising a structure to meet the special needs of children in Karamoja: 1)
Government health structure had collapsed and no effective intervention was
possible from this normally vital sector, and 2) the missionaries in the
area were severely stretched trying to cope with the growing numbers of the
destitute, and their limited resources could not be depended upon solely to
care for all the affected population.

UNICEF thus decided that the only feasible immediate intervention that could
be made was to establish a network of nutrition rehabilitation and feeding
centres. Voluntary agencies were approached to provide personnel to run
these centres and WFP immediately agreed to provide the required food aid.

By late in 1980 eleven centres and three subcentres had been established
and were being operated by three voluntary agencies--Save the Children Fund,
Medicins sans Frontieres and Concern. Altogether these centres could, under
maximum utilisation, cater for between 12,000 and 15,000 children, a sub-

stantive proportion of the estimated 40,000 under-five population. Other children along with other members of their families received food through the WFP general distribution programme.

Indications in October 1980 were that by December as many as 200,000 in Karamoja would be dependent on food aid from the outside. In order to prepare for such developments UNICEF decided to establish a food and medical supply base in Soroti. Recognising that inadequate vehicle maintenance is often an "Achilles heel" in relief operations of the kind anticipated, UNICEF also made arrangements to utilise the garage of the Ministry of Lands, Minerals and Natural Resources in Soroti as a central maintenance depot for the Vulnerable Group Feeding Program. Among other things, UNICEF also made a series of contacts within the UN family investigating the feasibility of a cooperative effort in fuel supplies, and continued vigourously to implement a programme of borehole repair both in Uganda as a whole and in Karamoja (where some 385 out of 481 boreholes were out of order).

ASSESSMENT

Specific Observations

Many aspects of the situation that developed in Karamoja in 1980-81 might be assessed. Tactics changed over time, more feeding centres were opened and so on. Some of the more easily identifiable difficulties involved, however, include the following. Firstly, the district commissioners who seemed to be doing their very best to assist were--to make an understatement--not informed about what was going on, especially with reference to the activities of the voluntary agencies.

Secondly, the task of coordinating the voluntary organisations was a very difficult one. There were definite frictions among them and frictions between them and coordinating agencies.

Division of labour was another problem. WFP was supposed to deliver supplies to the general public. UNICEF was supposed to concentrate on the child-feeding centres. Upon occasion the feeding centres were without food, even though WFP supplies were close at hand, because of formal restrictions.

Fourthly, transportation presented a severe problem, the discussion of which would require too much space in this report. The remarkable diversity of vehicles made the supply of spare parts much more difficult than it should have been. Maintenance procedures and facilities were far from adequate.

Fifthly, the supply of food generally presented a disaster within the disaster. The supplies distributed were usually only to some extent decided upon by competent field organisations, and in general decided upon without regard for the cultural and nutritional requirements of the specific situation.

Finally, the coordinating and advisory roles of agencies cannot be carried out effectively unless suitable personnel are posted to the field.

General Observations

Responses by international aid agencies to disasters such as the disaster in Karamoja must be quick, rational and experienced rather than prolonged, irrational and nonexperienced. This implies that such organisations must allow and encourage their staffs to be participant in "early warning systems". By this I do not mean any sophisticated computer system. The simple conclusion is that staff should be given the time and possibility to listen, interpret and react to disaster situations quickly. Involvement in planning and in the collection of information must be continuous and meaningful.

Secondly, organisations like UNICEF which are mainly created for long-term activities and the planning and programming that such a mandate supplies, are not efficient for rapid ad hoc responses to unforeseen events, nor are they well equipped to mobilise and reallocate necessary resources in terms of personnel, funds and equipment from resources available but already committed to ongoing programmes. To use a metaphor, such a rapid shift in activities and allocation would amount to demanding a shipping company to turn into an airline overnight.

There is an urgent need for a much clearer understanding of this organisational dilemma both at headquarter and at regional and national levels. Alongside, long-term and overall development efforts must be continuous preparations for unforeseen emergency operations.

RECOMMENDATIONS

Against the background of the somewhat fragmented specific observations as well as the more general observations made in this paper, the following recommendations might be formulated.

Firstly, the headquarters of agencies such as UNICEF, in close contact with regional and country offices and as soon as possible, should plan for stand-by emergency forces. Experienced professional personnel should be accessible almost immediately in the major areas of general emergency logistics and field operation coordination, supply, transport and maintenance, health, nutrition and water and sanitation.

Adequate auxiliary personnel should also be available. Apart from professional and practical experience the groups should occasionally work and train together so that they can be moulded into efficient teams. During periods when their services in emergencies are not needed the personnel of these groups could be posted to countries and regions to assist in long-term activities. They should, however, be additional to the otherwise needed core personnel so that ongoing work is not hampered by their quick mobilisation.

In an emergency the group should either operate autonomously or under the leadership of a qualified country representative who could provide valuable context-specific knowledge and contacts. If this is not feasible, a high-ranking executive with maximum delegated power from headquarters should be posted temporarily to the emergency area.

Furthermore, preparedness in terms of financial capacity and equipment must be improved. This could be achieved by setting up a special emergency fund with less strict auditing and other constraints. Questions of supply, transport and maintenance must be rethought with the view to the increase of efficiency and speed.

Finally, an improved "ethic" for disaster operations must be developed. This should include:

     - increasing the political will of the affected nation (in

Uganda political will was almost nonexistent at the time of the Karamoja disaster);

- advocating the responsibility of the international community to respond quickly;

- raising the ability for the responsible field organisation itself to plan and decide upon the nature of the food and other supplies needed;

- "dumping of surplus" benevolence should be rejected;

- improving the understanding in the international community that losses of supplies and other difficulties in a rapid-response operation ought to be accepted. If they were, there would be a decrease in the naive application of "cost benefit" judgements detrimental both to public support and operational speed.

CONCLUSION

Much more could be written about Karamoja and about the activities of the international agencies that responded to the 1979-81 period of disaster in Karamoja. This is not necessary here. In conclusion it is only necessary to stress again that overly generalised interpretations of the backgrounds and causes of disasters do not facilitate effective responses, and that each disaster must be approached in terms of its own distinctive outlines. At the same time, frameworks that allow for new conceptual orientations and new practical responses to disaster situations must be developed.

REFERENCES

Dyson-Hudson, N.(1958). The Karamojong and the Suk. Uganda Journal, 22: 173-80.
Dyson-Hudson, N. (1959). The Present Positon of the Karamojong. Colonial Office, London, mimeographed.
Dyson-Hudson, N. (1966). Karamojong Politics. Clarendon Press, Oxford.
Hjort, A. and G. Dahl (1978). Having Herds. Stockholm.
Gulliver, P. H. (1952). The Karamojong Cluster. Africa Cluster, 22: 1-22.
Turpin, E. A. (1948). The Occupation of the Turkwell River Area by the Karamojong Tribe. Uganda Journal 12: 161-65.

Section 4

Perspectives

Population Access to Hospitals, Health Centres and Dispensary/Maternity Units in Uganda, 1980

D. J. Alnwick, M. R. Stirling and G. Kyeyune

INTRODUCTION

The provision of comprehensive and accessible health care services ranks highly among the multitude of development objectives proclaimed by most developing countries at independence. Recognising that access to health services is the primary prerequisite to improved community health, newly independent governments have prepared comprehensive health development plans, identifying targets in terms of population to health infrastructure resource ratios (people to beds, doctors, hospitals and so on), and launched ambitious programmes to create and equip health units.

In Uganda the commitment to expand the number of health facilities was not genuinely taken until 1966 since under the first development plan (Uganda, 1961: 44) the conscious decision was made to divert "available resources to purposes aimed at economic growth." This severely limited the resources available for the development of health services.

With the overall objective of "bringing about a more even geographical distribution of hospital beds in relation to population" and "availing comprehensive health services to Ugandans," the second plan (1966-71) sought to establish 327 new health centres--in pursuance of the long-term goal of locating a health centre in every gombolola (subcounty)--and erect twenty-two new one-hundred-bed hospitals "to be sited in places where hospital services are most needed with even distribution between the regions" (Uganda, 1966: 151).

By 1975, as Table 1 indicates, eighteen new government hospitals had been constructed and an additional fifty-one health centres registered. A number of subordinate health units (dispensary maternity units, dispensaries, sub-dispensaries and aid posts), both government and voluntary, were also established. While the construction of health centres proceeded at a slower pace than planned they were relatively evenly distributed between the four regions, and siting followed the one per subcounty plan. It was recognised in 1971, however, that "defects in the planning of the rural hospital programme had resulted in an unbalanced geographical distribution of health facilities" (Uganda, 1971: 309).

TABLE 1:   Growth in Government Health Units, 1962-80

Health Unit	1962	1965	1970	1975	1980
Hospital	24	24	36	42	48
Health centre	17	20	43	71	91
Disp/Maternity	31	41	50	43	59
Maternity unit	2	2	4	3	5
Dispensary	85	76	81	65	63
Subdispensary	38	57	104	204	287
Population (1000s)	7,016	7,551	9,806	11,549	12,636

TABLE 2:   Inventory of All Government and Voluntary Health Units

Health Unit	1965	1970	1975	1980
Hospital	50	62	69	76
Health centre	20	46	74	91
Disp/Maternity	55	65	60	80
Maternity unit	17	20	16	20
Dispensary	83	103	92	88
Subdispensary	77	110	211	293

On this planning problem it is worthwhile quoting at length the observations of the 1977 Commission of Inquiry into Medical Services (Uganda, 1977: 35-36):

> The distribution of the twenty-two rural hospitals was not equitable. One would have thought that for equitable distribution, account should have been taken of, among other things, the population, the then existing medical units, and the size of the districts at the time.
>
> As it transpired however, a district like Masaka densely populated as it was and still is, never benefited from this exercise at all. On the other hand, however, such districts like Bukedi and Bunyoro got two hospitals each though the corresponding population of either district does not in any way come near that of Masaka. One would also have expected a vast district like Karamoja with the population which needed medical services even more to have had more than one hospital like its large sister district Ankole, which got two.

The Commission further observed that some units were built in apparent disregard of the population density and concluded that the natural result of the maldistribution of the new units was that the very purpose of taking services nearer to the people in the rural areas had been partly defeated in that some of these hospitals were evidently underutilised, whereas health centres in the vicinity where hospitals should have been situated were overcrowded with patients.

This example of "defective planning" emphasises the need for a thorough knowledge of the communities which require health care and of the alternative means of providing for those health needs. In the above case of the new hospitals it is suggested that a prime cause of their maldistribution

was the absence of detailed demographic data and a simple inventory of the
health infrastructure to assist health planners and politicians in the
placing of hospitals.

OBJECTIVES

To provide a working tool for planning health services this study was undertaken in 1983 by UNICEF, with assistance from the staff of Makerere University's geography department, to map at district level Uganda's population in
relation to major health units (hospitals, health centres, dispensary-
maternity units). A complementary objective of the exercise was to estimate
the proportion of the population with access to "comprehensive health
care".[1]

METHOD

To estimate population access to health facilities all government and voluntary hospitals, health centres and dispensary-maternity units were plotted
on large scale population density maps originally prepared by B. Langlands
(1972) using 1969 parish-level census data. In 1969 one dot designated five
hundred people and was carefully plotted taking into consideration uninhabited areas such as swamps, lakes and mountains. When updating the maps the
new district boundaries were redrawn and the number of people represented by
each dot in 1980 was estimated on the basis of the ratio between the 1980
and 1969 populations of each district.

For most districts of Uganda, where the population has remained relatively
stable over the eleven-year period, the maps present a reasonably accurate
reflection of present population distribution. However, changes in migration and settlement patterns, which may have occurred between censuses, will
undoubtedly be reflected less accurately. The maps may also oversimplify
complex geographical features. For instance, some people marked as being
within, say, ten kilometres of a health facility may in fact be much further
away in terms of walking distance or transport networks because of swamps,
rivers or hills.

To present an indicator of access a circle was drawn around each health unit
on the map having a radius equivalent to ten kilometres. The population
within this circle was then estimated by counting the dots within the circle.

The ten-kilometre radius was chosen since it represents the maximum likely
catchment area for a rural health centre and most hospitals in that it takes
a healthy adult approximately two hours to walk ten kilometres and about
twice as long for a sick person or child (Gish, 1978). F. Bennett (1968)

---

[1] For the purpose of this exercise "comprehensive" health service is
defined as a service offered by a health unit which operates general outpatient and at least a limited inpatient/maternity service and maternal and
child health services inclusive of immunisation, care of children under five
and antenatal care, health education, etc. By definition therefore, this
study is limited to hospitals, health centres and dispensary-maternity
units since it is widely considered that health units below the level of DMU
are insufficiently staffed, equipped and supervised/supported, so as to be
able to provide basic health services.

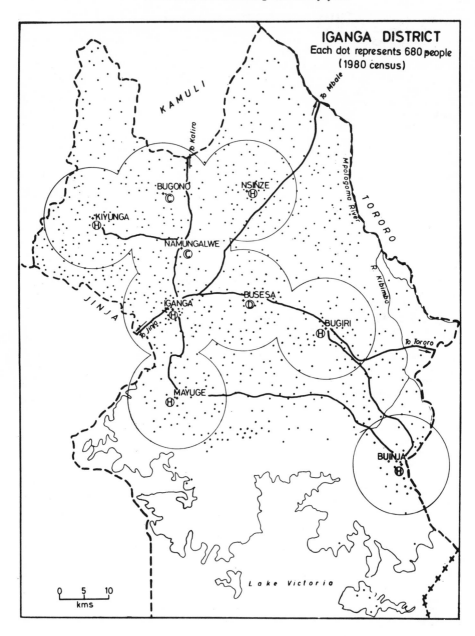

Figure 1 Iganga district

noted at Kasangati Health Centre that:

> Women with small babies and especially with toddlers, are unable to come
> to the centre frequently if they have to carry the children long distanc-
> es. Old people are very poor attenders, hardly coming at all for treat-
> ment if they live far away . . . The decline in attendance with distance
> also varies with certain illnesses. A serious painful condition, such
> as pneumonia, would bring a patient to the clinic even if he lived five
> miles away (although probably late in the course of the illness), whereas
> a trivial condition, such as a common cold, would only be seen at the
> centre if the sufferer lived nearby. Similarly there is poor attendance
> from distant villages for preventative nonurgent measures such as ante-
> natal care and immunisation of children.

Other studies confirm the Kasangati experience. For example, while R. Jolly
and M. King (1966: 2-7) found that in the Mubende area few patients were
prepared to walk more than eight kilometres to a health facility, M. Moffat
(1969), working in what is now Mbarara District, states that "although
parents may bring a seriously ill child a long distance for medical care, in
practice we found that for preventative services like child welfare or
immunisation clinics very few families travel more than six kilometres."
These studies suggest that the proportion of the population living within
five kilometres may provide a better indicator of physical accessibility to
medical and maternal and child health services.[2]

RESULTS

This exercise revealed that 12.6 million Ugandans were served by seventy-six
hospitals and 170 health centres and dispensary-maternity units. Table 3
presents a summary of these health units by type and operating agency. In
national terms it is indicated that the ratio of health units capable of
offering comprehensive health care to population stood at 1:56,000 in 1980.
This represents a slight deterioration over the 1962 ratio of 1:51,600.[3]
Concerning regional distribution the less heavily populated northern and
eastern areas of the country have proportionally more health units per thousand people than the more densely populated southern, central and western
regions.

While such ratios are important measures for monitoring national progress in
increasing health coverage, they do not indicate population access to the
health delivery infrastructure. Analysis of the district population/health
unit maps does, however, enable objective comment on the accessibility of
Uganda's health services to Ugandans down to the community level. This
information for each of Uganda's thirty-three districts is summarised in
Table 4.

Approximately 27 percent of Ugandans live within five kilometres of a hospital, health centre or dispensary-maternity unit, and 57 percent live within
ten kilometres of those same units. Regionally it is clear that Eastern
Region is the best served with 66 percent of the population being within ten

---

[2]In view of such observations the defined area at Kasangati was limited
to approximately a three-mile radius.
[3]The ratios in 1970 and 1975 were 1:43,600 and 1:48,300 respectively.
By 1980 only 25 percent of the planned objective of establishing a health
centre per gombolola had been achieved.

D. J. Alnwick, M. R. Stirling and G. Kyeyune

kilometres of a comprehensive health care facility. The East is followed
by Southern Region with 60 percent, Western Region with 57 percent and
Northern Region with 43 percent.

TABLE 3: Health Units in Uganda, and Population of Regions

	Region				
	Eastern	Northern	Southern	Western	Uganda
Population 1980 (1000s)	3237	2424	3582	3392	12636
Government hospitals	11	12	13	10	46
Government health centres and dispensary-maternity units	44	30	31	42	147
Mission hospitals	3	10	8	10	31
Mission dispensary-maternity units	10	6	6	1	23
Total units	68	58	58	63	247
Population per unit (1000s)	48.0	41.5	62.5	55.5	50.0

In twenty-two of the districts more than half of the population live within
ten kilometres of a health unit, but in four districts (Apac, Kitgum, Luwero
and Mbarara) less than one-third of the population live within this distance
of a health unit.

Further analysis of these data also indicates that while the northern areas
of the country may have a lower population:health unit ratio than the rest
of the nation, the dispersed nature of that population in relation to the
health units means that, on average, only 43 percent of the population have
a health unit within ten kilometres compared to the national average of 57
percent. The most deprived districts of the northern region (Kotido,
Kitgum, Apac) have only about 28 percent of their populations within ten
kilometres of a health unit. To contrast, eight of the better served districts have over three-quarters of their population within ten kilometres of
a comprehensive health care unit.

CONCLUSION

In Uganda as a whole about 30 percent of the population live within one
hour's walk, and 60 percent live within two hours' walk of a health facility
staffed, equipped and potentially capable of offering a comprehensive health
care service. Available maternal and child health (MCH) activity returns,
however, suggest that only a very small proportion of these facilities
presently offer promotive and preventative health services: immunisation,
growth monitoring and nutrition advice, antenatal care, health education and
so on. Efforts to improve and extend the availability of community health
services must therefore address the issues of, firstly, stimulating and
strengthening the ability of the existing infrastructure of 250 health units
to provide a higher quality and more reliable service, and secondly, to develop appropriate means of taking services to the five or so million
Ugandans presently under- or unserved.

The first issue of quality of health care is currently being addressed by
the Ministry of Health and donor agencies through the promotion of an inte-

TABLE 4:   Access to Health Facilities by District and Region

DISTRICT Region	No. Units	Population 1980	Population within 5 km of unit (%)	Population within 10 km of unit (%)
IGANGA	9	643,881	22	58
JINJA	7	228,520	38	77
KAMULI	13	349,549	36	89
KAPCHORWA	5	73,967	51	78
KUMI	5	239,539	17	51
MBALE	9	556,941	43	89
SOROTI	8	476,629	14	35
TORORO	12	668,410	24	63
Eastern	68	3,237,436	28	66
APAC	6	313,333	8	28
ARUA	9	472,283	23	52
GULU	8	270,085	29	54
KITGUM	9	308,711	13	28
KOTIDO	6	161,445	9	27
LIRA	7	370,252	17	47
MOROTO	6	188,641	18	43
MOYO	2	106,492	15	38
NEBBI	5	233,000	20	53
Northern	58	2,424,242	18	43
KAMPALA	9	458,503	100	100
LUWERO	4	412,474	10	31
MASAKA	9	631,156	21	50
MPIGI	12	661,208	24	62
MUBENDE	6	510,260	15	40
MUKONO	11	634,275	22	54
RAKAI	7	274,558	33	80
S/Central	58	3,582,434	32	60
BUNDIBUGYO	3	112,216	48	79
BUSHENYI	8	524,669	21	53
HOIMA	10	294,301	29	60
KABALE	7	455,421	30	66
KABAROLE	10	519,821	31	60
KASESE	4	277,697	46	62
MASINDI	5	223,230	22	39
MBARARA	6	688,153	12	31
RUKUNGIRI	10	296,559	37	87
Western	63	3,392,067	27	56
UGANDA	247	12,636,179	27	57

grated immunisation (UNEPI), oral rehydration therapy (ORT), growth monitoring, drug management and health education programme which is envisaged to
act as the vanguard to the reintroduction and strengthening of comprehensive MCH services in rural Uganda. In taking health services to more people
a number of alternative avenues of development are available. In the
1960s, for example, a trust in the efficacy of the referral system and the
network of lower level health units (dispensary, subdispensary, aid post)
prompted the advocacy of mobile services to extend health coverage to remote
underserved rural areas. Many of these earlier programmes were vertically
managed and separate programmes focused on specific problems--for example,
TB and leprosy control or smallpox eradication--and are not in keeping with
the current philosophy of providing appropriate low-cost integrated health
services.

Possibly the most practical and realistic means of improving access to
comprehensive health care is to aim at the accepted government objective of
establishing one health unit with health centre services in each subcounty
or gombolola (average population of about 20,000 people)(Uganda Government,
1982). Complementing the expansion of the health infrastructure, the health
centre's ability to train, supervise and support community health teams
working within the subcounty area must be promoted.[4] Through such a strategy the health centre could effectively act as a community health resource
and referral centre providing supplies and advisory services to community
health workers and to the community as a whole.

---

[4]A community health team (CHT) consists of a primary health care worker
(PHCW) and a traditional birth attendant (TBA). The plan is to have a CHT
for an average population of 1000 people which geographically corresponds
roughly to a subparish.

REFERENCES

Bennett, F. J. (1968). An Evaluation of Health Education at Kasangati
    Health Centre. Children in the Tropics, 52: 14-34.
Gish, O. (1978). Planning the Health Sector: The Tanzanian Experience.
    Groom Hill, London.
King, M. (1966). Medical Care in Developing Countries. Oxford University
    Press.
Langlands, B. W. (1972). The Distribution of Population in Uganda. Uganda.
    Occasional Papers Nos. 26-42, Department of Geography, Makerere Uni-
    versity.
Moffat, M. (1969). Mobile Young Child Clinics in Rural Uganda: A
    Report on the Ankole Preschool Protection Programme, 1967-69. Mimeo-
    graphed, Kampala.
Uganda, Republic of, Ministry of Health (1961). The First Five-Year
    Development Plan: 1961-2 to 1965-6. Government Printers, Entebbe.
Uganda, Republic of (1966). Work for Progress: Uganda's Second Five-Year
    Plan: 1966-71. Government Printers, Entebbe.
Uganda, Republic of (1972). Uganda Plan III: Third Five-Year Develop-
    ment Plan: 1971-1976. Government Printers, Entebbe.
Uganda, Republic of, Ministry of Health (1977). Report and Recommendations
    of the Commission of Inquiry into the Medical Services of Uganda."
    Government Printers, Entebbe.
Uganda, Republic of, Ministry of Health (1982). National Plan of Action on
    Primary Health Care. Government Printers, Entebbe.

Social Change and Lugbara Subsistence Agriculture in West Nile District

Virginia Lee Barnes Dean

The Lugbara people live in West Nile District of Uganda and the contiguous area of Zaire. Their traditional territory straddles the gentle continental divide of Africa and consists of a rolling plateau which varies in elevation from about 1000 to 1500 metres. The plateau is drained by small streams which flow into larger streams which in West Nile District eventually flow eastward into the Nile but in Zaire find their way into the Congo River. The year is divided into two main seasons: the dry season, from December until early April, and the rainy season, from April to November. During the dry season there are occasionally short rains in February called "grass rains" because they provide much needed grazing for Lugbara cattle; the rainy season is also biphasic with a drier period during the middle. The plateau supports scrub savannah vegetation and the occasional large groves of trees which have grown up around the graves of Lugbara ancestors. The people live in mud-walled, circular and thatch-roofed houses which are clustered on the landscape and surrounded by cultivated and fallow fields and outlying bush. Houses are situated near water sources and as often as possible near granite outcroppings which are used for threshing grain and other activities involved in food preparation.

The Lugbara traditionally lived in dispersed patrilineages headed by an elder who was the previous elder's oldest male child by his first wife.[1] The residential group was governed by the elder and the other senior male heads of households in the patrilineage. Marriage was patrilocal, with a very abrupt transition for a girl from the status of daughter to the status of wife. Perhaps for this reason Lugbara men, and Lugbara society in general, have two very different conceptions of women. Women as sisters were treated as equals and were expected to be emotionally close to their siblings; women as wives were considered creatures of nature rather than of culture and were said to be be "behind" their husbands (who were often much older than their wives because of their need to postpone marriage until they had accumulated bridewealth). Wives were responsible for the feeding and reproduction of their husband's lineage but were not socially fully incorpo-

---

[1]For thorough background material on the Lugbara people and their territory, see Middleton (1960 and 1965). I carried out the original research reported here in 1972-73.

rated into it. When women became menopausal they were said to be "like men"
and might often return to their own patrilineage, sometimes to acquire considerable political and ritual power.

The brief description of traditional Lugbara social organisation given above
provides the context for an examination of the traditional agricultural system and the changes which have occurred since the Lugbara have been incorporated into the world economy.

TRADITIONAL LUGBARA AGRICULTURE

Land among the Lugbara was trationally allocated by the elder in consultation with other male heads of household of the patrilineage. Land was al-
lotted to a head of household according to his political acumen and the number of his dependent wives and children. Although Lugbara wives were
peripheral to their husband's patrilineage in many ways, it was in the interest of Lugbara men to lobby the elders and other senior men on their
wives' behalf, because Lugbara women performed about 75 percent of the agricultural labour.

Each wife needed some of three kinds of fields: "home fields" which were
fertilised with ashes and manure and used to grow crops--such as the white
sorghums used in the preparation of beer--which made the most demand on the
soil; "outside fields" which were less intensively cultivated and were
planted with staple crops such as finger millet, sorghum, sesame, beans and
pigeon peas; and "fields at the water's edge" (or irrigated fields) which
were independent of the dry season/rainy season cycle and were used to grow
sweet potatoes, maize, sugar cane, bananas and beans (Middleton, 1965: 10-
11).

Lugbara men prepared the land for planting by hoeing the field two or three
times, and were responsible for sowing seeds. Women working in reciprocal
work parties were responsible for all of the pre-sowing raking and seed bed
preparation, and the weeding and care of the crops until they matured. Both
men and women did the harvesting, after which the crops from any given field
belonged to the woman who had use rights in the field for the season. Women
fed their husbands and children from their granaries.

The traditional staple carbohydrate crop was finger millet (Eleusine
coracana). Finger millet is well suited to growing conditions in West
Nile. It has a small seed which dries out completely in the field before
harvest and is easily stored. It tolerates dry spells in the early stages of
its growth and so can be sown after the grass rains in February, germinate
and still be viable without further rain until the main rains start in early
April (Acland, 1971: 114-117).

Millet growing, however, is very labour intensive. Seeds are tiny and seed
beds must be very carefully prepared. The first weeding, done when the
seedlings are four to five inches tall, is difficult because the roots of
the seedlings are delicate. Several additional weedings are necesary before
harvest; when the millet has matured it must be protected in the fields from
weaver birds; harvests require the participation of all available persons.

Relationships between men and women in traditional Lugbara society were
complementary rather than competitive. Men were motivated to acquire good
lands for their wives to cultivate, and had no alternative use for the land.
Patterns in the division of labour were well established.

THE COLONIAL PERIOD

The Lugbara were spared the ravages of the slave trade, and their early contacts with the outside world were more gentle than they were for many tribal groups in Africa. Nevertheless the colonial period led to an extensive transformation of Lugbara society. The first significant contact with Europeans occurred in 1900 when Belgians began to administer the region. The people who came forward to deal with them were followers of Rembe, a Kakwa who had come into Lugbara country from the north to start a cult in response to European penetration, and were marginal members of Lugbara society; nevertheless the Belgians appointed them as "chiefs" and paid them well in cattle.[2] In turn these "chiefs" were able to marry well and acquire a great deal of power, which contributed to the erosion of the traditional power structure of the patrilineages.

In 1908 West Nile became part of the Sudan; in 1914 it was incorporated into Uganda and the first British administrator arrived. In the 1920s the Protestant African Inland Mission and the Catholic Verona Fathers sent missionaries to establish schools in the area. Until independence these schools provided the only Western education in the district and were important in the transmission of the Western ideas and skills necessary to enter the Ugandan governmental structure.

Events outside of West Nile also had a profound influence on the evolution of Lugbara society. With the development of cash cropping in Buganda to the south, opportunities arose for young Lugbara men to work as wage labourers for Baganda or Indian landlords. The higher areas of the Lugbara plateau were approaching a population density of 250 people per square mile (which is relatively dense for a subsistence agricultural population), and one way of easing the shortage of land was for young men to leave the district for a time.[3] When they returned home with their savings they no longer had to wait their turn at the lineage's cattle herd to obtain bridewealth but instead could go out and purchase cattle, marry a wife and present themselves to lineage elders as household heads in need of land because they had dependents. In short, labour migration, like the Belgians' setting up of Rembe's followers as "chiefs" with payment in cattle, also served to lessen the traditional authority elders had over younger males within the patrilineages (see Middleton, 1965: 12-13, 90).

A third major change which took place in West Nile prior to 1973 was the development of cash cropping in the district itself. The colonial administration had been anxious to have Uganda as a whole produce a surplus, and in West Nile several different cash crops had been introduced: coffee, cotton and tobacco. Cotton only grew well at the lower altitudes of the district, in the area along the Nile, and coffee was only successful in the extreme southwestern part of the district where the elevation is around 2000 metres. But most of the central Lugbara plateau proved very suitable for tobacco farming, and in the 1950s tobacco cooperatives were set up for drying the tobacco leaves, changing tobacco growing from a small-scale effort mostly for home consumption and occasional sale under the control of the lineage elder for the lineage's cash needs, into a major enterprise. Those who

---

[2]Older Lugbara told Middleton (1965: 3-7) that the new "chiefs" started the practice of using cattle for bridewealth. Previously the Lugbara had used lumps of iron and unfinished hoes.

[3]Middleton (1960: 3) reports that 19 percent of adult Lugbara males were outside the district in 1951.

joined the cooperatives were mostly younger men who felt comfortable in
associations not based on lineage, perhaps because of their experience as
migrant labourers in southern Uganda. The development of tobacco growing
made it possible for men to acquire cash income for the payment of taxes and
their children's school fees (primary education was not free), and for the
purchase of trade goods such as bicycles and radios, right at home in West
Nile District with relative freedom from their elders' control. Meanwhile,
with husbands now utilising part of the land for growing tobacco, both the
amount and quality of land available to Lugbara women for other farming was
diminished.

The changes just referred to took place primarily in the economic sphere as
a direct result of colonial policies and had far-reaching impact on the
social organisation of the Lugbara people. The compulsory growing of cassava (Manihot esculenta) as a famine relief crop was also significant.

It is not known when cassava was introduced to West Nile. After the
widespread famine of 1942-43, however, the Lugbara were required to grow
one-third of an acre of cassava per household each year (Middleton, 1965:).
Since then cassava has increasingly replaced millet as the staple carbohydrate crop.

Cassava is planted as the last crop in the farming rotation and is usually
intercropped with a close-spaced planting of groundnuts. The cassava crop
requires almost no weeding. It is mature and ready for harvest at the same
time as the millet and the other crops, but can be left in the ground
unattended for another six months and harvested at any time during that
period. Cassava is extremely drought resistant, and desert locusts do not
eat cassava leaves. Perhaps most importantly, cassava has a higher caloric
yield per acre than either sorghum or millet.

DECISION-MAKING

Lugbara women, faced with the changes in the structure of Lugbara society
which have taken place over the past decades, and the resulting changes in
the subsistence economy of their people, are faced every year with decisions
about how much millet and sorghum and how much cassava they are going to
plant. The decision-making process invariably involves a traditional preference for millet. The women say they prefer to make enya, their staple
carbohydrate steamed bread, from millet flour alone because it tastes better
and gives them strength. Cassava is thought of as a good crop because it
eliminated the famines that used to plague Lugbaraland. But the women say
they do not like the taste of cassava flour without millet or sorghum mixed
in. When one probes a little deeper, the women say they grow cassava
because millet is too much work.

Is cassava really less work to grow and prepare for cooking? Up until
planting time, the labour of field preparation is essentially the same for
both crops. The millet seeds are broadcast and then raked in, while cassava
cuttings must be individually buried in the ground. The millet has to be
weeded three times between planting and harvest, while cassava needs no
weeding. The millet must be protected from weaver birds for about one week
before it is harvested, then must be harvested and stored in a granary.
Before it is ground into flour, millet must be threshed and winnowed. Cassava tubers, on the other hand, can be harvested when and as desired within
a six-month period. The tubers are peeled and then fermented under wet
leaves for three days. After the three days, the tubers (now covered with

a surprising variety of moulds) are scraped and pounded with a stick to break them into lumps. Then the resulting mixture of cassava lumps is dried in the sun. When the mixture is dry it can be stored in the house or one of the granaries for several days until it is needed for grinding into flour.

The statement of Lugbara women that millet is more work to grow has as much to do with the the quality and timing of the work involved as it does with the actual expenditure of energy. Millet cultivation must be done on a fairly rigid schedule, from planting to harvesting; only after harvesting can one choose when to grind it into flour. With cassava the schedule is the other way around; there is little rigidity in the tasks involved in its cultivation until it is harvested, after which it must be processed vigourously for four days. Lugbara women would rather be tied to a rigid schedule for four days in return for the flexibility cassava offers at other stages of the cultivation process.

The first reason for this preference derives from the fact that there has been an increasing tendency for wives in a polygynous household to have their own separate compounds because co-wives tend to quarrel (Middleton, 1965: 10-12). The dispersal is also related to the need to utilise land more efficiently in an area of increasing population pressure. The dispersal of household compounds also means that women are much more socially isolated than they were from each other; i.e. that in forming agricultural work groups women now have less access than they did to each other's labour. Getting together on granite outcroppings to process cassava has become one of their primary times of social interaction.

Secondly, women have had less and less access to the labour of young girls to carry and care for their infants because of the physical separation of households, and because primary school attendance has increased. It is difficult to do any of the agricultural tasks associated with millet cultivation while caring for a one- to three-year-old child. The work of cassava processing on the granite outcroppings near homesteads is much more easily integrated with infant and toddler care.

Besides the above-mentioned issues of scheduling flexibility and social networking, there is the fact that an average acre of millet under subsistence conditions will yield from 200 to 400 kilogrammes of dried grain per acre, while an acre of cassava will yield 500 to 650 kilogrammes of dried cassava (Acland, 1971: 37, 116). Millet provides slightly more calories per unit weight (Jelliffe and asociates, 1962: 41), but this is relatively insignificant when compared to the greater yield per acre of cassava.

DISCUSSION

The changes described above have had an important impact on Lugbara society and must be considered in relation to the overall welfare of the population. As Africa opened up and Uganda became an independent state the Lugbara were brought into the spheres of influence of both the national economy and the world economy. The development of tobacco cash cropping and the related increasing reliance on cassava as a staple crop has nutritional implications of far-reaching significance, especially for very young children.

In 1961 a team from Makerere Medical School headed by D. B. Jelliffe undertook a general survey of child health and nutrition among the Lugbara, and the nutritional content of Lugbara food (Jelliffe and associates, 1961: 41).

They found that by eighteen months of age over half the children were eating
mostly adult food, and that by two years of age most children were on an
essentially adult diet supplemented by breast milk for the 41 percent who
were still nursing. Many of the children were anaemic, almost 50 percent
had positive malaria smears and most were quite retarded in growth in comparison with other Ugandan populations.

In 1973 a sample of twenty-six families from all over Lugbaraland were
interviewed about their crops and their children's diets.[4] Every family
listed cassava as a main crop; only 30 percent listed millet or sorghum as a
main crop. Only five families did not list millet or sorghum as a consti-
tuent of their child's staple food. One family reported making millet
gruel--traditionally fed to weanling children and to pregnant mothers for
breakfast--for their children. All families reported eating legumes daily.
Seven families reported eating meat or fish between once a week and once a
month; the rest, but for one, ate meat or fish less often than once a
month.[5]

The traditional Lugbara staples--millet, sesame and beans--were combined in
a diet that was nourishing and well balanced. Millet and sesame are both
high in iron content, an asset in an area where anaemia (whether from
malaria, hookworm or some other cause) is widespread. Both crops are also
high in calcium, making them an ideal weaning food in a milkless culture
(the Lugbara do not milk their cows). The traditional diet was also adequate
in protein.[6]

Unfortunately, if the trend of substituting cassava for millet and sorghum
continues, it is likely that a deterioration in the adequacy of the diets of
the Lugbara, particularly the diets of children, will also occur.

The taste conservatism of the Lugbara people has so far led them to continue
growing millet even though cassava is more productive and involves a more
comfortable kind and amount of labour input, and even though the growing of
cash crops in the area continues to be encouraged. But the population of
West Nile District doubled between 1950 and 1973, and there is no doubt that
the pressures which led to change in traditional cropping patterns will
continue.

Cassava originated in the New World, but Africa now produces more cassava
than any other continent. Where cash crops have disturbed traditional
cropping systems, cassava has often filled the gap in food production. Its
productivity, however, could be a mixed blessing for the Lugbara in the long
run.

----

[4]The families were the matched controls for a case-control study of
children with Burkitt's lymphoma, a cancer of childhood occurring in the
Lugbara area.
    [5]This agrees with Middleton's statement that meat was an unimportant
part of the diet of the Lugbara people (Middleton, 1965, p. 7).
    [6]While millet is deficient in the amino acid lysine and sesame is defi-
cient in both isoleucine and lysine, beans are rich in lysine and only moderately deficient in isoleucine. Millet is 6 percent protein, cassava only
1 to 2 percent protein.

REFERENCES

Acland, J. D. (1971). East African Crops. Food and Agricultural Organisa-
ation, Rome.

Jelliffe, D. B., F. J. Bennett, H. R. White, T. R. Cullinan and E. F. P.
Jelliffe (1962). The Children of the Lugbara: A Study in the Techniques
of Paediatric Field Survey in Tropical Africa. Tropical and Geographic
Medicine, 14: 33-50.

Middleton, John (1960). Lugbara Religion. Oxford University Press.

Middleton, John (1965). The Lugbara of Uganda. Holt, Rinehart and Winston,
New York.

Purseglove, J. W. (1968). Tropical Crops: Dicotyledons 1. Longmans, Green
and Company, London.

Republic of Uganda, Department of Lands and Surveys (1967). Atlas of Uganda
(Second Edition). Government Printers, Kampala.

Recent Health Surveys: Towards a Morbidity and Mortality Baseline

Cole P. Dodge and Peggy L. Henderson

Medical research and reporting systems broke down throughout Uganda in the period between the liberation war and 1984. The cessation of immunisation led to a rise in communicable diseases, bringing increased demands on health care providers. Shortages of medicines and the breakage and looting of basic equipment, in addition to paper shortages and the disruption of communications, exacerbated the situation. As a result of such circumstances official statistics on health conditions in Uganda are no longer based on current data but on trends projected from the 1970s and from the reports of a few institutions.

The purposes of this paper are to report on four surveys that were carried out in the first half of 1984 in relation to health project planning and the definition of baseline data, and to compare the results of these recent surveys with results from earlier surveys and with health survey information for the country as a whole. The survey methodologies employed in the recent surveys are reported briefly. While national averages cannot be derived from any of the surveys, their results do provide relevant baseline data.

BACKGROUND

The areas in which the surveys referred to were conducted--northern Karamoja (Dodoth County), Luwero District, Mbale District and the Kasangati Health Centre catchment area on the periphery of Kampala--vary considerably in ecology, stage of development and degree of economic and civil disruption suffered in the 1970s and at present. Karamoja, the poorest region of Uganda, is inhabited by pastoralist tribesmen and has low population density (see the article by Alnwick in the section on Karamoja in this book for background information on Karamoja). Medical services performance and literacy rates are lower in this area than in any other part of Uganda (Uganda, 1982a; Alnwick, Stirling and Kyeyune, "Population Access to Hospitals . . . ", in this book). Various international organisations have been providing assistance to the region since the famine of 1979-81, in recognition of the fact that food security has been seriously disrupted in the area and that its people are again vulnerable to famine.

The population of Luwero District north of Kampala has been under severe

TABLE   1:   Age and Sex Distributions of the Populations   Surveyed Compared with Earlier Data for Uganda

Survey and Year	Age Group	Sample Size	Males %	Females %	Total %
Uganda Census 1969	<1	272,808	1.5	1.5	3
	1-4	1,554,296	8	8	16
	>5	7,618,442	41	40	81
Uganda Census 1980	all ages	12,636,179	50	50	100
Karamoja 1969	0-4	44,215	8	8	16
	>5	239,561	42	42	84
Karamoja 1984	<1	155	-	-	6
	1-4	436	-	-	18
	>5	1,862	-	-	76
Kasangati 1984	<1	161	2	2	4
	1-4	821	9	10	19
	>5	3,408	37	40	77
Mbale District 1984	<1	477	-	-	4
	1-4	2,018	-	-	17
	>5	9,657	-	-	79
Luwero District 1984[a]	<1	30	1	1	2
	1-4	177	7	7	13
	>5	1,117	36	49	84

*Source: Uganda 1969 (Uganda, 1969), Uganda 1980 (Uganda, 1982b), Karamoja 1969 (Uganda, 1973), Karamoja 1984 (Pearson, 1984), Kasangati 1984 (Namboze and associates, 1984), Mbale (UNICEF/Uganda, 1984), Luwero (Economist Development Report, 1984; ICRC, 1984).
[a]Numbers extrapolated from limited reported data.

stress from the large-scale displacement of civilians since 1982 (Africa Confidential, 1984; Johnston, "The Luwero Triangle . . . ", in this book). Emergency relief programmes were initiated in the area in June 1983.

Mbale District is situated in eastern Uganda on the lower slopes of Mount Elgon. It did not suffer any direct disturbances in the aftermath of the liberation war in 1979, and its organisational infrastructure has remained reasonably intact despite the turmoil in other parts of the country in recent years.

Kasangati is a small rural trading centre located six miles north of Kampala.   The health centre here has been a teaching centre for many years. In 1983 UNICEF and the American voluntary agency, Minnesota International Health Volunteers (MIHV), established a programme of assistance to this health centre under the Institute of Public Health, Makerere University, to improve the physical facility and to resume teaching and medical service delivery to the population in the catchment area.

METHODOLOGY

The reported surveys in Kasangati (Namboze and associates, 1984) and Mbale (UNICEF and Uganda, 1984) were carried out in 1984 to establish baseline figures for programme planning and evaluation, while the reported surveys in Karamoja (Pearson, 1984) and Luwero (Economist Development Report, 1984; ICRC, 1984) were carried out in order to monitor the health situation in areas under stress. The Kasangati and Karamoja surveys used a standard random sampling methodology. An innovative survey design was used in the collection of the Mbale data, with only households likely to be reached by expanded health facility services (according to definitions here, households within one kilometre of the health unit) included in the sampling procedure. Finally, the Luwero study subjects included only female heads of household who were Red Cross beneficiaries in camps or halfway houses for displaced persons, plus a few Red Cross workers.

RESULTS

The age and sex distributions of the populations surveyed, in comparison with data from selected other surveys, are shown in Table 1. In Table 2 infant, child and crude mortality rates determined in the four surveys are given, again in comparison with the results from selected other surveys.

The chief causes of death were identified in two of the surveys. Measles and gunshot trauma, in order, were discovered to be the chief causes of

TABLE 2:   Infant, Child and Crude Mortality Rates, Uganda 1984

Source and Year		Infant Mortality Rate[a]	Child Mortality Rate[b]	Crude Death Rate[c]
Uganda Census	1969	120	–	19 females 21 males
Official Uganda	1984	120	17	19
Karamoja	1980	607	305	212
Karamoja	1984	134	23	22
Kasangati	1966	73.7	–	10.5
	1967	41.2	–	11.3
	1968	28	–	5.5
	1969	27	–	4.8
	1970	27.5	–	6.4
	1971	29.8	–	8.1
	1984	93	–	17
Mbale District	1984	95	25	–
Luwero District	1984	305	39	22[d]

*Source: Uganda 1969 (Uganda, 1969), Uganda 1984 (Uganda, 1984), Karamoja 1980 (Biellik and Henderson, 1981a), Karamoja 1984 (Pearson, 1984), Kasangati 1966-68 (Matovu, Bennett and Namboze, 1971), Kasangati 1969-71 (IPH, 1972), Kasangati 1984 (Namboze and associates, 1984), Mbale (UNICEF/Uganda, 1984), Luwero (Economist Development Report, 1984; ICRC, 1984).
[a]Number of deaths aged less than 1 year per 1000 live births (in some cases estimated under 1 year) per year.
[b]Number of deaths aged 1-4 years per 1000 children aged 1-4 per year.
[c]Number of deaths divided by total population.
[d]Extrapolated from limited reported data.

death during the period in question in the Kasangati survey (with malaria, tuberculosis and diarrhoea also being identified as significant causes of death). According to the Mbale data, 69 and 41 percent of the deaths of children aged 1-4 could be associated with diarrhoea and measles, respectively, and 16 percent of infant deaths could be attributed to neonatal tetanus. (Such results can be compared with data for the causes of death in Ugandan hospitals, as given in the article by Alnwick, Stirling and Kyeyune, and included in this book, "Morbidity and Mortality in Selected Ugandan Hospitals".)

Five percent of the population under 5 years of age in northern Karamoja in 1984 were found to be moderately or severely malnourished (less than 80 percent of the international WHO/CDC (World Health Organisation/Center for Disease Control) reference median). This finding may be compared with the 4.8 percent similarly identifiable as moderately or severely malnourished in southern Karamoja in 1980 (Biellik and Henderson, 1981a), and the 0.2 percent so identifiable in North Teso adjoining Karamoja in 1980 (Biellik and Henderson, 1981b).

The top ten causes of morbidity as reported for the previous two-week period were identified in the Kasangati survey and are shown in Table 3.

TABLE 3: **Reported Causes of Morbidity in Kasangati for All Ages 1984**

Cause	Number Reporting	Percentage
Fever/malaria	545	36
Respiratory infection	205	14
Abdominal pains	134	9
Headache	90	6
Measles	78	5
Diarrhoea	62	4
Body pains	63	4
Backache	50	3
Heart disease	33	2
Skin infections	30	2

*Source: Namboze and associates (1984).

Recent estimates for immunisation coverage for the country as a whole are compared with the results from the two surveys (Kasangati and Mbale) in which such findings were determined, and are given in Table 4. Immunisation services in Karamoja have been carried out by mass campaign since 1981, and coverage rates are believed to have reached reasonably high levels. The district's medical officer, Dr. L. Rossanigo (1983), estimates that about 60 percent of the children in the district were covered with at least one antigen in 1982-83.

CONCLUSION

The four surveys briefly referred to above covered very different populations and used different methodologies. They were designed to meet different purposes and their findings are not generalisable to the country as a whole. Such surveys would not be necessary were it not for the virtual

**TABLE 4:   Percent   Immunisation Coverage of Population   under   5
Years of Age**

Antigen	National 0-4	Kasangati 0-4	Mbale <1	Mbale 1-4
BCG	7	32	48	58
DPT-1	-	16	50	58
Polio-1	-	16	51	58
DPT-2	-	5	39	51
Polio-2	-	5	39	51
DPT-3	3	7	28	41
Polio-3	4	7	28	41
Measles	4	12	33	52
Fully immunised	-	1	21	38

*Source: The national data are from Uganda (1984), the Kasangati data from
Namboze and associates (1984) and the Mbale data from UNICEF/Uganda (1984).

nonexistence in recent years of reliable information generated on a regular
basis by the Ministry of Health. Given the situation, however, their
findings are important, and more such studies will be necessary (and are
underway) in order to fill the current health information gap. It is hoped
that through the accumulation and interpretation of such survey results a
picture of present patterns of morbidity and mortality throughout the
country will emerge. The government, assisted by various nongovernment
agencies, is to rehabilitate its own health information system in the meantime, and hopefully, in the not-too-distant future, will again provide the
chief means of acquiring reliable figures for planning and evaluating health
programmes in the country.

REFERENCES

Africa Confidential, 17 (1984). Uganda: For Whom the Bell Tolls. 15 Au-
    gust: 1-3.
Biellik, Robin J. and Peggy L. Henderson (1981a). Mortality, Nutritional
    Status, and Diet During the Famine in Karamoja, Uganda, 1980. Lancet,
    ii (12 December): 1330-1333.
Biellik, Robin J. and Peggy L. Henderson (1981b). Mortality, Nutritional
    Status and Dietary Conditions in a Food Deficit Region: North Teso
    District, Uganda, December 1980. Ecology and Food Nutrition, 11: 163-
    170.
Economist Development Report (1984). Uganda Horrors. August.
Institute of Public Health, Makerere University (1972). Report of Kasangati
    Health Centre. Mimeographed. Kampala.
International Committee of the Red Cross (1984). Note on Infant and Child
    Mortality Survey. Mimeographed, ICRC, Kampala.
Matovu, H., F. J. Bennett and J. Namboze (1971). Kasangati Health Centre:
    A Community Approach. In Clifford G. Gould (Ed.), Health and Disease in
    Africa. East Africa Literature Bureau, Nairobi.
Namboze, J., B. K. Asaba, R. Biritwum, J. Mafigiri and N. Nickerson (1984).
    Community Health Survey of Kasangati Defined Area. Mimeographed, Insti-
    tute of Public Health, Kampala.
Pearson, R. (1984). A Survey Providing Baseline Data for the Future Evalu-

ation of the Departments of Education and Agriculture School Agriculture Project. Mimeographed, Save the Children Fund/World Food Programme, Kampala.

Rossanigo, L. (1983). Annual Report of the District Medical Officer. Mimeographed, Moroto.

Uganda, Republic of, Statistics Division (1969). Report of the 1969 Population Census: Volume IV, The Analytic Report. Ministry for Planning and Economic Development, Kampala.

Uganda, Republic of, Statistics Division (1973). Report of the 1969 Population Census: Volume III, Additional Tables. Ministry for Planning and Economic Development, Kampala.

Uganda, Republic of (1982a). Educational Statistics. Ministry of Education, Kampala.

Uganda, Republic of (1982b). Report on the 1980 Population Census: Volume I, The Provisional Results by Administrative Areas. Ministry for Planning and Economic Development, Kampala.

Uganda, Republic of (1984). Ministry of Health, Planning Section, personal communication.

UNICEF and Republic of Uganda (1984). Report of Baseline Morbidity/Mortality Survey, Mbale District, June 1984. UNICEF, Kampala.

Child Health Crisis at Mulago and Makerere

C. Ndugwa, D. A. Hillman and E. S. Hillman

The impact of the health crisis in Uganda on services for children was felt throughout the country. By 1979 little remained of the comprehensive network of health services for children that had been recognised twenty years earlier as the best in Africa (Bennett, 1981).

Facilities broke down and supplies became nonexistent. Many essential health care providers left the country. Others became totally immersed in the problems of day-to-day survival.

The net result of these problems was that the complex plumbing, electrical and sewage systems on the paediatric wards of the new University Hospital ceased to function, rendering the wards totally unacceptable to deliver care to children or to serve as models and teaching facilities.

Medical education that had been seriously eroded during the Amin era became inadequate and incapable of providing the training, evaluation and planning essential to the establishment of an effective health care system.

SOCIAL PAEDIATRICS

In response to Makerere University's decision that support of child health and paediatrics was the priority need in the Faculty of Medicine, Canadian medical schools supported by the Canadian International Development Agency developed a Child Health and Medical Education Programme (CHAMP) to provide essential faculty and other support as a first step in overcoming this aspect of the health crisis in Uganda.

The purpose of this programme is to support a new concept called "social paediatrics" on a special ward where service and teaching are related to the critical needs of Ugandan children.

The objectives and operation of this ward are consistent with the recommendations developed at the Karachi Conference in 1981 orienting service, education and health care research to a defined community adjacent to the hospital (The Role of Hospitals in Primary Health Care, 1981). This community, Mulago village, is typical of underserviced poor urban communities recognised as an ever-increasing problem in the delivery of health services (WHO, 1981).

The ward, an old reconditioned one-story hospital building surrounded by grass and gardens, is simple to operate and maintain and can be easily reproduced in hospitals throughout Uganda.

The social paediatric ward provides a focus for the teaching of comprehensive paediatrics. As trainees on this ward medical students and postgraduates acquire the necessary knowledge and skills to function as consultants while also learning to play key roles in the operation of a health care team. Major emphasis is placed on the prevention of disease and on the promotion of health, and students learn to develop and evaluate programmes designed to meet community needs (Walsh, 1979 and Parry, 1983).

The six aspects of child health care given particular emphasis are as follows.

Immunisation

All children are immunised within twenty-four hours of admission and immunisation of siblings is completed on the ward during the sick child's hospital stay or during the home visit at the time of discharge. Mothers of childbearing age are given tetanus immunisation.

Nutritional Assessment and Support

The vital importance of breastfeeding is stressed and dietary supplements are provided to breastfeeding mothers. Nutritional histories and careful measurements of height, weight and arm circumference identify those children at risk who then receive special supplements. All mothers receive instruction on appropriate local weaning foods, and nutrition counselling. Height, weight, immunisation and any special risk factors are entered on a growth chart which is frequently referred to by the ward staff and explained to the mother. At the time of discharge the growth chart is given to the mother to take home and serves as the ongoing record of her child's health.

Health Education

Members of the ward team conduct daily teaching sessions at which they discuss management of minor illnesses, cuts and burns, the prevention of accidents, the use of oral rehydration therapy in the home treatment of diarrhoea, and family planning.

A Problem-oriented Record System

Essential medical and demographic data on each patient are recorded in a ledger at the time of discharge. This enables immediate recall of information needed for follow-up care or readmission of individual patients. It also facilitates an ongoing tabulation of accurate ward statistics. During hospitalisation and immediate follow-up, the patient's chart, kept on the ward, provides a comprehensive listing of the problems that have been identified. The list includes not only the one or more medical problems that led to admission but also the nutritional, social, developmental, immuni-

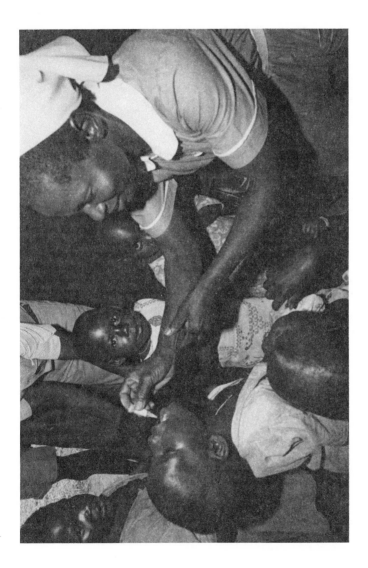

Figure 1 Polio immunisation, Mbale, 1982
(Photograph courtesy of UNICEF/D Heiden)

sation and other problems that may be of even greater importance than the
"presenting" complaint.

Follow-up of Discharged Patients

The child, when ready for discharge, is taken home by the medical student
who has been involved in the case. The student who walks home with the
mother is able to see firsthand any problems faced by the family in the
village. He answers questions about the illness, follow-up and prevention,
and often immunises neighbourhood children, provides family planning counselling and nutritional advice and checks on latrines while in the area. He
encourages the family to be increasingly self-reliant and to take responsibility for the health of each member.

Management Skills

The role of physicians as key participants in educational, referral and
supervisory systems is stressed (Lathem, 1977). Cost-effectiveness attitudes are emphasised, and problems of excessive and irrational use of drugs
and costly investigations are closely monitored and corrected. Few of the
students realise that expenditure on drugs constitutes up to 60 percent of
the health budget in developing countries, and that as the majority of drugs
are imported this would represent a major drain on foreign exchange for
Uganda (Yudkin, 1980). No opportunity is missed 1) to encourage members of
the ward team to support mothers in acquiring a personal responsibility for
health of their families and 2) to mobilise community leaders to take
a more active role in promoting health and financing the health services
rather than relying passively on a government health system (Evans, 1981).

Following a recent survey of Mulago village, our catchment area, the results
were presented and discussed with chiefs and elders who have themselves
taken responsibility for improving sanitation and water supplies to the
area and have requested our help in the initiation of an immunisation programme that they will organise and advertise throughout the area (Morley,
1974). Our students, with supervision, are responding to this request. In
addition, during the long vacation break this year more than forty senior
medical students completed surveys of the child health care needs in their
home villages or large urban centres. These projects will be discussed with
the paediatric faculty in consideration of the problems identified and the
solutions proposed.

We recognise the need to provide health care and distribute medical
resources on the basis of the real needs of the people, whether rural or
urban based (Hendrickse, 1977), and believe this University Hospital-asso-
ciated ward serves as a model for the teaching and practice of primary and
comprehensive paediatric care for the population of a poor urban community.
The need for such a model is underlined by the WHO estimate that by the year
2000, 44 percent of the developing world's population will be living in
cities (WHO, 1981 and Ebrahim, 1983).

WARD ORGANISATION

Rennovation of the ward was easily accomplished with a major cleanup in
which all the staff participated, followed by minor electrical and plumbing
repairs. Coloured health posters and instructional material--such as the

"Thinness Chart" (Save the Children Fund, 1980)--and an illustrated daily quiz for the staff brighten the walls. Mothers are taught and encouraged to undertake crafts such as mat and basket weaving, and take pride in keeping the ward clean. A fresh bouquet of flowers decorates the central desk. A large but simple tearoom for all the staff has been a great success in developing team spirit on the ward and provides a friendly setting for formal and informal teaching sessions. A major obstacle to providing better service to patients in hospital has been the general sense of discouragement felt by all staff at the seemingly insoluble problems of supplies, security, low wages and low standards. The most obvious effect of the social paediatric ward has been a major boost to the morale of all the staff involved who feel a real sense of pride in the part they have played in the planning and operation of "their ward". Simple motivational techniques such as ward competitions with prizes and health promotion buttons and posters have been very well received. A weekly meeting at which only good news and successes are discussed serves as a pleasant change from the usual department business meetings which tend to consist of a litany of problems with few solutions. A great deal of credit goes to an enthusiastic head nurse whose leadership and devotion to patients and staff has provided an ideal role model.

CONCLUSION

The approach to improving child health care in the University Medical Centre has been enthusiastically received and supported by the students, faculty, patients and members of the hospital administration.

The medical school at Makerere University once provided leadership in academic medicine and biomedical research to the developing world. We believe this leadership can be effectively reestablished and directed not only to resolving the current health crisis in Uganda but also to developing health care research and demonstration models focusing on the essential interrelationships between hospitals and primary health centres. Curricula must be revised so that medical graduates will acquire the knowledge, attitudes and management skills necessary for more effective and efficient health care in the developing world.

REFERENCES

Bennett, F. J. (1981). Uses of Community Diagnosis in East Africa. Israel Journal of Medical Sciences, 17: 129-137.

Ebrahim, G. H. (1983). Primary Care and the Urban Poor. Journal of Tropical Paediatrics, 29: 2-3.

Evans, John (1981). Health Care in the Developing World: Scarcity and Choice. New England Journal of Medicine, 305: 1117-1127.

Hendrickse, R. G. (1977). Paediatrics. Proceedings of the Royal Society of London: 73-82.

Lathem, W. (1977). Medical Education: Reform for Developing Countries. Medical Education, 11: 65-70.

Morley, David (1974). Some Steps through which Hospitals may become more deeply Involved in Community Health Care. Contact, 20. Christian Medical Commission of the World Council of Churches.

Parry, E. H. O.(1983). The Future of Medical Education in East Africa. Postgraduate Doctor: Africa, 212-215.

The Role of Hospitals in Primary Health Care (1981). Report of a conference sponsored by the Aga Khan Foundation and WHO co-sponsored by the Canadian International Development Agency. Mendham Bowen Ltd.

Save the Children Fund, U. K. (1980). The Weight for Height Wall Chart for the Assessment of Thinness.

Walsh, J. (1979). Selective Primary Health Care. New England Journal of Medicine, 301: 967-973.

WHO (1981). Primary Health Care for the Urban Poor. WHO Document SHS/HSR/81.2.

Yudkin, J. S. (1980). The Economics of Pharmaceutical Supply in Tanzania. International Journal of Health Services, 10: 455-477.

Primary Health Care in Teso, 1980–1984

Dick Stockley

This report on primary health care (PHC) in Teso District is largely anecdotal. It is derived from my own experience. I arrived at Ngora Mission Hospital in 1980 and worked for one year in the paediatric and outpatient departments, transferred in 1981 to become full-time director of the PHC project run by the hospital. I left Ngora in 1983 to become director of the Karamoja diocese PHC project in Kotido.

BACKGROUND

A village health programme was started by the hospital in one of the nearby subcounties in 1978. Village health workers (VHWs) were selected by the hospital for each of the eight parishes. All were men and educated to at least secondary school grade four. They were paid at nursing aid rates by the hospital. The focus of their work was nutrition, hygiene and health education. The only equipment they were given was a spring balance Salter scale with which they were expected to weigh each parish child monthly.

When I arrived in 1980 many of the VHWs had not been seen for months and only appeared at the hospital to collect their salaries. My first contact was with two who came for recommendation letters to support their applications to join the army. At the first formal meeting, the unanimous request from the eight was for bicycles, uniforms, milk powder and "injections", my second warning that something was wrong. Gradually I learned that most of the VHWs were selling the simple medicines issued by the hospital and profiting on the side. Whenever I treated a patient with a malnourished child who had come to the hospital from that subcounty, I made enquiries about the VHWs there and was surprised that no one seemed to know about them. It was not hard to conclude that the hospital's VHW project was in complete disarray.

To fortify the VHW project and get more outreach started, we re-started a community health project later in 1980. The original eight VHWs were included in a maternal child health (MCH) mobile clinic schedule of monthly visits to four subcounty headquarters. MCH clinics were also held at the hospital twice each week.

I went on the mobile clinics weekly for eight months, and kept detailed nutrition records for five months as one main platform of the clinic routine. Health education at each clinic was first presented to all mothers (though this was seldom carried out if I was not present), then each child was weighed and the weight plotted on the child's "Road to Health" chart. Immunisation was then done and recorded.

Nutritional status in the first six months of life followed a regular distribution of 40 percent over the standard line, 40 percent within the Road to Health and 20 percent below.[1] When the children reached nine months of age, however, 36 percent of them fell below the 80 percent line, and by one year to one and a half years of age 50 percent of the children fell below the line.

On closer scrutiny I found that attendance dropped markedly as the children grew older. That is, very few children attended the MCH clinics after one year of age, nutritionally the worst time. In talking to mothers and staff I found further that it was the better motivated among the mothers who did attend the clinics, not those with malnourished children. This led me to the conclusion that the nutritional situation in the general public was probably worse than among those children examined at our clinics.

I had hoped to see an improvement in the nutritional status of children in the five-month period over which records were kept, but no statistical changes could be seen. The children who attended in November as well-nourished six-month-olds were malnourished eleven-month-olds by April. For all practical purposes we concluded that all our weighing, recording, assessing, advising on nutrition through the mobile MCH clinics had made no difference. Why?

Immunisation is dramatic, quick and appreciated by mothers. Nutrition is a bore and difficult, and the purposes of Road to Health charts are seldom understood. Once a child was fully immunised, mothers saw no reasons for return visits. Though nutritionally deteriorating noticeably, the children who did come were only treated for clinically diagnosed illnesses when what they really needed was food (particularly proper weaning food).

My conclusion was that MCH mobile clinics organised by professional outsiders (hospital-based medical workers) was a waste of time. It seemed to me a better use of resources and time to use the hospital's vehicle and staff for mass immunisation three or four times per year while tackling the malnutrition problem from a more indigenously meaningful perspective.

Over the period we conducted mobile MCH clinics in the subcounty headquarters, we experienced high mortality rates in the paediatric ward of the hospital. I examined the causes and found that the inpatient mortality rate for measles was 25 percent in some months. Among the twenty-two children with measles who on admission were visibly malnourished in one month, eleven died, while among the twenty-five who were well nourished when admitted during the same month, only one died. The mortality rate for malnourished measles cases was 50 percent compared to only 4 percent for the well-nourished measles cases.

---

[1] That is, 40 percent were above 100 percent of the expected weight-for-age, 40 percent were between 80 and 100 percent of the expected weight-for-age and 20 percent were below 80 percent of the expected weight-for-age. See UNICEF (1983).

In July 1981 I visited all the chiefs in the area and asked them to call public meetings to discuss Community-Based Health Care (our first title for what later became PHC). Enthusiasm was high, meetings were held, committees elected and young unemployed men recruited by the committees to be trained as PHC workers. Rumours had circulated that bicycles and salaries would come from Ngora Hospital. I repeated that this was not the case. Nevertheless, a host of recruits met me at every village, and inexperienced and enthusiastic as I was I immediately agreed to start training as soon as I had visited each village.

My village visits were made on bicycle to emphasise that the programme envisaged was to be village based.[2] Quickly, however, enthusiasm lapsed, committees dispersed, and I was left with twenty-two newly trained PHC workers. The local bases of the programme had not been well established.

While all of our workers had supposedly been selected by their committees as suitable PHC workers, two were very young and most were the sons or daughters of chiefs, political party chairmen or other "big" men from their communities, classically, as I was to learn, the wrong sorts of recruits for PHC work.

Only four VHWs from two villages survived the training and the initial six months of work. These four were backed strongly by their committees and their committees had wide community support.

All of the original committees, but for the two just referred to, were bogus, created for my benefit only. Eventually, however, memberships changed as community members not so far included became involved. The most common reason given for ousting a former member was, "He's a drunkard."

Many problems were encountered. But gradually a number of good committees emerged and by January 1984 viable PHC programmes had been established in six of the twelve villages in which they had been initiated, plus in four other subcounties.

SOME LESSONS LEARNED

Each of the villages in which we worked had a young child clinic once a month run by local health workers with the assistance of workers from neighbouring villages. These clinics were supervised by a bicycle-mobilised midwife who lived at the subcounty headquarters. Children were weighed by the visiting health worker, then seen by the resident health worker for advice if the child was under the expected weight-for-age, had an enlarged spleen or appeared anaemic. Mothers were advised to buy tablets for treatment of intestinal worms, and other appropriate medicines. They were counselled by their own PHC worker rather than instructed by outsiders as had been the case in the previous mobile clinics.

PHC workers were paid from funds raised by the local committee. The Road to Health cards were sold at a price fixed by the committee. By 1982 we required a prospective village committee to demonstrate its commitment to the efforts we were encouraging (and the commitment of the local community) by raising USh 10,000 before we would include them in the PHC programme.

---

[2] An "aid" mentality gripped the area at the time as relief convoys passed along the main Mbale-Soroti road destined for Karamoja.

PHC workers were taught to give routine immunisations by the local midwife. Several PHC workers expressed an interest in delivering babies and were taught basic procedure. Three of the villages in one subcounty had PHC workers who became proficient in deliveries. One worker with only primary grade four education and very poor English delivered seventy-five babies in her village in 1981, all without a hitch. The midwife in the area did all the antenatal clinics; difficult cases were advised to go to her or the hospital for delivery.

As regards nutrition, we saw slow but significant results. I once found a very malnourished child in a clinic and asked the PHC how she could allow this in her village. She promptly replied that the child was not one of hers but came from a neighbouring village. The nutrition surveys PHC workers were encouraged to do, did not produce usable statistical results, but did serve to increase awareness about the existence, causes and treatment of malnutrition. Whereas about 250 children attended our old mobile MCH clinics each month, some 500 now attended the clinics established.

But our real triumph was in the area of immunisation, and before long a clinic with 100 children produced only fifteen or so in need of immunisation. In 1981-82 most of the PHC villages reported no measles while Ngoro Hospital continued to treat large numbers of measles cases.

What made such results so gratifying was that results in our mobile clinic immunisation attempts had been much less successful. We began our earlier attempts in 1981 by scheduling an immunisation day in a particular parish, then asking the local chief for help in "getting the people out". And for the first round we generally had good results with perhaps 80 percent of the mothers with infants in attendance. But by the time the second round was announced all of the chiefs had been dismissed and the turnout was dismal. In turn, the new chiefs appointed could not produce the crowds that the former chiefs could. Overall we estimated that we covered between 70 and 80 percent in the first round, only 20 to 30 percent in the third round in this approach.

The aspect of the PHC programme we were most troubled with concerned drug treatment. Drugs issued were often sold or misused. To address this issue we devised a testing procedure on the management of diagnosis and prescription of each drug made available to PHC workers. Then, after I had tested them on the use of the drugs, the district medical officer licensed them in the prescription of those drugs in relation to which they had demonstrated suitable understandings. Some workers were licensed to prescribe only one or two drugs. Others were licensed to prescribe all seven of the drugs we stocked.

In the treatment of diarrhoeal diseases, we taught all PHC workers how to mix oral rehydration salts. Workers in turn taught mothers.

One problem with the distribution of drugs was record-keeping, and we never overcame this problem completely. We devised a simple procedure whereby workers collected their drugs the day before a clinic and returned money the following day. While this procedure was suitable for our purposes, it was in fact cumbersome and would hardly work well if a large number of PHC workers were involved.

We noticed that persons with at least some formal education tended to be more effective than persons without education in the organisation of committee responsibilities, that women tended to be better PHC workers than men and that committees with no women members tended to be far less successful in their efforts than committees with women members.

SOME REFLECTIONS AND CONCLUSIONS

Our biggest initial mistake was one of attitude. We thought that we could run programmes if people would cooperate with us. The fact is that programmes initiated from the outside simply do not work. In the end we tried to portray ourselves as resources to be tapped by the committees and the workers in the development of their programmes rather than as initiators and supervisors who looked to community leaders as resources in programmes brought in from the outside.

Such an approach caused considerable resentment from hospital staff. They wanted to be "in charge" in a vertically established PHC programme and seemed to resent the organisation of an independent and self-sufficient PHC programme.

Finally, should the morale of PHC workers be lowered through the replacement of village clinics by mobile hospital clinics, the introduction of big aid programmes or the introduction of great numbers of free ORS packets and other free supplies, or should the committees themselves be treated as irrelevant, with the assumption that more and more professional committees should be formed, then, whatever we have managed to marshall in terms of local pride and initiative will be lost.

REFERENCE

UNICEF and Republic of Uganda (1983). How to Use the Weight Chart. Government Printers, Entebbe.

Breast-feeding in and Around Kampala

Charles A. S. Karamagi

INTRODUCTION

The decline in breast-feeding that occurred first in the more industrialised countries is today occurring also in developing countries. It involves first elites, then certain sections of the general population in urban and periurban areas.

Reasons for the decline in breast-feeding include the adoption of Western lifestyles, the movement of people into urban areas, the increasing employment of women outside the home and the vigorous promotion and marketing of breast-milk substitutes by multinational corporations.

Breast-feeding is still clearly the principal method of infant feeding in the rural areas of developing countries (Niehoff and Meister, 1972; Gebriel, 1981). Unfortunately, here too a decline in breast-feeding has been observed, for example in Chile, Costa Rica, Mexico, Nigeria and Kenya.

Recognising the advantages of breast-feeding for children and the problems in the uncontrolled promotion of breast-milk substitutes, international and national agencies have taken measures to halt the decline of breast-feeding. In May 1974 the World Health Assembly recommended strongly the promotion of breast milk as the ideal baby food. In May 1981 the Assembly endorsed a WHO code designed to regulate the marketing of breast-milk substitutes. WHO and UNICEF have strongly encouraged the promotion of breast-feeding in programmes designed to expand primary health care services around the world. In their own interests in promoting health wherever possible, other international bodies--for example FAO, ILO and the International Paediatric Association--have joined in the promotion of breast-feeding.

Steps in the implementation of the WHO code in Uganda have involved the use of existing legislation and the proposed enactment of new legislation to control the promotion of infant feeding products in the country. They have also involved voluntary arrangements between manufacturers and their local representatives, and officials.

A seminar on child nutrition in Uganda was held in Kampala in March 1983 (UNICEF, 1983). Its purpose was to expose politicians and policy makers, civic leaders and the general public to current understandings of the advantages in breast-feeding and the dangers associated with the indiscriminate marketing of breast-milk substitutes. The Minister of Health proposed in conclusion that a committee involving government, nongovernment, voluntary and international agencies be responsible for the collection and analysis of information about different aspects of breast-feeding, weaning and the sale of breast-milk substitutes in Uganda. The study reported here is one of the results of the proposal.

OBJECTIVES AND METHODS

The objectives of this study were:
1. To establish the extent to which mothers in and around Kampala breast-feed their children;
2. To investigate weaning practices and factors associated with lactation failure among mothers;
3. To investigate the relationship between breast-feeding and the clinical nutritional status of the child.

The subjects included in the study were mothers with children aged 2 and younger who attended the paediatric units in Mulago Hospital between 1 September 1982 and 31 January 1983.

The background information collected for each child included: age, sex, birth weight and place of birth; age, parity, tribe, education and marital status of mother; antenatal care, mode and place of delivery; method of infant feeding and reasons for choice; weaning practices; problems with breast-feeding; occurrence of diarrhoeal disease in the child requiring hospital attendance; occupation of mother and head of household, number of rooms in house, food storage and cooking facilities. The physical examination carried out on each child to assess clinical nutritional status included all standard measurements and observations. Next, examining the clinical nutritional status of each child in comparison with the Jellife (1966) standards, the children were divided into normal, underweight, marasmic and kwashiorkor groups. Finally, associated diseases were noted. Children unaccompanied by their mothers and children with congenital abnormalities were excluded from the study.

Four socioeconomic classes were identified among the 926 mothers interviewed during the study in consideration of the occupation of the mother, the occupation of the head of the household to which the mother belonged and the family's food storage and cooking facilities. The classes identified were: urban elite, urban middle, urban poor and rural. In general identification: members of the urban elite class were those with political and/or economic power, members of the urban middle class those at the level of civil servants, members of the urban poor class those with very low incomes and members of the rural class those who came to the hospital from rural areas.

RESULTS AND DISCUSSION

Urban and Rural Mothers

All but two of the 926 mothers interviewed during this study initiated breast-feeding upon the birth of their children, and virtually all of the mothers were still breast-feeding at the end of 6 weeks.

After one year dramatic differences were observable. Now only 3 percent of the urban elite mothers, 42 percent of the urban middle class mothers, 36 percent of the urban poor mothers and all of the rural mothers continued to breast-feed their children. The mean duration of breast-feeding for the different classes, in the same order, came to 8.5, 13.1, 12.7 and 16.1 months.[1]

In short, the initiation of breast-feeding by women in and around Kampala is universal from birth through the first six months.[1] During the next six months breast-feeding is much less well maintained among mothers with urban, and particularly urban elite, rather than rural backgrounds.[2] Economic factors are no doubt involved in the differences that occur. So are differences in cultural values and differences in exposure to the influences of urban life, advertisements for breast-milk substitutes and so on.

Introduction of Solids

The early introduction of solids into an infant's diet impairs a mother's lactation by decreasing the infant's appetite and therefore vigour to stimulate the nipple and elicit prolactin and milk let-down reflexes (Applebaum, 1970). Thus, as M. Latham (1982) has pointed out, supplementary food for a baby may in fact be a cause rather than a "cure" for insufficient milk.

The age for the introduction of solids into an infant's diet has been decreasing in many parts of the world, particularly the West. Here many infants receive their first solid food within the first month of life (Hambraeus, 1977).

Among the mothers who were interviewed in our study, 7.7 percent started their children on solids before they were 3 months of age. Of this number, more than half came from the urban elite. Most babies were started on solids sometime between 4 and 6 months of age. The most common reason given by mothers for starting solids (a reason given by 41.5 percent) was insufficient milk.

Illness

Mothers who discontinued breast-feeding because of the illness of their children most commonly identified measles (74%) and gastroenteritis (12%) as causal. Discontinuance under such conditions is most unfortunate. Both illness conditions are largely preventable with immunisation and good sanitation; a switch in the feeding of an ill baby is especially difficult for the child; considering the significance of hydration, sick babies should be encouraged to drink more not less.

The manual expression of the breast must be encouraged by mothers of sick children until the baby is strong enough to suck again.

---

[1]Similar studies in Nigeria and Ethiopia have shown that the initiation of breast-feeding here too is universal. See Gebriel (1981).

[2]Comparatively, only 67 percent of the urban and 85 percent of the rural mothers were still breast-feeding their children when they were 6 months of age. In Ethiopia 90.7 percent, 98 percent and 100 percent of mothers in appropriately comparable UE, UP and R classes were still breast-feeding their children at 6 months.

Pregnancy

Pregnancy was given as the reason for stopping breast-feeding by 17.4 percent of the mothers involved in this study. The mean duration of lactation amenorrhoea was six months for the urban elite and eleven months for all others. The reasons why the contraceptive effect related to breast-feeding is of shorter duration among wealthier mothers, and among urban rather than rural mothers, in this study are not difficult to identify. Wealthier and urban mothers are more likely than their poorer and rural counterparts to be able to purchase supplementary food for their children, and their contraception is impaired as the sucking stimulus of their children is reduced (Jellife and Jellife, 1978).

On the other hand, pregnancy was given as a cause of lactation failure by a considerable percentage (17.4) of the women interviewed. Part of the reason here has to do with cultural understandings among at least some of the mothers that a continuation of breast-feeding after conception can poison an unborn baby. Part of the reason has to do with the nutritional burden put on poor pregnant mothers.

Age of Mother

None of the fourteen mothers in this study who were 15 years or younger, and none of the twenty-two mothers over 35, breast-fed their children for more than one year. The young mothers were not married, and their child-rearing was neither planned nor welcome. The disapproval, neglect and anxiety they probably experienced as a result might have affected their desire and capacity to continue breast-feeding their children. Among more elderly mothers the capacity to breast-feed decreases as breast tissue atrophies.

Parity of Mother

Only 22 percent of the mothers who had given birth to four or five offspring breast-fed their children for more than one year, while none with parity of six or more did so. The decrease is related to increase in age. It is also associated with a decreasing capacity for breast-feeding, particularly among women with poorer nutritional backgrounds (Jellife and Jelliffe, 1978).

Antenatal Clinic Attendance and Promotion of Breast-Feeding

Antenatal care is important in the promotion of breast-feeding. Doctors have the knowledge and influence to promote breast-feeding if they choose to do so. So do others with formal responsibilities in health education. Unfortunately, not one of the mothers interviewed in this study mentioned the mass media, school educators or doctors as sources of information concerning breast-feeding.

Weaning

Some mixed feeding was initiated by most of the mothers involved in this study when their children were around 4 months in age. Supplementary food commonly consisted of varying proportions of fresh or powdered cow's milk mixed with maize porridge. Tinned powdered milk was used only by members of the urban elite and upper middle classes, and at these levels by fewer than 10 percent of the mothers.

Nutritional Status of Baby

One-third of all of the children involved in this study were undernourished, and 14 percent had frank Protein Energy Malnutrition (PEM). Almost all of the undernourished children (90.9 %) were from the poorest families. Such populations have very low incomes and live commonly in crowded estates and slums. Sicknesses and inadequate diets often result in malnutrition.

CONCLUSIONS AND RECOMMENDATIONS

The initiation of breast-feeding for babies is still universal in and around Kampala. The factors investigated in this study that can be associated with the duration of breast-feeding include socioeconomic status, age, parity, illness and early feeding with supplementary foods.

Problematically, a large percentage (33.5) of children under 2 in this study were found to be malnourished. The difficulty here has to do with weaning practices and is commonly a problem in Uganda. It is related not so much to problems in breast-feeding as to problems that arise in relation to the introduction of weaning foods.

In consideration of the findings of this study, I strongly recommend that:
1. Breast-feeding be promoted by all agencies in a position to influence public opinion and effect public policy, in the maintenance of high levels of breast-feeding;
2. Health care providers be encouraged to mount programmes to improve weaning practices, as current practices are clearly often problematic;
3. Further appropriate laws and regulations be devised to monitor the marketing and distribution of breast-milk substitutes in Uganda.

The use of breast-milk substitutes was not found to be a cause for concern in this study. Very few people can afford them. With economic improvements, however, breast-milk substitutes could begin to flood the market.

REFERENCES

Applebaum, R. M. 1970. The Modern Management of Successful Breast-Feeding. The Pediatric Clinics of North America, 17: 203-225.
Gebriel, Z. W. 1981. The Breast-Feeding Situation in Ethiopia. Assignment Children, 55/56: 201-209.
Hambraeus, L. 1977. Proprietary Milk Versus Human Breast Milk: A Critical Approach from the Nutritional Point of View. The Pediatric Clinics of North America, 24: 17-36.
Jellife, D. B. 1966. The Assessment of the Nutritional Status of the Community. WHO monograph No. 53, Geneva.
Jellife, D. B. and E. F. P. Jelliffe. 1976. Human Milk in the Modern World. Oxford University Press.
Latham, M. C. 1982. Insufficient Milk and the World Health Organisation Code. East African Medical Journal, 59: 87-90.
Neihoff, A. and N. Meister. 1972. The Cultural Characteristics of Breast-

Feeding: A Survey. _Journal of Tropical Pediatrics and Environmental Child Health_, 18: 16-20.

Wenner-Van Der Mey, C. A. M.   1969.   The Decline of Breast-Feeding in Ni-Nigeria.   _Tropical and Geographical Medicine_, 21: 93-96.

UNICEF.   1983.   The Code Considered.   AMREF, Nairobi.

Family Planning in Difficult Times

Mary Okello

Modern family planning services were not really a casualty of the general breakdown of services that commenced with the advent of the military regime in Uganda in 1971. The Family Planning Association of Uganda (FPAU) was barely on its feet at the time and established only in urban centres. Here, by circumstance rather than intention, it catered primarily for the urban few, and particularly for Indians and expatriates. The majority of the population had not yet been reached in any meaningful way.

The health crisis of recent years, however, has buffeted traditional practices in family life and has had tragic consequences for mothers of child-bearing age and their children. It has also significantly retarded the expansion of family planning services at a time when they have become increasingly important.

In the pages that follow I will briefly review the story of modern family planning in Uganda, then review some of the constraints to the introduction of more effective family planning services. I am encouraged by what I believe is an increasingly favourable climate of public opinion towards the spacing of children--and even the limitation of their numbers--in Uganda. I fervently hope that such developments are not simply the result of the severe economic pressures so many families face at the present time.

FAMILY PLANNING

Modern concepts in family planning are relatively new in Uganda. The FPAU was established in 1957 as a result of the initiatives taken by a number of European and Indian women, and consolidated largely by the efforts of an American doctor at Makerere Medical School, and his wife. While the first African doctor joined the association in 1957, very few Africans were at first attracted. Part of the reason was their reluctance to join what they considered to be a European/Asian organisation in which an African might not be comfortably received. Part of the reason was the burgeoning nationalism of the time which tended to see family planning more as "birth control", and quite possibly as a Western plot to limit the number of Africans.

The view of family planning as foreign and alien was erroneous, for child-

233

spacing practices had traditionally existed in most if not all of the ethnic groups in Uganda. The practice of sexual abstinence during the period of breastfeeding was commonly understood to be beneficial both to mother and child and often observed. The use of abortifacient herbs was more common in birth control than in child spacing, but was widespread.[1] Various rituals--for example, "cursing" a young girl or hiding away her first menstrual blood--were practised by particular ethnic groups to prevent unwanted pregnancies.[2]

"Again and again spoils the drum," the Langi have commonly said of a woman who produces children too frequently, recognising that continual childbearing undermines a woman's health. Continual childbearing has also been traditionally disapproved by the Langi because the preceding child is thus weaned too suddenly and early for the child's well-being.

But while the history of family planning in Uganda does not begin with the birth of the FPAU, the story of organised modern contraception does, and it begins with the efforts of foreigners in the country. Along with the emphases of nationalism, however, Africans soon began to demand and accept a bigger voice in the affairs of the FPAU. The association gained international recognition as a member of the International Planned Parenthood Federation (IPPF) not long after independence. Official Ugandan approval was at least implicit when the First Lady of the time, Mrs. Miria Obote, agreed to become patron. The 1960s saw the association gain strength and extend its area of operations as clinics were opened upcountry from Kampala and as a number of well-known persons became active as volunteers.

In a struggle for power within the association in 1969, the executive secretary, Mrs. Sigra Visram, was ousted and a number of the early organisers of the association resigned in protest. Mrs. Visram had served the association well, but the times were now historically ripe for African leadership. The dust from this episode was just barely settled, in turn, and the association had just been officially charged by the government with the duty of acting as the main agent of implementation for its newly enunciated policy in family planning matters, when the military coup of 1971 turned back the clock.

In its third five-year Development Programme (1971-76), the ousted Obote Government had expressed concern over the high rate of population growth and its consequences for attempts to increase per capita income and improve social services. Noted also with concern in the Programme was the effect of the high rate of population growth on maternal and child health. Though it was not concluded in the Programme that Uganda's rate of population growth would soon outstrip available resources, it was considered "necessary to institute a programme of advice to women on family planning and child spacing matters."

In the implementation of the new programme, FPAU was to receive a recurrent

----

[1]Such herbs were sometimes used by jealous wives in the prevention of the pregnancy of a co-wife. Perhaps such past practices help form the basis of the widely prevalent belief that the use of contraceptives brings about sterility.

[2]How effective traditional methods were in preventing and spacing the birth of children, in practice, cannot be easily ascertained. Even today, however, many modern and educated young women in Uganda opt for traditional rather than modern methods of contraception.

subvention from the government and was to operate clinics in all government medical institutions, while the Ministry of Health (MOH) was to take over gradually the coordination and administration of the family planning programme throughout the country. Mobile clinics were to be established, staff were to be trained and information on family planning was to be disseminated in rural areas. The main aims of the proposed government efforts at this time were to make people aware of the benefits of child spacing and to make family planning services available to those who desired them.

The programme was moderate enough in its aims and hardly likely to bring about any immediate or notable changes in the reproductive behaviour of the average rural Ugandan. Yet it found great disfavour with the military regime, and in 1972 the then permanent secretary of the MOH directed that all health units which provided family planning services should cease doing so. Another permanent secretary reversed this directive in 1975, but few medical superintendents heeded the new instruction. In the climate of fear at the time it was better to let sleeping dogs lie.

The FPAU lay low during this period; its activities too found little favour with the authorities. But it did operate some clinics and employ fieldworkers, and in 1976 it undertook to supply contraceptives and train staff in those hospitals which had elected to heed the 1975 MOH directive to integrate family planning with maternal and child health services. Thus in a small way it was able to fulfill the role which the ousted Obote Government had assigned itself.

But the FPAU did not escape the strife that characterised life in Uganda at the time. Staff-volunteer relationships were poor, and as a result of gross mismanagement the association in 1979 was very nearly expelled from the IPPF movement. The solution to the problem was to dissolve the volunteer body and to set up an advisory committee of volunteers to work with a newly appointed administrator. The volunteer structure was not revived for another two years, by which time the elected government had formulated its population and MCH policies and strategies. The FPAU was then not only able to embark on managerial reorganisation but also to find fertile ground for the expansion of its activities with the full support of, and in cooperation with, the government.

The 1980 Census revealed a population of 12.8 million in Uganda and a growth rate of 2.8 percent per annum. Growth was highest in the northern and western parts of the country and among poorer families, thus creating the highest dependency ratios in just those regions of the country and sectors of society which were least able to cater for the social and other needs of their young. Noting the percentage of the population under fifteen years (43.5 percent in 1969 and 45 percent in 1980), and the implications of this concentration for social, welfare and economic provisions in the years ahead, the government in 1981 defined the objectives of its new population policy as follows (Article 13.11):

> Over the 1981-95 period, Government will attempt to influence mortality and fertility rates and adopt other measures with a view to: (1) lower the population growth rate from the currently projected 3 percent per annum to 2.6 percent per annum and (2) increase the quality of the population in terms of physical, mental and social capacity of the people, their educational status and access to adequate recreational, cultural and other social services.

Among the strategies outlined in pursuance of the objective of lowering the population growth rate, the government committed itself to "strengthen the family planning services delivery system and design and integrate them fully with the national health service delivery system." Thus it planned within the available budget to establish a family planning services network in all hospitals, rural medical units and aid posts owned by government, missionary and private institutions, merging them as far as feasible with nutrition and MCH services in the expectation that in combination these services would have a greater impact than they would have in isolation. Other strategies included nonformal population education (responsibility for which was assigned to FPAU and MOH staff); population education in primary and secondary schools and teacher training institutions; support for health and nutrition education for women; promotion and encouragement of formal education of women; discouragement of early female marriage. While the overall coordination and administration of all aspects of health and family planning were designated the responsibility of the MOH, the FPAU's continuing role was guaranteed by the government in its commitment to liase with the FPAU and other agencies in the development of "coherent national health and family planning programmes, projects and activities."

CONSTRAINTS

Some of the constraints in the implementation of the government's programme in family planning are institutional. Others are cultural and socioeconomic. Institutional constraints can be summed up in one word, LACK: lack of funds, lack of facilities and lack of manpower. Buildings and equipment are often unavailable. Workers in government institutions today generally lack initiative and interest in their work. Medical school and training institute curricula fail to include maternal and child health, and family planning components. Requisite drugs are frequently unavailable. Economically pressed midwives and others often require of clients unofficial but significant charges for services. Clinics are often overcrowded.

MOH strategy is to establish family planning clinics in twenty hospitals annually. Whether or not this target is achieved, FPAU will continue to serve large numbers of clients because of continuing problems in funding and supply in the delivery of family planning services in government hospitals.[3] FPAU has continued to act as a catalyst in spurring MOH efforts to train medical personnel in family planning methods and delivery, and in spurring the Ministry of Education to produce a family life education curriculum for use in secondary and training institutions. FPAU has strengthened its management capacity and plans to expand its services to the public but sees its efforts only as supportive of government efforts. In the FPAU view the ideal situation would be for the association to have to redefine its role as the government takes over operation of the service delivery system.

Cultural and socioeconomic constraints in family planning are more varied than are institutional constraints. To tackle them effectively will require innovative thinking, hard work and funds, and perhaps a social revolution.

Children are greatly desired in Africa, but when children are considered, numbers often seem to be more important than the quality of life possible for them. This general orientation—in combination with a high mortality rate among children, ignorance, the breakdown of both curative and preven-

---

[3]In 1984 the FPAU operated sixty clinics throughout the country: twenty-three in their own premises and thirty-seven in government hospitals.

tive health services, a frequently fatalistic attitude to the survival of children, the absence of social services and the realisation that children serve as a form of "insurance" for parents in their old age--tends to result in a much higher birth rate than is compatible with maternal and child health and social and economic progress.

This is particularly true in the northern and western sections of Uganda. Here more than in the central parts of the country parents place a greater value on the early marriage of their children, pressures from elders and among wives in polygamous households tend to encourage reproduction, women are likely to have little if any education, and a woman's sense of value to herself, her husband and society is still derived largely in relation to her motherhood.

On top of this is the still strongly prevailing ethos of male supremacy and the bride-price tradition. Even a university graduate wife will still usually expect her husband to make all of the important decisions in her household and will understand that she is required to produce children to compensate for her bride price. And even when a wife desires to regulate her fertility--as is now often the case--her husband will often, if not usually, override her wish.

Government strategies in the implementation of family planning policies take no consideration of the critical fact that the man, for better or for worse, is still the decision maker in the Ugandan family, and thus the fact that men must be educated into an understanding of and sympathy with the needs of women and children before any family planning programme can have hope of significant success. FPAU, in recognition of such facts, has adopted a policy of approaching men's groups and trying to influence opinion leaders-- for instance, through seminars for district commissioners, but so far has had almost no impact. The government will have to take the lead.

To the north in Uganda, arguments for family planning are often met with stubborn resistance because of the strongly felt belief that sons who were lost during the period of the military regime must now be replaced.[4] In the less economically advantaged areas of the country--and once again, particularly in the north--a trend has begun towards earlier marriages among school-leaver boys who have failed to find employment opportunities. Such youthful marriages can occur only in areas where bride prices are provided by father or clan; in an area such as Bunyoro where a man works for his bride price himself, and where there is pressure on available land, the trend is towards later marriages. Among in-school youth in all areas a factor militating against the effectiveness of even an efficiently imple- mented family planning programme is the breakdown of older family practices and understandings. The high incidence of schoolgirl pregnancies today is exacerbated by ignorance, the notion of male supremacy and, especially among schoolboys, an increasing lack of any sense of responsibility for one's actions. There can be no doubt that eduction for Uganda's youth in popula- tion and family-life matters must be strongly encouraged.

In areas of Uganda where there is a higher level of socioeconomic develop- ment--including higher rates of education among females--older cultural and social patterns that encouraged higher birth rates have been undermined by the demands of modern living. Thus in the economically more advanced cen-

---

[4]This has been especially important to ethnic groups who still cherish an image of themselves as military peoples.

tral region--where, additionally, population pressures on available land are greater than they are to the north--acceptance of family planning is noticeably higher than it is in more disadvantaged areas of the country.

CONCLUSION

The prospects of persuading the Ugandan population to regulate its fertility are at best uphill and at worst hopeless. However, it is also possible to report a trend which began about the beginning of 1983 and appears to be continuing: a sharply increasing rate of attendance at family planning clinics in large urban centres such as Kampala, Jinja and Mbale, and a noticeably more favourable response to family planning emphases even in rural areas. FPAU clinic attendance figures for the country over the period 1975-83 show a historically explainable sharp increase in attendance in 1976, a historically explainable drop in 1979 (the year of the liberation war) and a sharp rise in attendance in 1980. The 1983 sharp increase of 36 percent over the previous year is related to the fact that in urban centres there is now a strong tendency to limit family size; children have simply become too expensive for many in contemporary Uganda.

The increasing rates of attendance at FPAU clinics is encouraging. There is no cause for complacency, however, for even at an accelerated rate of attendance and acceptance only 2 percent of the women of reproductive age in Uganda are currently receiving family planning services. Older constraints in the implementation of family planning policies will have to be tackled. New strategies will have to be devised in breaking down male resistance to family planning. Services will have to be provided more efficiently than has so far been possible. Education will have to be encouraged.

The implementation of the family planning component of the government's population policy will require a will on the part of all concerned, government and nongovernment workers alike, to ensure that the people are reached and not disappointed.

The Delivery of Primary Health Care in Uganda Today: Some Problems and Opportunities

Klaus K. Minde and Israel Kalyesubula

INTRODUCTION

Recent political and economic difficulties have drastically affected the availability of primary health care in Uganda. While the number of physicians and ancillary health care personnel decreased significantly over the years of Amin's dictatorship, there is less information about possible changes in the quality of care provided by those working within the field. Questions pertaining to quality are of particular interest as the quantity of health care facilities and staff in the country probably will rise only slowly over the coming years, placing a special responsibility on presently available personnel. Furthermore, it may be useful to know to what extent the present reconstruction of all health services should concentrate on the provision of more manpower and equipment or on the upgrading and support of those workers who have remained at their posts.

This study then is an attempt to look at this issue by examining the workings of two primary child health care centres (Facilities A and B). Our interest was to learn something about the quality of care these facilities provided and the level of satisfaction they engendered in their clients. It was also to make some inference about the morale of the staff in each clinic and possibly to come up with some suggestions which might prove helpful to health care providers in Uganda.

Facilities A and B seemed especially suitable for such a study as they were differently structured yet served the same population. Both facilities also provide primary as well as secondary health care services, assisting families through health and nutritional education, immunisation and reproductive counselling as much as through direct medical intervention.

DESCRIPTION OF FACILITIES

Clinic A is an outpatient health care facility situated between Mulago Hospital and the adjacent Mulago village. It serves some 150 to 180 children a day and is staffed by three medical assistants, an intern, a clerk and two nurses. Patients attending Clinic A come primarily from six to eight villages situated within seven miles of the facility, but some 15 percent of

239

the children seen live in neighbouring small towns and some children are brought in from as much as twenty-five miles away. While two small church-sponsored clinics within the major catchment area do provide health services for children, the closest primary health care facility with a paediatric consultant is some ten to twelve miles away. Children who cannot be readily diagnosed by medical assistants are referred in theory to Facility B for more detailed examination or for direct admission to the paediatric inpatient unit. No physician works regularly at Facility A. Facility A is open from 8:00 a.m. to 2:00 p.m. but patients are seldom seen before 10:30 a.m.

Facility B is situated within Mulago Hospital proper and serves some 120 to 150 children per day. It is staffed by various teams, each of which includes two to three interns, a senior house officer in paediatrics, up to two attending physicians in rotation, nurses and a clerk. Medical students are regularly assigned to Facility B for practice under the supervision (limited though it often is) of more senior paediatricians.

Most of the patients in Facility B as in Facility A come from nearby villages. However Facility B also assesses and treats children who have been brought to the emergency department or are referred from Facility A or any other speciality clinic within Mulago Hospital. Nurses work at Clinic B around the clock. Children who need any kind of care after 2:00 p.m. are automatically brought to this facility.

PROCEDURE

All children who attended either the A or B facility during a two-week period in December 1983 and who lived in two villages (K and M) were included in the study.[1] The two villages were chosen because they furnished the biggest percentage of patients to the two clinics under consideration and had very similar population characteristics.

Village K is situated about four miles west of Facility A. Its population of some 12,000 consists primarily of working class men and women employed in certain minor local industries or in the city of Kampala. The village has long been a place in which people moving into the city from the country have first settled. It is relatively crowded and has only limited public health facilities. In late 1983 it had an elected group of elders and its inhabitants were generally knowledgeable about the need for primary health care.

Village M has a population of some 11,000 and is situated within half a mile of Facility A. Many of its inhabitants work in nonprofessional capacities within Mulago Hospital or the Makerere Medical School. Again this village is overcrowded and has insufficient rubbish removal. Elected elders here were politically active during the time of study and had a plan to set up a new health care facility in their village.

If the patient arriving at Facility A or B satisfied the criteria of our study, the mother was interviewed for some ten minutes by one of two fourth-year medical students hired and trained for this purpose. This interview enabled us to obtain information on each of the patients, including birth-

---
[1]This study could not have been done without the assistance of Messrs. Patrick Bassajjasubi and Michael Buyinza. Their assistance in collecting the original data is very much appreciated.

date, tribe, socioeconomic grouping, previous medical history, immunisation status and present complaints. Enquiry was made about the child's previous contacts with physicians, hospitals or native healers and any treatment already received for the current illness. Interviewers noted the time of the child's arrival at the clinic and assessed the apparent severity of the illness of the youngster on a three-point scale (mildly, moderately or severely ill). The socioeconomic background of the child's family was also broadly identified at three levels in consideration of the principal occupation of the household head, as follows: 1 = professional or senior civil servant; 2 = small independent businessman, middle or lower civil servant; 3 = small cultivator or unskilled worker.

Our assistants next recorded the time the child was called by the physician or the medical assistant, the length of the consultation and the details of the services offered. In a short interview with the mother after the consultation they next obtained details about laboratory investigations suggested, medications prescribed (type, dosage and length of treatment suggested), follow-up appointments given and any possible referrals to other clinics or for inpatient admission. Our assistants finally noted the appropriateness of the treatment given and the satisfaction with the clinic visit expressed by the adult accompanying the patient.

The students helping us with data collection were introduced to clinic staff simply as assistants in a study of certain epidemiological details of the children and their families attending the clinic.

RESULTS

A total of 167 children were involved in the study. Of these, 127 were seen at Facility A and forty at Facility B. The background data given in Table 1 indicate that the children from villages K and M and those attending Facilities A and B did not differ particularly much from each other on the variables identified.

TABLE 1: Background Data

		Clinic A Village		Clinic B Village	
		K N=67	M N=60	K N=20	M N=20
Age in years					
	Mean	2.3	2.0	1.6	1.6
	S.D.	2.2	2.1	1.8	1.2
Sex					
	Male	29	31	11	10
	Female	38	29	9	10
Number of children in family					
	Mean	2.6	3.1	3.3	3.5
	S.D.	2.1	2.2	2.5	2.6
SES					
	Upper	4	3	3	4
	Middle	20	15	5	4
	Lower	43	42	12	12

The previous and present medical conditions of the two groups of children
are shown in Table 2. The figures indicate that the children brought to
Facilty B differed from those brought to Facility A in three ways. They had
a lower rate of immunisation, had more often seen other health professionals
for the same illness and were considered to be more seriously ill. The
difference in immunisation status may be a reflection of the children's
slightly younger ages at Facility B, while their more serious medical condition and the higher rate of previous medical contact indicate that mothers
use Facility B when their children are more seriously ill and/or have not
been helped by other practitioners.

TABLE 2: Medical History

	Clinic A Village		Clinic B Village	
	K	M	K	M
Present immunisation status (%)				
DPT	58	40	30	35
BCG	70	55	55	55
Polio	62	43	35	30
Measles	33	39	25	30
Toxoid	20	31	0	0
None	28	40	45	40
Previous treatment for same condition (%)				
Other M.D.	6	12	50	45
Clinic or hospital	15	6	10	5
Native healer	0	0	15	0
None	79	82	25	50
		($x^2 = 34.7$	p < .001)	
Seriousness of condition (%)				
Mild	67	75	25	40
Moderate	31	25	60	60
		($x^2 = 22.9$	p < .001)	

Table 3 summarises the actual contact of the children with the respective
clinic staffs. As children from villages K and M waited and were seen
equally long in both facilities, the data from the two subsamples have been
combined.

TABLE 3: Length of Waiting and Duration of Consulation

	Clinic A	Clinic B
Waiting		
Mean	188.2 min.	119.9 min.
S.D.	47.1 min.	67.9 min.
	(t = 7.5	p < .001)
Consultation		
Mean	1.9 min.	11.1 min.
S.D.	1.3 min.	7.7 min.
	(t = 12.6 p < .001	df = 165)

It is clear from Table 3 that children on the average waited for more than three hours to be seen in Clinic A and that once they did see a health professional, history taking, examination and discussion lasted on an average only 1.9 minutes. In contrast children coming to Facility B waited for only about two hours and were seen for an average of 11.1 minutes. The difference in both waiting and consultation time is statistically highly significant.

Table 4 examines the treatment received by the children. The child attending Facility A received an average of 3.1 drugs, only 24 percent of which were considered to be appropriate, 28 percent partially appropriate and 48 percent inappropriate or even harmful. The figures for Clinic B were somewhat more reassuring. Children here were given fewer drugs (2.3 per child) although equally few were thought to be appropriate (32 %) or partially appropriate (18 %). The decision about the treatment's appropriateness was obviously rather crude and had to be interpreted liberally. For example, if a child complained of diarrhoea and vomiting for three days, had no fever and was given penicillin and chloroquin injections and phenergan syrup, the treatment was considered inappropriate. However, if together with the foregoing treatment Darrow's solution was prescribed, the treatment was considered to be partially appropriate.

TABLE 4: Treatment Received

	Clinic A	Clinic B
Number of drugs		
Mean	3.1	2.3
S.D.	1.2	1.0
	$(t = 3.2 \quad p < .01$	$df = 165)$
Appropriateness of medication (%)		
Appropriate	24	32
Partially appropriate	28	18
Not appropriate	48	50
	$(\chi^2 = 2.5$ NS)	

In addition to the general overuse of medication at the time of the clinic visit, the children usually received only one single injection of intramuscular medications. Even when oral medication was prescribed the amount of drug handed to the patient's mother on average was sufficient for only 1.8 days. There was also no systematic screening of the children by the clerk in either facility, with the result that severely ill children or infants waited as long as did those with only minor troubles. Referral, consultation or admission was also quite rare. For example, in Clinic A only fourteen of the 127 children seen (11 %) were referred anywhere, and only four parents were asked to bring their children back for further observation. This would seem to be a very low number, especially when one considers that the mothers on the average had been given such a meagre supply of medication. In Clinic B, 35 percent of all children were either admitted or referred and 25 percent were asked to come back for further checkups. This undoubtedly reflects the more serious types of disorders presenting to Clinic B. Most astonishing, however, was the fact that despite the generally mild nature of the illnesses and the relatively poor immunisation status of the children seen in Clinic A, not one of the children here was immunised nor did any mother receive any instruction about general health care, nutrition or family planning during her clinic visit.

In contrast, 15 percent of all children attending Clinic B were immunised, while 32.5 percent received some sort of educational counselling. Not surprisingly, 74 percent of the mothers attending Clinic A considered the care they had received to have been inadequate or very inadequate, although 65 percent had not expected more comprehensive treatment prior to their visit. Only 36 percent of attending mothers thought Clinic B had provided them with inadequate or very inadequate care, and 72 percent had not expected better care than they had received.

DISCUSSION

It should be emphasised that the review of comparatively few cases in only two health facilities cannot be seen as a reliable reflection of Uganda's present-day difficulties in the provision of health services. The fact that two-thirds of all the interviewed mothers in Clinic A had not expected more comprehensive treatment, however, suggests that many parents in this sample could not think of a place where they would have received better care for their young children. Thus the findings of this study may in fact be fairly representative of much present-day health care in Uganda for children from nonprivileged families.

A further cautionary note must refer to the validity of the study's findings. We have no hard data which tell us whether the medical practice in the same primary health care facilities at Mulago Hospital ten years earlier, say in 1973, or in other developing countries, differs markedly from that reflected in this study.

But keeping such methodological limitations in mind, two themes seem to speak especially forcefully from the data presented. Firstly, the apparent ease with which expensive medications were dispensed to children who most likely did not need them was striking. About 65 percent of all the children seen in Clinic A received penicillin injections, 50 percent received injections of chloroquin and 20 percent were given broad spectrum antibiotics even though many of the infants and children seen had only mild viral disorders with little or no fever.

On the other hand, Clinic A immunised no children and provided no guidance and assistance to mothers. Virtually all of the mothers expected some concrete signs of treatment (such as a pill) during their clinic visit and generally indicated that they would have been pleased if their children had been immunised. In short, it seems that our data rule out a consumer resistance towards preventive medical care.

The second message of this paper appears to be the brevity of contact between patients and clinicians, especially in Clinic A. It is obviously impossible to take a proper history and do an examination in less than two minutes. While the exact reason for this type of care-giving is not clear, it is suggested that the lack of professional contact or in-service training and consequent absence of stimulation of the medical assistants in Clinic A have led to decreasing interest in patients, among professionals, and the consequent shrinkage of clinic hours. As the professionals in Clinics A and B were paid nearly identical salaries and yet provided different services, one can speculate that the apparent demoralisation of staff at Clinic A was not due primarily to external reasons but was related to lack of professional and emotional support. Clinic B was manned by physicians who spent only part of their day at the clinic. At other times they worked on an inpatient ward, attended lectures and had at least some opportunity to discuss the problems they encountered with colleagues and supervisors. While it may seem plausible to blame the difference in medical training for the variations in care provided, the medical assistants who worked at Clinic A were highly competent individuals who had all worked at Mulago for more than ten years and clearly "knew" about immunisations, follow-up visits and the appropriate treatments for viral diseases.

This suggests that the loss of human qualities such as curiosity and pride in addition to the present shortage of equipment and drugs in Uganda should be seen as a primary deterrent to good health care, and that it is the human equipment which needs most urgently to be restored. This can be done by organising case conferences for medical assistants in local hospitals at regular intervals, publicly acknowledging the importance of their work and providing them with other means of recognition. As such efforts would be comparatively cheap and cost no foreign exchange, the present external restrictions in the physical growth of Uganda's health services may provide an ideal time for internal renewal.

Medical Education in Uganda Today

William Parson

We are honouring the memory of Sir Albert Cook today, and the Uganda Medical Association has chosen the topic of its annual lecture, "Medical Education in Uganda".*

Sir Albert was a splendid doctor and an extraordinary man. We know this from the testimony of his patients, peers and friends, and from his meticulous case notes and clinical reports preserved in the Albert Cook library. Sir Albert was the pioneer Western-trained doctor in Uganda. He has remained a teacher to all of us who have followed him. Great teachers teach by precept and Sir Albert's teaching model has been splendid.

Medical education is tested after qualification. The critical period comes after the discipline of medical school and the experience of hospital training are complete, and the doctor is weighed down by clinical responsibilities. The properly educated doctor must continue to be a student, read current journals and new texts, attend conferences and advance his understandings. The medical world moves along quickly and the doctor who stands still is left behind.

Despite his relative isolation and difficult working conditions, Sir Albert was a lifelong student. He continued to purchase new preclinical and clinical books over the years, and from his marginal notes you will know that he made use of them.

The need for continuing medical education is widely accepted today. Indeed continuing medical education in many places has been changing from a voluntary activity to a mandatory requirement.

Unfortunately the pace set by Sir Albert in the continuation of his own education has not been possible during the past painful decade in Uganda. Despite the heroic efforts of the Uganda Medical Association in holding regional meetings and attempting to publish a journal, current journals from other countries have been unavailable, transportation has been difficult and

---

*Editors' note: This is an edited and shortened version of the author's Sir Albert Cook memorial lecture given in Kampala in 1982.

faculty numbers have shrunk, all at a time when understandings in the medical/scientific world in general have been exploding.

The lack of continuing medical education and medical rejuvenation courses is a critical problem that must be faced today by the Uganda Medical Association, Makerere University and the Ministries of Health and Education. A coordinated effort must be directed toward bringing medical practitioners, specialists and teachers in the country back up to date.

MAKERERE'S DISTINCTION

Sir Albert first attempted to train Ugandans in Western medicine at the turn of the century. His first recruits were grateful patients who received food and clothing while they trained. But this didn't work well and Sir Albert had to confess after ten years of effort that he "could only point to four thoroughly trustworthy male assistants." His new vision never left him, however, and he persisted with the idea of a medical faculty to be based in a projected Mengo University.

Mengo Medical School opened in 1917 with seventeen students and offered a three-year course qualifying African dressers and dispensers. The much larger and more complete School of Medical Training was initiated at Mulago in 1924. Under the Mulago programme, two years were to be spent at Makerere University in general studies, then four years in medical studies at the School of Medical Training, the end result being the achievement of a standard in training equivalent to the standard at the Asian subassistant level. Not until the late 1940s was the standard achieved equivalent to a full British qualification, and not until this time was the Diploma of Medicine (Diploma of Medicine, East Africa) awarded locally.

Ultimately, in 1964 the medical qualification earned at the University of East Africa was recognised by the General Medical Council in the United Kingdom and the M.B., Ch.B. was awarded locally to graduating students. When the University of East Africa was dissolved a few years later, this degree was awarded by Makerere University. By the end of the 1960s roughly 100 students were being admitted into the Makerere University Medical School for training as doctors. Makerere's rapid rise to distinction in the quality of its medical programme was built on the high quality and keenness of its students, the talent and enormous industry of its developing Ugandan faculty, a first-rate expatriate staff and generous donor support.

For my part, because I needed a change from my home university in 1964, I wrote my former chief, Professor Robert Loeb, who had just been on a worldwide tour of medical institutions, and asked for suggestions concerning a suitable place in which I might work for a year. He wrote back promptly to extol the virtues of Makerere Medical School and ended with the comment that if he and his wife were younger they would choose to work here.

I pursued Professor Loeb's suggestion, and since have spent nine years teaching at Makerere. I had the good luck to be in the right place at the right time—in Makerere when the East African nations agreed to establish a postgraduate programme here to train future teachers and consultants locally rather than overseas. I have never regretted my decision to travel to Uganda. In 1975 I wrote to a graduate of the first M.Med. class (1970), Charles Olweny, to ask what had become of the first four graduating classes at this level. I have saved his detailed reply. It included the following details:

1970 - 2 Consultants (Mulago and Mbale);
     - 1 Practitioner (Masindi);
     - 2 Asian graduates on medical school faculties
       in the United States;
     - 1 Director of the Ugandan Cancer Institute,
       and Assistant Professor, Makerere;
1971 - 2 Senior Lecturers (Dar es Salaam);
1972 - 2 Lecturers at Makerere;
1973 - 4 Lecturers at Makerere;
     - 2 Lecturers in Nairobi;
     - 1 Lecturer in Zimbabwe.

The results for the first four classes at the postgraduate level at Makerere were most gratifying. But in the 1970s Uganda went deeper and deeper into trouble.

THE CURRENT SITUATION

For the past two years (having arrived at emeritus status at the University of California), I have worked as hard as I know how, teaching clinical medicine in Uganda. I have used methods that have worked in the past. But these haven't worked this time, and I have a personal sense of failure. A teacher who shares the successes of his students must also share their failures.

Medical education in Uganda is at a critical stage. My seniority and years of proven devotion to Uganda allow me to speak with candour. We've just been through another examination period, with dismal results. Examiners are trying to retain standards. Growing internal and external pressures have been erosive.

Many factors have contributed to the problems of the current situation. Uganda has lost many of its talented and well-trained physicians. Education at preliminary levels in the country has deteriorated badly. Teaching staffs have been depleted in most departments. Paper, books and stethoscopes are unavailable. The breakdown of hospital facilities and services has been catastrophic. Drugs are in very short supply or not available at all.

Have I said too much? The list is familiar to all of us who have worked in Uganda in recent years. It is compounded by insecurity, family tragedies, transport problems, financial hardships and widespread _magendo_.

A Need to Cut Back

Many of Uganda's problems today are national problems. It is not my task to comment on such except to wish the government success as it grapples with an enormous task. But there is one feature of medical education I must comment upon for it is something that has cut down on the effectiveness of all clinical teaching: For the size of the patient population, which shrinks intermittently because of lack of transport and diminished facilities and drugs--and for the size of the effective teaching faculty, which has shrunk because of economic and security problems as well as career frustrations-- there are currently far too many students for proper bedside teaching.

There was a time at Mulago when four of us stood around a patient's bed and

each observed, palpated, percussed and auscultated. At that time splendid
bedside teaching was a Makerere tradition and a mark of our graduates. At
that time there were enough teachers to do the job effectively.

Today the combined number of Makerere and Mulago teachers in medicine is
down to about half of the previously effective level, with the size of the
Makerere faculty itself down to about one-third of the established number of
posts. As a result it is no secret that teachers are no longer working at
even close to full effectiveness. In short, we are dealing today with an
unworkable equation, with fewer than half of the faculty members necessary
for the number of students enrolled.

The problem would be resolved if the reservoir of interested and trained
Ugandan teachers overseas and elsewhere in Africa were to return, or if
there was sufficient foreign exchange to hire expatriates. And perhaps
something along such lines will happen in due time.

In the meanwhile there is an urgent logic to cut down the number of medical
students to approach equilibrium with the diminished faculty. The issues
surrounding this topic are complex and sensitive, and my response to the
problem at hand sounds simplistic--almost like a surgical attack on a complex medical problem. But simplicity here may be a virtue. Such an approach would certainly improve the morale and effectiveness of our teachers.
It might serve as an opportunity to tighten the band of productive teachers
by releasing those whose other commitments are too great, while possibly
permitting better financial supports for those who remained. It would
result in more manageable teaching schedules. It would certainly make our
programme more attractive in the recruitment of new colleagues.

It is common knowledge that there is considerable wastage from our larger
classes with reference to those who run away from Uganda as soon as they are
qualified or as soon as they have completed advanced training. Perhaps
smaller classes where the students selected are carefully screened for
personal and intellectual qualities, and where morale is sustained by high
quality teaching and a recognition of the medical professional as a national asset, would lead to a situation where fewer doctors would run away.

No decision for retrenchment is likely to be popular. Yet the history of
great campaign victories teaches us of the wisdom of the strategy of retreating occasionally in order to regroup forces before again moving ahead.
The ultimate purpose of medical education in Uganda must be a healthier
Uganda. Building strength elsewhere as the number of doctors is diminished
may help us achieve this goal more effectively.

The Health Personnel Pyramid

Let us think of the trained health personnel of Uganda in the traditional
fashion as a pyramid, with a small group of leaders at the apex and a broad
base of practitioners and auxiliaries. In reference to the apex there is
little controversy. Any medical education system that does not replenish
its leaders--that does not train teachers, investigative scientists and
consultant clinicians--inevitably grows stunted, withers and dies.

By the same token I don't need to remind you that a successful postgraduate
programme built with talented, highly motivated and well-trained students
who are taught by an up-to-date faculty, encouraged by opportunities for
continuing education and supported by suitable terms of service, is essen-

tial. Such a programme does not currently exist in Uganda. But there is no
argument that this is what is desirable and should be worked out again as
quickly as possible.

But mainly, I would like to discuss the base of the pyramid which would
certainly be diminished in numbers if class sizes were cut. That is, if we
are to take cuts seriously we are forced to ask the question: What are
Uganda's priorities in health care?

In order to establish perspective here, let me refer to the Report of the
Sanitary Commission of the State of Massachusetts presented to the state
legislature in the middle of the nineteenth century. The report identified
the basic health problems at the time in Massachusetts as follows: immunisation and communicable disease control, promotion of child health, environmental sanitation training of community-oriented health manpower, public
health education, promotion of individual responsibility for one's own
health and so on.

Industrialised nations today have a list of health problems just as long as
ever, but their nature has changed. Meanwhile, the problems of health care
in Massachusetts in the middle of the last century now prevail in most of
the low-income countries of the developing world. In such countries, as J.
Evans (1981) once pointed out: Life expectancy at birth averages fifty-one
years whereas it averages seventy-four years in industrialised nations;
mortality rates for children between one and four years of age are ten to
twenty times higher than they are in industrialised countries, and nearly
one-half of all deaths occur before five years of age; the major causes of
death--diarrhoeal disease, respiratory infection, tetanus and childhood
contagions--all can be controlled by measures already available in the
industrialised nations; and malnutrition and short birth intervals contribute to poor chances for survival.

It is not difficult to conclude that the problems of scarcity and choice in
health care that existed in Massachusetts in the last century are similar to
the problems in health care in Uganda today. With the breakdown of health
services in recent years, Uganda has been forced to depend mainly on health
auxiliaries, few as these auxiliaries are in number and sadly deficient as
is their training, supervision and support.

In recent years evidence has been marshalled to show that that the base of
the medical pyramid should be skilled workers inexpensively trained at the
community level, rather than expensively trained conventional doctors whose
skills are likely to be unused and who tend to lose morale under difficult
conditions. We see in Uganda today that doctors have tended to gravitate to
the cities to open private practice, or emigrate to other countries. In
fact our friends in preventive medicine, public health and social paediatrics have waved this banner for years and now wave it with the support of
WHO, UNICEF, the World Bank and the IMF. Since first coming to Uganda
eighteen years ago, I have been sympathetic with such a point of view. My
training, experience and skills, however, are in scientific medicine and the
care of the individual patient. But I've carried a sense of guilt for doing
so little for the broader problems of health care in Uganda over the years.

CONCLUSION

To bring the strands of this presentation together, I believe that 1) a reduction in the number of medical students is an urgent practical step that

can be taken now to rescue the quality of medical education in Uganda, 2) that an expansion and improvement of the training of health auxiliaries will more than make up for any gap in medical services that occurs as a consequence of a cut-back in the training of doctors, and 3) it will be advisable to adapt the medical curriculum to a changing role for the doctor which should include skills in managerial and supervisory functions in working with auxiliaries.

My wife and I returned to Uganda this time because we wanted to take part in the rebuilding of Makerere. Perhaps we shall return again. But things haven't worked out this time exactly as we thought they would. As I have indicated, I've been disappointed in the relative ineffectiveness of my teaching activities.

But I shall end on a more positive note. One of my postgraduate students in saying goodbye said he wanted to thank me for what I had taught him. I thanked him for his gracious remark but looked at him a bit dubiously. "Yes," he said, "you've taught me to love my patients." I'm sure that would have pleased Sir Albert Cook as much as it does me.

REFERENCE

Evans, John (1981). Health Care in the Developing World: Problems of Scarcity and Choice. New England Journal of Medicine, 305: 1117-1127.

Voluntary Agencies and Health Services: AMREF in Uganda

Christopher H. Wood

The first and most obvious element in the breakdown of medical care in Uganda was the failure of curative services. These services were provided by various organisations and were disrupted at different times through neglect during the Amin regime, destruction during the war and looting afterwards. The less obvious but in the long run more serious breakdown occurred in those services concerned with promoting health and preventing disease, provided to some extent by the same organisations. Other important breakdowns occurred in services such as water supplies, agriculture and education. The reconstruction of these services together with the morale, discipline and law and order necessary to maintain them still poses a major challenge.

Historically, the first medical care in Uganda was provided by the private practice of traditional healers. This was later augmented by a government health service started during the colonial regime, initially caring for civil servants and slowly extending to the rest of the population. Even after independence this service had still not reached its target of coverage for the total population.

Another very important source of medical care was the missions who first looked after themselves and their congregations and then the catchment population around them. Private practice based on "Western" medicine has also grown up in the major towns, and also caters for the more educated and wealthy people in the villages.

Against this varied background of medical care services a number of other voluntary agencies have started providing services. These are generally international agencies, each concerned with a specific aim--preventing blindness, saving children, care for leprosy, first aid, etc. These agencies establish local national branches and develop their services.

Increasingly important on the medical care scene are funding agencies. These may be private, national or international, and they may sponsor both government and nongovernment health care programmes. Sometimes they carry out services themselves but more often they channel funds through field officers for project implementation.

Where in this mixture of organisations does the African Medical and Research
Foundation (AMREF) lie? What are its special features that help or hinder
it in making a contribution to the overall health care picture? This paper
considers these questions.

AMREF

AMREF was conceived and developed in eastern Africa. Twenty-five years ago
a group of surgeons saw a need for the improvement and extension of surgical
and emergency care. One of the first, best-known and longest-lasting servi-
ces--the Flying Doctor Service--was founded. Based in Nairobi, this service
reached out to each of the former East African Community countries. It
provided radio communication and visits by surgeons to isolated rural hospitals, with the possibility of medical evacuation if necessary. From these
beginnings and on the back of the Flying Doctor Service all the other AMREF
activities have been developed. In the early days funds to cover activities
were obtained mainly through individual well-wishers and small private
foundations sought out by fund-raising offices set up in New York and
London.

A health education unit was the first nonclinical activity to be started.
This was followed by a training department and a community health department. With the addition of these diverse activities the Foundation began to
grow quickly. More requests for assistance were received from more places,
wider sources of funding were found (AMREF established offices in seven
other countries), and a larger staff with a broader range of experience was
acquired. As these activities expanded a reputation for "getting things
done" was established.

In the early 1970s the AMREF programme in Uganda included specialist visits
to eight outlying hospitals, an eye disease programme in Busoga and occasional lecturing at Makerere Medical School. The eye project was established and handed over to the local services. Gradually, as problems with
security became more severe, the radios installed at the hospitals visited
were removed and visits had to be stopped. Ugandan staff continued to be
invited to AMREF seminars and workshops and a small number of books continued to be supplied to health auxiliary training schools, but programmes
in general had to be curtailed.

After the liberation war AMREF was one of the first organisations invited
back to Uganda, and it soon returned with support from EEC. A plan was
drawn up to supply emergency drugs and vaccines, a seven-ton delivery truck,
spare parts for other incapacitated vehicles, books and stationery for five
schools, and typewriters and other office equipment to the Ministry of
Health. A detailed plan of requirements allowing for what was best provided
by others was made, and logistics problems were organised.

With a supply system in operation, other donors joined in to provide books,
stationery, medical supplies and equipment from small contributions through
AMREF. The Government of Uganda turned to AMREF in assisting seventy-five
nurses who were stranded in Libya, opening the door for longer-term project
involvements.

As the last part of this emergency programme an AMREF team accompanied by a
Ministry of Health official undertook a survey of health facilities and
training schools in the eastern, southern and western parts of the country
to evaluate the emergency supply programme and to identify further needs and

possible areas for future assistance.

Four main areas for which AMREF might be able to raise funds and provide
assistance were identified--training, drugs and medical supplies, health
planning and medical equipment repair. The Ministry of Health approved the
list of projects proposed, giving priority to assistance with the development of a planning unit.

Shortly after this a Canadian delegation arrived, wanting to offer assistance to Uganda. They were having difficulty in establishing a mechanism
for doing so as no Canadian High Commission existed in Uganda at the time.
After discussion it was agreed that they would sponsor AMREF in assistance
to the planning unit in MOH, the creation of a continuing education unit
within MOH and the emergency renovation and reequipment of fifteen auxiliary training schools.

A detailed proposal was quickly prepared and approval was promised within
three months. In practice, final approval of the proposal took more than
twenty months. In the meantime AMREF was asked by the Carl Duisberg
Gesellschaft (CDG) from Germany to work with them on a health training programme. In anticipation of the long-term continuing education programme to
be funded over five years by CIDA it was decided to make a start with CDG.
This was done in October 1981.

The rationale for the continuing education programme was that there were
many staff in the rural health facilities who had "qualified" five, ten or
twenty years previously and who had had no opportunity to update their
knowledge and skills. Despite the acute shortage of equipment and drugs,
and knowing that staff were often absent from their posts either to grow
food or earn much needed additional money, it was decided to go ahead with
the programme. Emphasis was to be put on raising morale and introducing
appropriate technology to overcome shortages as well as refreshing knowledge
and skills.

District health teams made up of the district medical officer, district
nursing officer and district health officer and sometimes the hospital
superintendent of all the districts in the Eastern Region were invited to a
workshop to alert the district teams to the decline in standards of care in
their districts and to help them learn how they could run appropriate
refresher courses for their own staff. After general discussions on needs
and appropriate methods of adult education, each team made specific plans
for their own course. It was assumed that funds would be available to
sponsor these courses.

The initial workshop was, according to all present, a great success. To the
author it revealed that however severe the malfunctions of the health services had been, you only had to scratch just below the surface to uncover
many committed persons who were exasperated by the conditions and constraints under which they worked. When during the workshop the constraints
were removed, the enthusiasm for getting the job done was enormous.

Many delays were experienced in the acquisition of the CIDA grant due to
uncertainties in Uganda. There were two changes in government during this
period, and the shilling was floated during the negotiations.

To maintain momentum with the district health teams for developing their own
district programmes, funds were sought and obtained from the Canadian High
Commission in Kenya, Brot fur die Welt and CDG. AMREF staff were borrowed

from Tanzania and Kenya to run the Uganda Project. In all, ten district refresher courses were held and upon AMREF advice the new school in Mbale was
designated the Centre for Continuing Education. The second phase of the CDG
assistance to training took place in October 1982. This time instead of
assisting district health teams start their own refresher courses, a seminar
for auxiliary and paramedical training school teachers was organised.

The CIDA grant was finally confirmed at the end of 1982 and the agreement
was signed in early 1983. The initial implementation step was staff recruitment, and locating people with appropriate qualifications, experience
and the personality to fit the role of secondment to an MOH, plus working
with a counterpart, proved to be difficult. The security problems in Uganda
gave the country a bad image. Being an African-based NGO, it is AMREF's
policy to recruit as many people from within the country as possible, with
those from other parts of Africa as second choice, and from outside Africa
as a last resort. AMREF's salary structure is somewhat above local government salaries but well below UN or bilateral agency rates, or what can
be made in private practice. Two of the unresolvable consequences of this
policy are the danger of attracting some of the best national staff out of
government employment and, at the same time, not being competitive in the
international job market. In most circumstances an agency that does take
national staff is accused of poaching and disrupting the national programme
which it attempts to support. But if it does not do so, it is accused of
relying on temporary expatriates who, after gaining valuable experience,
leave the country. Steering a course between these extremes requires great
care and time in selection of staff. In discussions with the MOH it became
clear in this instance that they would prefer non-Ugandan staff who would
work with Ugandan counterparts.

DISCUSSION

In its early days AMREF was concerned mainly with short-term and clinical
activities. Over twenty-five years it has grown and broadened its range of
activities and the areas in which it works. It has become more involved
with development programmes requiring baseline information, feasibility
studies, pilot projects, training, operational research and evaluation.
What are the advantages and disadvantages of such activities being undertaken by voluntary agencies? Are they the responsibility of governments and
therefore best left to them? Or is there a role for organisations such as
AMREF in the health care delivery system of Uganda?

AMREF has become an African-based, international, multipurpose, health care
nongovernment organisation. It has no national, political, or religious affiliations. The organisation and its staff have extensive experience of
working in eastern Africa and are known to governments, UN, international
and other more specialised voluntary agencies. AMREF derives its funds from
diverse sources--local national governments and voluntary contributions, and
from overseas governments, foundations and voluntary contributions in ten
different countries (USA, Canada, UK, Germany, Holland, Sweden, Denmark,
France, Norway and Switzerland). AMREF's characteristics give it opportunities to respond to requests from other organisations or to identify needs
itself over a wide range of activities in East Africa. AMREF is an operational agency. It has tried to balance providing service with research,
consultancy, training and publications, but always with an emphasis on
actually doing the job. It is currently funded on a project-by-project
basis, however, and has no funds of its own to develop programmes until it
has prepared proposals and sought and obtained sponsorship. Thus it is

acting as an agent, and preparing proposals and seeking sponsorship can mean considerable delays in getting started. Its broad range of activities from community-based health care to reconstructive surgery, from health behaviour studies to training and parasitological research, and its support services of printing, radio communications and air transport, may contribute to a broad--and hopefully balanced--approach; it can, however also lead to dilution of skill in a particular field. While AMREF may bring an understanding of the organisation of health care and training to a specialist programme such as eye disease control, it may lack some of the technical skills and experience available to more specialised agencies.

The question of whether there is any need for "public" organisations-- somewhere between government and private--is partly philosophical and partly political. We believe that public organisations such as AMREF do have an important role to play. They are a manifestation of one form of self-help and community participation. They are a little freer from the bureaucracy and conservatism associated with any government establishment, of whatever political persuasion, and from the exploitation for personal gain often associated with purely private enterprise. They are therefore more able to respond to changing needs and changing technologies faster than government and still be in the public interest.

Voluntary agencies, however, each with their own objectives and separate funding, may develop their own vested interests, and cooperation between them and other organisations may be no better than between government ministries. The organisational framework for constructive coordination between voluntary agencies, and between them and government, is only slowly emerging.

Index